P9-BJM-393

Deutsches Museum

VON MEISTERWERKEN DER NATURWISSENSCHAFT UND TECHNIK

German Museum
of Masterworks of Science and Technology

Editors: F. Heilbronner (supervision),
R. Gutmann (production, coordination), B. Heilbronner, P. Smith
Photographs: R. Zwillsperger and H.-J. Becker; Maps: B. Boissel

Authors: K. Allwang, F. L. Bauer, A. Brachner, J. Broelmann, G. Filchner,
J. Fischer, S. Fitz, F. Frisch, G. Hartl, F. Heilbronner, S. Hladky, Z. Hlava,
H. Holzer, G. Knerr, O. Krätz, W. Kretzler, H. Kühn, K. Maurice, L. Michel,
G. Probeck, W. Rathjen, K. Rohrbach, E. Rödl, M. Seeberger, L. Schletzbaum,
H. Schmiedel, R. Schwankner, H. Straßl, F. Thomas, H. Tietzel, M. Weidner
(all from the Deutsches Museum)

English translation by V. Maasburg and J. Peryer

Deutsches Museum

Guide
through the Collections

Published by the
Deutsches Museum

Verlag C. H. Beck Munich

Published by the Deutsches Museum, Museumsinsel 1, D-8000 München 22,
Telephone (089) 21791

Release of the aerial photograph on the cover by the
Government of Upper Bavaria, no. G 30/11066. Photograph by M. Prugger

With 232 illustrations, 130 of which in colour,
and 54 floor plans

CIP-Titelaufnahme der Deutschen Bibliothek

Deutsches Museum von Meisterwerken der Naturwissenschaft
und Technik (München):
Deutsches Museum : guide through the coll. / publ. by the Dt
Museum. [Ed.: F. Heilbronner (supervision) … Photogr.: R.
Zwillsperger and H.-J. Becker. Maps: B. Boissel. Authors: K.
Allwang … Engl. transl. by V. Maasburg and J. Peryer]. –
München : Beck, 1988
    Dt. Ausg. unter demselben Titel
    ISBN 3 406 31761 8
NE: Heilbronner, Friedrich [Hrsg.]; HST

ISBN 3 406 31761 8
© Copyright Deutsches Museum and
C. H. Beck'sche Verlagsbuchhandlung (Oscar Beck), Munich 1988
All rights to the illustrations reserved by the Deutsches Museum
Reproduction of the illustrations by Brend'amour, Munich
Composition and printing by Appl, Wemding
Paper: BVS° matt, wood-free, mat coated illustration printing paper, 100 g/m²
by Papierfabrik Scheufelen, 7318 Lenningen
Binding by Großbuchbinderei Monheim
Printed in Germany

Contents

Introduction

This guide is intended to invite you to the Deutsches Museum, to welcome you in the Museum and to help you to make yourself acquainted with it.

The guide was made up by members of the Museum staff, thus by persons who not only know the Museum in every detail, but also love it and want to pass something of their devotion on to you.

The Deutsches Museum is a vast museum, one of the world's largest. The exhibition housed in it makes demands on the visitor. This is why I would like to make two suggestions for your visit:

Don't try to see the whole Museum at once: the result of such an attempt would be fatigue instead of pleasure. Rather, make a choice that corresponds to the amount of time you have available.

And don't wander about desultorily, because this might confuse or discourage you. Rather follow the didactic arrangement of the collection departments.

It is a pleasure for all of us at the Deutsches Museum to see you here. We wish you a pleasant and profitable visit and trust that this guide will contribute to it.

Munich, July 1987   *Otto Mayr*
                                             Director General of
                                             the Deutsches Museum

Information for your Visit

Opening Hours
Museum and Library are open to the public daily from 9 to 17 hrs.;
on the second Wednesday of December from 9 to 14 hrs.
Museum and Library are *closed* on New Year's Day, Shrove Tuesday,
Good Friday, Easter Sunday, 1st May, Whit Sunday, Corpus Christi,
17th June, 1st November, 24th, 25th and 31st December.

Entrance Fees
Adults DM 5,–; school-children and students with a student's card
DM 2,– or year's ticket DM 10,–; groups (minimum 20 persons)
DM 3,50 per person; all-week tickets for school classes and groups of
apprentices DM 6,–; card of 10 tickets (also valid for Hellabrunn Zoo)
DM 35,–. Planetarium DM 1,50 extra per person (tickets at the infor-
mation booth in the Entrance Hall). Library and Special Collections:
entrance free.

Guided Tours and School Visits
For guided tours of the collections please apply to the "Führungswe-
sen" office, telephone (089) 21 79 25 2. Special guided tours (duration
2 hours) for groups up to 25 persons only upon written request at least
one week in advance. The fee of DM 100,– is to be paid in cash to the
guide. Guided visits of the Library are arranged on the 2nd Sunday of
every month at 11 hrs. and are free of charge (reading rooms, store
rooms, rare books).

Handicapped Visitors
can reach the Museum's displays (except for the planetarium, mines
and parts of the metallurgy section and the marine navigation department) by special ramps and elevators. A lavatory for handicapped visitors is on the 1st floor next to the hall of Musical Instruments; please
contact the Museum staff.

Restaurant and Snack-bar
are located within the Museum; during the summer months a dining-
car will welcome you in the outdoor exhibits area, tel. (089) 22 71 33.

The Museum Shop
in front of the Museum sells popular books on science and technology,
catalogues, posters, slides, as well as technical toys and souvenirs, tel.
(089) 29 99 31.

Photographs
(including flash photography) for private purposes may be taken free
of charge. Commercial photographs as well as filming, sound recording and television only upon authorization of the "Pressestelle", tel.
(089) 21 79 24 6; fees are charged.

Special Events
Matinées, lectures etc. are announced separately (please ask for the
quarterly programme, available only in German at the "Pressestelle").

Additional Facilities of the Deutsches Museum

Library
The library concentrates on the history of science and technology. It does not lend out books, and its entire holdings are available to the reader at any time. In 1988 it comprised about 700 000 volumes and 4900 periodicals, including 1750 current periodicals (280 foreign). The collection of the Libri Rari includes some 5000 valuable rare books, printed before 1750, on natural science and technology.

Special Collections and Archives
The special collections of the library hold non-book materials ranging from the complete papers of scientists, engineers and inventors to manuscripts, documents and autographs, technical sketches and illustrations, maps, posters, pamphlets and trade literature as well as to company periodicals, portraits, medals, trade-marks, watermarks and coloured paper stocks and finally to audiovisual material. Notable are the archives of aeronautics and astronautics. The photographic archives keep some 40 000 negatives at the disposal of the visitor.

Reserve Collections
About 50 000 additional devices, machines, instruments, models and samples are housed in the store rooms of the Reserve Collections. Only specialists are admitted by previous arrangement.

Kerschensteiner Kolleg
The Kerschensteiner Kolleg – named after the mathematician and physicist, Georg Kerschensteiner (1854–1932) – offers continuation courses for teachers, instructors, students and other groups, as well as symposia and tutorial classes for scholars and students from Germany and abroad. The college includes a dormitory accommodating 38 persons and a student laboratory with 36 bench places.

Research Institute
The *Research Institute for the History of Technology and Science of the Deutsches Museum* mainly deals with research in this field aiming at publication of scientific studies. By proximity and close cooperation, the Research Institute is linked to the *Institute for the History of the Natural Sciences of the Ludwig-Maximilian-University,* to the *Institute for the History of Technology of the Munich Technical University* and to the *German Copernicus Research Office.*

Congress Centre
The Deutsches Museum also has a large Congress Building, which consists of a congress hall accommodating 2400 persons for meetings, lectures and concerts and of four additional conference rooms for 60 to 320 persons.

Demonstrations and Films (only in German)

Meeting point at the sign-boards with the red dot. Numerous films are available; the film programmes may partly be chosen by the visitor. All announcements are subject to alteration; please ask at the information desk in the entrance hall.

Time	Demonstrations (Duration 15 to 20 minutes)	Floor	Films (appr. 30 minutes)
9.45	Mining (60 minutes)	Ground	
10.00	Model Railway	Ground	Mineral Oil and
	Aeronautics	1st	Natural Gas
(except	Brickmaking Plant (60 minutes)	2nd	
Wednesday)	Planetarium	6th	
10.30	Locomotives	Ground	
	Moulding and Casting of Metals	Ground	
	Aeronautics	Ground	
	Hand-made Paper	2nd	
	Marine Navigation	Ground	
10.45			Mining
11.00	High-Voltage Demonstration	Ground	
	Model Railway	Ground	
(Monday to	Chemistry Lecture with Experiments	1st	
Friday)			
	Astronautics	2nd	
11.30	Locomotives	Ground	Metallurgy
	Power Machinery	Ground	
	Processing of Plastics, Industrial Chemistry	1st	
	Agriculture	3rd	
12.00	Model Railway	Ground	
	Planetarium	6th	
13.00	Model Railway	Ground	
13.30	Locomotives	Ground	
	History of Photography (45 minutes)	2nd	
13.45	Mining (60 minutes)	Ground	
14.00	High-Voltage Demonstration	Ground	Mineral Oil and
	Model Railway	Ground	Natural Gas
	Aeronautics	1st	
(except	Brickmaking Plant (60 minutes)	2nd	
Wednesday)	Agriculture	3rd	
	Planetarium	6th	
14.30	Moulding and Casting of Metals	Ground	
	Aeronautics	Ground	
	Power Machinery	Ground	
	Marine Navigation		
14.45			Mining
15.00	Model Railway	Ground	
	Textile Technology	2nd	
(Monday to	Paper Making Machine	2nd	
Wednesday)	Astronautics	2nd	
15.30	Locomotives	Ground	Metallurgy
	Processing of Plastics, Industrial Chemistry	1st	
16.00	High-Voltage Demonstration	Ground	
	Model Railway	Ground	
	Planetarium	6th	
All day	Musical Instruments	1st	
	Glass Blowing	2nd	
	Ceramics	2nd	

OVERVIEW

The maps are intended as a help for your orientation in the Museum. The page numbers after entries indicate the beginning of the relevant chapter. For additional subject entries please see the index from page 285 onwards.

Explanation of Signs:

ℹ	Information	**☕**	Snack-bar
WC	WC	**🍴**	Restaurant
WC	WC for handicapped visitors	**✚**	First Aid
🛗	Elevator	**✎**	Room for Baby Care
🛗	Elevator for handicapped visitors	**🎬**	Films
→	Guide Line	**☎**	Telephone
			not accessible

Halls of Exhibition and Floor Plans

Ground floor/Basement*

* accessible only from the ground floor

Basement

Accessible only from the ground floor

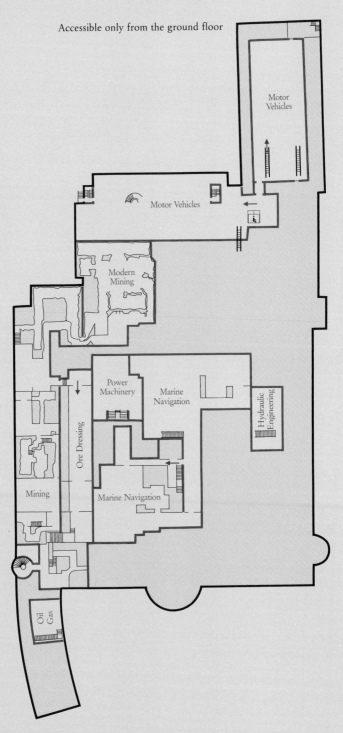

Motor Vehicles

Motor Vehicles

Modern Mining

Power Machinery

Marine Navigation

Hydraulic Engineering

Ore Dressing

Mining

Marine Navigation

Oil Gas

Ground floor

Display surface 18 400 sq.m.
(including the basement)

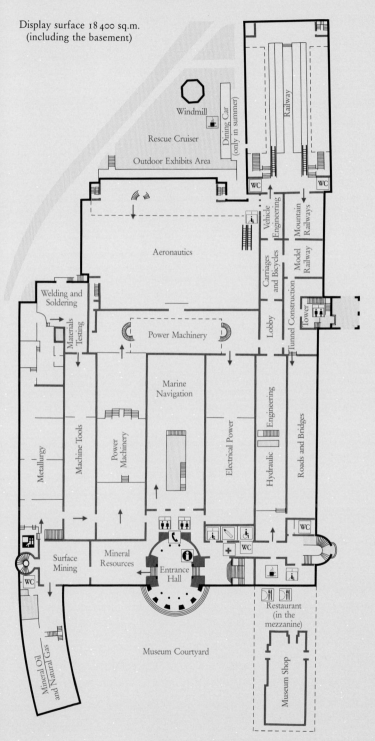

Windmill

Rescue Cruiser

Dining Car (only in summer)

Outdoor Exhibits Area

Railway

Aeronautics

Welding and Soldering

Materials Testing

Power Machinery

Vehicle Engineering

Mountain Railways

Carriages and Bicycles

Model Railway

Lobby

Tunnel Construction

Tower

Marine Navigation

Metallurgy

Machine Tools

Power Machinery

Electrical Power

Hydraulic Engineering

Roads and Bridges

Surface Mining

Mineral Resources

Entrance Hall

WC

WC

WC

Restaurant (in the mezzanine)

Mineral Oil and Natural Gas

Museum Courtyard

Museum Shop

First floor

First floor

Display surface 16 400 sq.m.

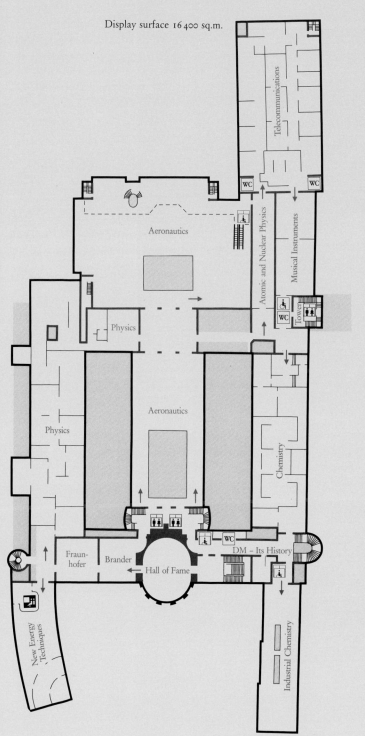

Second floor

Second floor

Display surface 3800 sq.m.

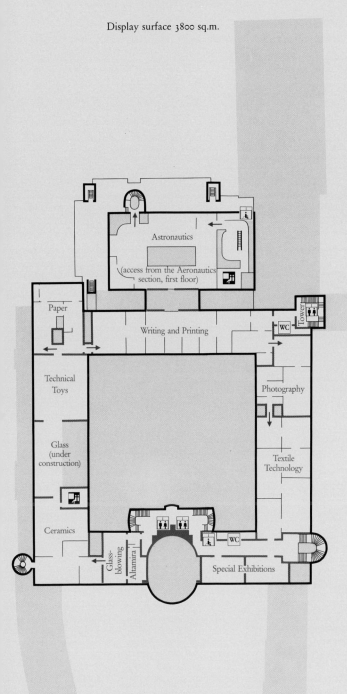

Astronautics

(access from the Aeronautics
section, first floor)

Paper

Writing and Printing

WC

Tower

Technical
Toys

Photography

Glass
(under
construction)

Textile
Technology

Ceramics

Glass-
blowing

Altamira

Special Exhibitions

WC

Third floor

Third floor

Display surface 3000 sq. m.

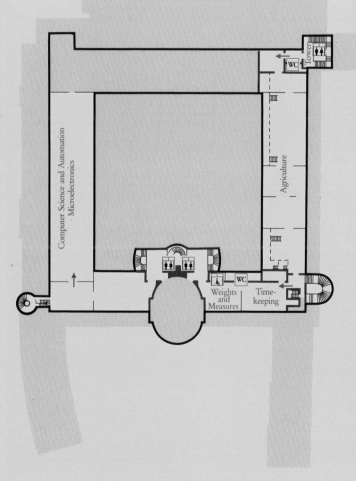

Computer Science and Automation
Microelectronics

Agriculture

Tower

WC

Weights
and
Measures

WC

Time-
keeping

Fourth floor

Observatory 284
Demonstration only by previous appointment (tel. 2 17 94 56). Access
from the Timekeeping Department on the third floor.

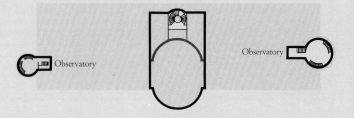

Fifth floor

Astronomy 279

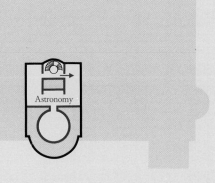

Sixth floor

Planetarium 283
Tickets at the information booth in the Entrance Hall. Simulation of
the celestial phenomena with a Zeiss projector.

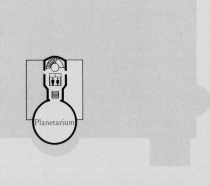

DESCRIPTIONS

On the following pages you will find a detailed description of all exhibition halls of the Museum, arranged by floor. Within every floor, the sequence represents a possible guide line.

Every description starts with a historical survey of the subject matter, followed by *"Information on the Exhibition"*.

Explanation of abbreviations in the captions:

(O)   Original
(R)   Replica or Reconstruction
(M)   Model
(P)   Presentation by Museum attendants
(Di) Diorama
(D)   Demonstration

Mineral Resources

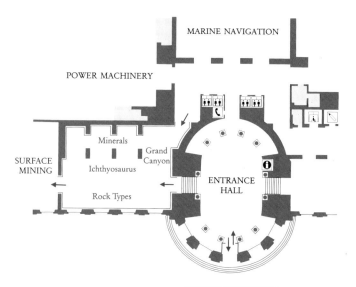

The science dealing with the material composition, the structure and the history of our Earth is geology. Complementary to geology there are branches of science such as mineralogy, petrography or petrology; further paleontology which endeavours to work out a consistent system of order in time and space from the petrified remainders of former plants and animals; then tectonics, the science of the structure of the Earth's crust; geophysics and geochemistry are branches which investigate in the physical properties and the chemical composition of the Earth.

Geology, i.e. the knowledge of our Earth, is not only a scientific end in itself, but also serves mankind daily in manifold ways. Catchwords like ore, coal, salt and mineral oil emerge in this context. The construction of roads, building underground and surface engineering, the sinking of wells, the supply of construction materials (sand, gravel, plaster, clay), the construction of tunnels and railway lines are all fields where geology is applied practically.

In recent years, the increasingly urgent problems of environmental protection have brought about new tasks for subsoil geology and hydrogeology. The search for the most advantageous location of household rubbish and special garbage without deterioration of the ground water is just one of the manifold problems. After 1945, another field of application was added to the traditional fields of geology: marine geology. The increasing need of raw materials required an extension of the exploration for raw materials to the ocean beds. Marine geology deals with the prospection, the discovery and the production of such raw material reserves as halobolites, phosphorite nodules, ore sludges and – above all – mineral oil.

But it is not only the endeavour for material and economic advantages that has prompted mankind for ages to investigate in the various rock types, the inner and outer forces of Earth, volcanoes, earthquakes and inundations. For Heraclitus (about 500 B.C.) there isn't anything solid and lasting in this world. Everything is changing. About the same time, Herodotus describes petrified concha of sea shells in the mountains of Egypt and hence infers that Lower Egypt was formerly covered by the sea. From Antiquity to modern times, scientists have continuously tried to answer the questions for the formation and structure of Earth, but only in 1765 the first mining school was founded in Freiberg/Saxony. Abraham Gottlob Werner was the uncontested authority of this first professorial chair of *geognosy*. More mining schools were founded subsequently: Schemnitz 1770; St. Petersburg 1783; Paris 1790. Leopold v. Buch, Horace Bénédicte de Saussure, Alexander v. Humboldt, James Hutton, William Smith, George Cervier, Alexander Brongniart and others followed Werner's example. Geology became an independent discipline.

The habitable, usable part of Earth is the Earth's outer crust. It reaches down about 35 km. It floats on the viscous plastic material of the upper mantle, followed by the inner mantle which ends at a depth of about 2900 km. There the dichotomous core begins, the outer part of which is liquid, the inner part solid. Temperatures here range between 2000° and 4000 °C. In the inner core, pressure is approximated to be more than 3,5 million bar.

Information on the Exhibition

The exhibition is situated at the beginning of the mining departments. You enter it by the lefthand stairs, coming from the Entrance Hall. A possible route through the following sections may be useful:

Minerals, Crystals, Rock types

Minerals are homogeneous, naturally formed, solid constituents of the Earth's crust. Almost all minerals develop specific crystal forms, i.e. bodies of material uniformity with a regular lattice structure of atoms, ions or molecules. They have a strictly geometrical shape and are bounded by mainly flat faces. The structure of the crystal lattice defines the external form, hardness, cleavability, fracture type, density and other features of the crystal.

The various crystal shapes are grouped in seven crystallization systems. There are over 2000 minerals, but only about 100 of them are of importance. Only about two dozen of the minerals have a substantial share in the formation of the different rock types. Minerals of mineral associations with a profitable yield of metals are called ore minerals. Rocks are aggregates of naturally originating minerals. They are divided into three main groups: Magmatic (igneous) rocks, sedimentary rocks and metamorphic rocks.

1. Igneous (magmatic) rocks originate from the magma, i.e. the viscous igneous melt of the Earth's interior. Magmas that intrude into the lower

part of the Earth's crust produce *plutonic rocks.* Magmas that reach the surface and extrude over it are called lavas and form *volcanic rocks.* Between both groups there are the dike rocks.

Plutonic rocks	*Dike rocks*	*Volcanic rocks*
Granite	Granite porphyry	Quartz porphyry
Syenite	Syenite porphyry	Trachyte
Diorite	Diorite porphyry	Porphyrite
Gabbro	Gabbro porphyrite	Basalt
Peridotite		Picrite

2. *Sedimentary rocks* are always produced by weathering of other rocks on the Earth's surface, i.e. the materials weathered from rocks are transported either in solid or in liquid form (by water or wind) and deposited elsewhere as sediments or as the result of chemical precipitation. Micro-organisms play an important role in chemical precipitation. An essential feature of nearly all sediments is bedding (stratification).

Grand Canyon (Di)
The Grand Canyon, the valley of the Colorado River in the southwest of the United States, offers an incomparable insight into protracted periods of the Earth's history. The fundamental complex of this 1 600 m thick pile of flat sandstone, marl and limestone layers consists of about 1 500 million years old mica schists. The limestones of the upper canyon edge are "only" 200 million years old. However, it would be wrong to think that the 1 600 m thick package of sedimentary rocks, offered to the visitor's eye by the Grand Canyon, represents a consistent history of marine and land sedimentation over 1 300 million years, since there were also intervals of erosion (about 1 000 m) between periods of intense sedimentation. This is why there are gaps in the history. Nevertheless the Grand Canyon shows an enormous period of our Earth's history.

Between the phase of unconsolidated sediments (clay, sand, gravel) and the state of solid sedimentary rocks (clay stone, sandstone, conglomerate, breccia) is the phase of chemical and mechanical consolidation, called diagnesis. Sinter rocks, saline rocks and carbonaceous rocks are special groups of sedimentary rocks.

Sinter rocks are formed where subterraneous waters come to the surface and the changes of pressure or temperature cause the precipitation of constituents (lime, silicate) dissolved in the water. Well-known are the porous calcareous tuffs (travertine) from the Sabine mountains near Rome (St. Peter's, Colosseum) or from the Bad Cannstatt area.

Saline rocks originate in cut-off lagoons of the sea in an arid climate. While the sea water, connected only temporarily with the open sea, steadily evaporates, the salts dissolved in the water remain and enrich the brine until the precipitation point is reached. The best-known saline rocks are rock salt, anhydrite and gypsolith, sylvinite, hartsalz, carnallite and kainite.

Carbonaceous rocks, called also *anthracides,* are of organic origin and therefore no true rocks in the proper sense. Since they mostly occur in such an altered state that their organic origin is hardly intelligible, they are nevertheless classified as sediments.

Items of the carbonization file	Contents of carbon (%)
Wood	50
Peat	60
Brown coal	73
Pit coal	83
Anthracite	94
Graphite	100

Limestone is the most widespread organogenic sediment. It is formed mainly in the sea with the contribution of organisms like algae, shells, foraminifers, corals, brachiopodes and snails. Singular freshwater limestones also occur in lakes. The said organisms build their skeletons from the lime dissolved in the water. When they die, they sink to the bottom, where lime sludge is formed by the calcareous parts. In many limestones the hard particles of former organisms can still be found (fossils). Such accumulation of organic relicts, along with the chemical and physical precipitation of calcium carbonate can make up stone packages several hundred meters high. The main constituent of limestones is the mineral calcite ($CaCO_3$).

Dolomite is closely related to limestone and formed by combination of lime with magnesium dissolved in the water. It is less common than limestone. It consists of the mineral dolomite ($CaMg\,[CO_3]_2$).

Siliceous rocks consist of relicts (skeletons) of diatoms, radiolaria and siliceous sponges. Chert, radiolite and flint derive from the consolidation of the original material, crystallization and recrystallization.

Petrifacts (fossils) are petrified relicts of organisms or traces of life. Thus organic parts are not directly transformed or conserved, but shapes and structural elements only are passed on. Petrified animals or plants which occur worldwide only in defined geological periods are called dominant (guide) fossils. They are important auxiliary means for the definition of the sequence of formations in the course of Earth's history.

Ichthyosaurus Stenopterygius quadriscissus Qu. (Fraas)
Age: Lias (about 140 million years). Location: Holzmaden/Württemberg (O)
The Posidonia shales, named after the Posidonia shell, a dominant (guide) fossil of an age of the Black Jura (Lias), are rich in petrified organic relicts from the former Jurassic sea.
Near Holzmaden/Württemberg several particularly beautiful petrifications, such as the Ichthyosaurus have been found.

3. *Metamorphic rocks* originate from the metamorphism of rocks by pressure and temperature. A distinction is made between contact metamorphism, caused by intrusion of magmatic material, and regional metamorphism, caused by the superimposing of stone material.

Typical examples of regional metamorphism are fruchtschiefer, garnet rock, hornstone and crystalline marble. With regional metamorphism, three formation zones are distinguished according to the intensity of pressure and temperature: the epizone, mesozone and katazone. If the parent rock is intruded even more deeply into the Earth's crust, another melting process (anatexis) takes place: the rock becomes part of the magma again.

Deposits

Usable materials in the earth, such as minerals, rock types, mineral oil, natural gas, hot springs and even ground water, are generally called mineral resources. Science prefers the expression 'deposits'. Deposits occur in various forms: seams, lodges, veins, domes, levels, impregnations, nests or placers. Just as with rock types, the distinction of the ores, i.e. of the proper ore minerals, is made according to their magmatic, sedimentary or metamorphic origin.

Precious stones and gems. Since Antiquity precious stones have been known and sought after. They were mainly used for the production of jewelry, sometimes also as remedies against sickness and black magic. Up to the 16th century gems were mostly worked up in their natural, uncut state. Facetting was achieved only in the 16th century.
There isn't any generally accepted definition of the term 'precious stones'. The most important features of gems are hardness, colour, transparency, reflection and refraction of light.
The unit of weight used in gem commerce is the metric carat (mct) = 0,2 g. Some confusion is due to the commercial names of precious stones which often do not correspond to the mineralogic definitions, e.g. Arkansas diamond (commercial name) = quartz (mineralogic name).

W. Kretzler

Surface Mining

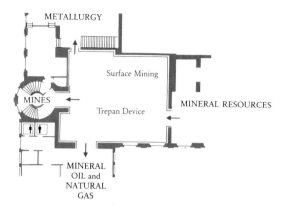

Surface mining probably is the oldest method used by man for the extraction of mineral resources for economic use. As early as the Meso-lithic Age, flint lumbs – to be used for arms – were mined in primitive surface mines. In modern times, too, ore deposits and coal seams were first mined where they cropped out to the surface.

About 70% of the world's ore and coal is nowadays produced in surface mines. Above all, coal is extracted in surface mines, in addition to iron, manganese, copper, chrome, molybdeniferous, bauxite and magnesium ores. The most important surface mines of the Federal Republic of Germany are in Rhineland, in the area between Cologne, Aachen and Düsseldorf, were brown coal reserves amount to about 55 billion tons. Other surface coal mines are run near Helmstedt (reserves of 120 million tons) and in Hesse.

Submersible motor-driven pump, 1976 (O)
Manufacturer: Wirth Maschinen- und Gerätefabrik GmbH, Erkelenz. Surface mines must be kept clear of water, so deep wells are sunk into the rock mass to be mined in order to lower the water table. Such wells can reach depths of 500 m and more. The pumped water is used either as fresh water or service water, or else fed into a water system. Drainage is done by means of submersible motor pumps with a capacity ranging from 0,8 to 1600 kilowatt. Alone in the Rhenanian Brown Coal District, about 1000 electrically operated submersible motor pumps are in use. The pumped water ratio to coal production was at times 14:1.

Extraction and Haulage of Brown Coal

Up to the turn of century, the brown coal of the Rhine District was mainly mined in small-scale deep workings and transformed into briquettes. The introduction of industrial raw lignite processing led to surface mining with the introduction of mechanization. Cable excavators and bucket chain dredgers were the forerunners of the bucket wheel excavators, generally used in surface coal mines today, giving a daily production of up to 240 000 tons.

As early as in the 18th century, the competent mining authorities required the recultivation of the scooped out diggings, and they still do it in our times. This means that the areas altered by coal mining must be returned either to their former use or to another type of utilization. The useless waste is carried by the excavators to large-scale belt conveyor systems and from there to the spreaders (stackers) which refill the exhausted surface mines with this material.

Information on the Exhibition

The different mining methods are demonstrated by models. The hall is dominated by a trepan device, Kind-Chaudron type, which belongs to the shaft boring display of the Mining Exhibition beneath. A more systematic arrangement is in the planning phase.

W. Kretzler

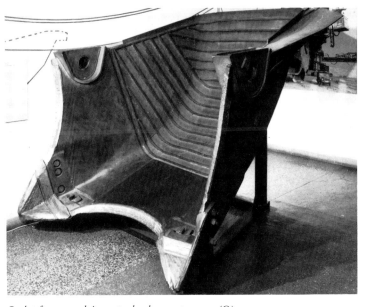

Bucket from a revolving cutter head excavator, 1977 (O)
The bucket on display is part of a bucket wheel of 17,3 m diameter. Ten such buckets, spaced equidistantly, are fitted to the cutter head. Excavators fitted with buckets of this size produce up to 100 000 m³ of coal or overburden per day.

Mineral Oil and Natural Gas

Gallery   Ground floor   Basement

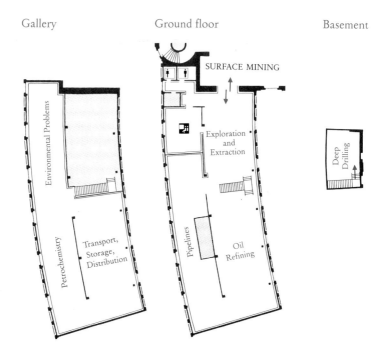

Utilization of Mineral Oil

Considering the history of mineral oil means at first, and has been for several thousands of years, the history of the native asphalt, bitumen or tar occurring in nature. It was, and still is, used as sealing and construction material and partly as a medicine (e.g. stone oil, ichthyol).

The temples and palaces of the Sumerians, built with air-dried clay bricks, were pitched with bitumen. It is said that the same construction method was used for the Tower of Babel built during the reign of Nebuchadnezzar II.

In Germany, tar pits in the area around Celle were first mentioned in a description of the boundary separating the diocese of Minden from that of Hildesheim. In the *Tegernsee Pamphlets,* of about 1440, the beneficial effects of the so-called *St. Quirin's Oil* were described. A list of buyers, dating back to the 16th and 17th century, gives – among others – the names of Queen Magdalena of Hungary (1571), Elector Ludwig of Heidelberg (1579), Duke Maximilian of Bavaria (1619) etc.

Up to the mid-nineteenth century, tar, petroleum, bitumen *(petroleum derivates)* were either collected from natural outlets or made accessible by flat wells.

The beginning of industrial development in Germany was also the beginning of the systematic search for raw materials. Among others, thirteen drilling projects were authorized by the Royal Hannoverian

Government and carried out under the supervision of Georg Christian Konrad Hunaeus, professor of geognosy at the Polytechnic School of Hannover. Three of these borings were intended to clarify the origin of the tar in the pits of Wietze, Hänigsen and Eidesse. The drilling work started early in April 1858 and ended early in May 1859 at a depth of 35,5 m with a considerable oil flow. This disproves the frequent assertion that the American Edwin Drake (Colonel Drake) had carried out the first oil-well drilling. Drake was drilling from the beginning of August until the 27th August, 1859. On the 28th August, his assistant Bill Smith discovered oil on the water.

Hunaeus' success gave rise to the so-called *German Oil Fever.* Profiteers and speculators turned up. The Grand Hotel of Peine was overcrowded and renamed New Pennsylvania. Real estate prices rose from 1 mark per German acre to 6 000 marks. From 1880 till 1883, over a hundred companies sank nearly 600 wells. This boom period was soon followed by disenchantment. It was not until the twenties of our century that Preussag took over the remaining workings and provided systematical exploration.

The exploration and production activities of the Upper Rhine Valley and in the Alpine foothills developed in a less spectacular way than those in Lower Saxony. A natural occurrence of bitumen near Pechelbronn and Lampertsloch in the Upper Rhine Trough had been known since 1498. In 1742, the Frenchman de la Sablionère started oil production from oil sand found in shafts of 30 m depth. For this purpose, he built a special preparation plant. From 1885 onward, bituminous shale was produced from the Messel pit near Darmstadt and distilled there.

Still in the 19th century, shafts and borings reaching down to a depth of 200 m were sunk in the Alpine foothills, near Robogen (Lake of Tegernsee), and on a petroleum outlet near St. Quirin's Chapel. 200 tons of oil were produced there.

Exploration drilling and production have been carried on ever since, with changing intensity and success, in Lower Saxony, Schleswig-Holstein, the Upper Rhine valley and in the Alpine foothills. During the past 125 years, about 20 000 wells were sunk in Germany.

Drilling Engineering

Drilling work was not an unknown prehistoric technique. The Englishman Feinders Petrie even furnished proof of a diamond-core boring method used for building the Gizeh pyramid. The reintroduction of this method is commonly considered as an invention of the 19th century.

When considering all those who ever dealt with the problem of earth drilling, even Leonardo da Vinci's name turns up.

The first construction of a deep-well drilling equipment of interest in engineering was probably that of Johann Bartels (1713), a machinist from Zellerfeld. It worked by the cable churn drilling method known already then. In 1714, Christian Lehmann's description of a boring device with rotary operation in upper depths and jump drilling in lower depths was published in Leipzig. The numerous positive evaluations of

Dahlbusch bomb-shaped rescue device (R) and rescue-pipe used at Lengede (O)
The application of deep drilling techniques in mine catastrophes has saved the lives of
many miners during the past decades. The rescue operation of Autumn 1963 in the
iron ore mine of Lengede-Broilstedt deserves particular attention. A fortnight after the
accident, 11 survivors were successfully rescued from a depth of 56 m using a Dahlbusch bomb-shaped rescue device.

contemporary specialized reviews show that the drilling technique
developed by Lehmann essentially stimulated the evolution of deep boring in the 18th century.

It may be assumed that percussion boring with stiff drill pipe – called
English method, and *German method* if a free-fall tool was used, during
the second half of the 19th century – goes straight back to Lehmann's
boring method.

Industrial growth and the increase in population in the 19th century
required a better utilization of the most important mineral resources:
salt, coal, ore and oil. In this context, Karl Christian Friedrich Glenck
(1779–1845) must be mentioned: he was the first German boring spe-
cialist who did systematic and successful exploration drilling for salt.
His work in the area of Weimar brought him into close contact with
Goethe who wrote down his impressions of Glenck's successful drilling
in a letter to his friend Zelter, dated 13th November, 1829.

It was the economic policy of the Prussian State that inspired all efforts
made in order to explore and utilize salt deposits or salt wells equivalent
to the South German ones, and to become independent of imports.

The maximum depth achievable by boring with stiff (rigid) rod systems
was about 400 m at that time. But greater depths were required. Carl
von Oeynhausen invented the drilling jars (1834) and thus overcame
the difficulties caused by the breaking of the drill stem in drilling with

stiff rods; greater depths became possible and increased the profitability.

The progress in drilling engineering, achieved in the second half of the 19th century by engineers and design engineers such as Karl Gotthelf Kind, Josef Kindermann, Joseph Chaudron or Friedrich Hermann Poetsch, also influenced coal mining.

The possibilities of large diameter (up to 4,3 m) shaft boring brought about the change from tunnel mining to deep mining in the Rhineland mining district.

The 2 000 m mark was first passed (2 003 m) during a drilling operation using Köbrich's drilling method (1893). The Mining Counsellor Köbrich used the flush boring system, invented in France in 1846, as well as the diamond drilling method by Leschot, shown at the Paris World Fair (1867), in combination with the proven freefall drilling equipment with working beam. In addition, he was the first to use Mannesmann pipes for the casing.

In 1886, the first volume of a six-volume manual series on deep drilling engineering by Theodor Tecklenburg was published. In 1894, the Association of Drilling Engineers was founded, and in 1895/96, Anton Raky made the epoch-making invention of a rapid percussion drill unit with the drilling-beam mounted on a flexible block, thus achieving an increase of drilling performance by nearly 100%. Raky was not only a brilliant engineer, but also a successful businessman. From 1895 to 1907, his drilling company achieved the enormous total drill-footage of 1 million meters. It used 120 steam-operated drilling rigs and employed 240 drill foremen and 3 000 borers.

The Origin of Mineral Oil and Natural Gas

Mineral oil is formed by accumulation of dead micro-organisms worked upon by bacteria in an environment lacking oxygen as well as under increasing pressure and temperature. The originating sapropel is then covered by calcareous or clayey sediments while the sea bottom is slowly sinking down. Pressure and temperature consolidate the sapropel over protracted periods and form oil mother rocks. The organic substance is thus transformed into liquid and gaseous hydrocarbons: mineral oil and natural gas. The pressure caused by overlaying rock strata displaces the oil and the gas out of the oil mother rock and into the porous reservoir rock, where it accumulates at the highest points. The objective of geological and geophysical exploration is the search of such places: mainly flexures, foldings and inclinations of rock strata, at the tops of which oil and gas may possibly have formed reservoirs. The search for such places – and not for oil or gas itself – is the task of exploration. Geological and geophysical – primarily seismic – prospecting methods are auxiliary means for the detection of potential bearing structures underground.

1. From its beginnings, *drilling engineering* has been closely linked to oil production. Though it is true that the historic roots of drilling techniques were in mining, the most essential development and improvement are due to oil. First reports of drilling down to depths of 500 m are

known from China. The same method, i.e. cable (rope) drilling, was still in use in the 19th century for the opening of oil deposits in North America (Pennsylvania). At that time, however, stiff (rigid) drill rods were already used for drilling in Europe.

In rotary drilling, the most common drilling method since the beginning of the 20th century, the rock isn't crushed by a free falling bit, but crushed by a rotating drill bit. New roller bits and diamond bits, special circulation (flush) fluids and other innovations make possible drilling advances of up to several hundred meters a day under favourable conditions.

Travelling block, swivel and rotary machine of a Rotary Drilling Unit, 1976 (O)
The central part of a Rotary Drilling Unit is the rotary table; by the quadrangular kelly, it sets the drill rod, hanging from a travelling block, in rotary motion. Diesel engines drive the plant.

While the oil companies of the first decades of oil production were satisfied with the quantities flowing from the well because of the pressure in the reservoir, oil well pumps were used later and the pressure on the deposit was increased by injection of water – in recent times, of steam and chemical additives – in order to release the oil from the reservoir rock.

Because of the increasing demand for oil and gas, more and more undersea (submarine) deposits have been opened up in recent years. Special equipment and plants were developed and constructed: measuring ships, drilling platforms, drilling ships, production platforms, pipe laying barges, small submarines etc.

2. *Oil transportation* used wooden barrels (1 barrel = 159 l) until the first cast-iron pipeline was laid from Titusville (Pennsylvania) to the nearby railway station. Today, pipelines and big tankers are the exclusive means of transport for mineral oil and natural gas, the latter being utilized only recently.

3. *Crude oil,* as it occurs in nature, is a mixture of many chemical compounds. Its main constituents are compounds of carbon and hydrogen (hydrocarbons). In order to obtain consumable products from crude oil, it is necessary to treat it according to one of the following four processing methods:

Distillation, i.e. the separation of the constituents of crude oil according to their higher or lower boiling-point (e.g. gasolines, petroleum, diesel fuels).

Cracking of the distillation residues, which produces additional fuel types and middle distillates.

Refining of crude oil derivates.

Reforming for better fuel qualities.

4. *Storage* is of vital importance for the consumer's supply with oil and gas and their products. For this purpose, large tank farms are mostly used, but also underground storage in depleted oil and gas reservoirs in recent years.

5. *Distribution* of oil and oil derivates is based on water, railway and road transportation. Pipelines take over this task for supraregional distribution.

Natural gas is almost exclusively transported by piping systems.

6. For the past 30 years, the *utilization* of oil, gas and their derivates has mainly served the energy demand. An ever increasing demand for products, the basic materials of which are oil or gas, developed at the same time. The petrochemical industry produces plastics, synthetic fibres, solvents, detergents etc.

7. The *lubricating oils* are often overlooked when speaking of the significance of oil for our daily life. However, many technical processes are absolutely inconceivable without the use of these highly specialized lubricants.

The path starts with exploration and prospection. Then the guide line turns right and makes a loop back to the stairs leading to the gallery, where mainly environmental problems are dealt with.

Exploration and Extraction

A general survey of the origin, prospection and extraction of mineral oil and natural gas is given in this section; an exhibition on deep drilling, located in the basement, also belongs to this section. Another section illustrates the construction and operation of pipelines.

Refinery Processes

The refinery processes section gives a synopsis of crude oil processing in the refineries. Flow-charts and models visualize the single steps of the processes.

Transport, Storage and Distribution

Surface storage in tank farms, subterranean storage in storage reservoirs and ship transport of liquefied natural gas are shown in this section, as well as petrol supply by horse-drawn vehicles around the year 1900.

Offshore discovery of mineral oil and natural gas, 1976 (M)
During the past decades, an increasing number of plants, special ships and equipment have been developed for offshore drilling and production:
– measuring ships and location methods
– drill platforms of various construction types
– drilling vessels for exploration and research purposes
– underwater completion and production equipment
– pipe laying barges and underwater excavators
– surveying, safety, and supply ships
– small submarines etc.

Oil and Gas as Fuels

This section shows the possibilities of energy utilization in private homes and industrial plants.

Petrochemistry

Petrochemistry, an industrial branch particularly linked to the daily needs of man, is explained by diagrams, models and petrochemical products.

Lubrication (in the planning phase)

Environmental Problems

The consequences of careless use of the raw materials oil and gas are demonstrated in this section. At the same time, however, alternative and protective measures are presented here.

Deep Drilling

The set-up and the operation of a drilling site depend on the drilling purpose (foundation test boring, prospection for ores, oil and salt etc.). We distinguish between prospection boring, exploration drilling and production wells. Relief wells and drilling for rescue operations take a special position in deep drilling. Auxiliary equipment helps to secure the drilling sites.

W. Kretzler

Mining

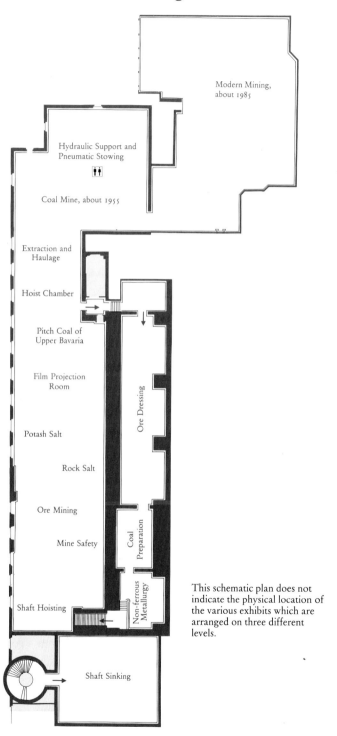

Modern Mining, about 1985

Hydraulic Support and Pneumatic Stowing

Coal Mine, about 1955

Extraction and Haulage

Hoist Chamber

Pitch Coal of Upper Bavaria

Film Projection Room

Potash Salt

Rock Salt

Ore Mining

Mine Safety

Shaft Hoisting

Shaft Sinking

Ore Dressing

Coal Preparation

Non-ferrous Metallurgy

This schematic plan does not indicate the physical location of the various exhibits which are arranged on three different levels.

Like the history of agriculture, the history of mining is as old as mankind. The hardest material available to man during the Stone Age and used for the fashioning of hunting implements and tools was flint. It had either to be collected or dug out. This is confirmed by numerous excavations, e.g. in England.

Cultural items and jewelry of gold, silver or copper, dating back to early history, prove that these were the first metals man found to be usable and durable. The reason for this was doubtless the fact that these metals occurred in pure form in brooks and rivers and thus didn't require any smelting process.

Between 7 000 and 2 500 B.C., probably somewhere in the Near East, it was discovered that it was not only possible to work occasionally found pieces of pure gold, copper and – less frequently – silver with stone tools and remelt them, but also to melt copper straight from appropriate ores.

Thus the fundamentals of systematic ore mining were known. The Sumerians got their copper ore from the mountains of Makan, an area which is probably identical with the northern parts of the Sultanate of Oman of today, a mountain region rich in copper ores. The civilization of ancient Egypt mainly secured their copper supplies by mining expeditions to the Sinai Peninsula (among others, to Timna, north of the seaport of Eilat of today).

Evidence of prehistoric and ancient mining activities in Central Europe is found especially near Mitterberg, in the Province of Salzburg and at the Kelchalpe near Kitzbühl. In this district, copper ores were mined

since the early Bronze Age until late in the Iron Age (between 1900 and 600 B.C.).

Economic and political importance of mining first appeared clearly in Antiquity. The Laurion silver extracted from lead ores with a silver content, or else the silver of the archaic mines of Sifnos, an Island of the Cyclades, played a role in the Aegean-Greek economic sphere similar to the role the rich Spanish silver ore deposits played in the western part of the Mediterranean and in the economic life of Carthage and Rome.

A considerable stimulus to mining was due to the introduction of the coinage system. Minted precious metals (silver, gold) used as tender, such as the Attic tetradrachma, raised the mining industry to an instrument of political and economic policy.

The Romans had come in contact with mining only during their territorial expansion. A Roman mining industry or mining engineering didn't exist until then. Their ability to take advantage of the knowledge of subjugated nations enabled them to contribute to the engineering techniques of their time. So they set up the first school for mining trainees in Rio Tinto (Spain).

The fall of the Western Roman Empire was accompanied also by a decline of mining engineering, and it is made clear only seldom that Roman mining engineering and – increasingly – Islamic knowledge were conserved and passed on by the mining and smelting industries of Central Europe. The over 1000 year-old mining activities of the Rammelsberg in the Lower Harz give manifest evidence of this fact. After a period of flourish, during which German mining specialists in particular

Reversible wheel (R)
In the 15th century, the reversible wheel was developed for shaft hoisting purposes. It was a water wheel installed in surface as well as in underground water wheel stations. The wheel had a double bucket rim, so that the direction of rotation could be changed by directing the water flow to one or the other. The wheel master could vary the speed by regulation of the water flow and by means of a brake acting on the wheel rim.

were highly in demand in the neighbouring countries (Italy, France), the mining industry stagnated, locally even broke down completely, in the 13th and 14th century.

The rising demand for silver, copper and tin, above all, led to ever-deeper galleries, shafts and faces. As a consequence, the problem of mine drainage grew steadily and had to be coped with, but couldn't be resolved with the technical means of that time.

The Renaissance brought about a new boom. Middle-class pioneers, eager for innovation, intervened actively in industrial production. The most eminent written evidence of Renaissance mining is doubtless the work of Georg Agricola (1494–1554) of Glauchau, Saxony.

Reference must be made here to the Tyrolian mining activities, and particularly to those of Schwaz in the Lower Inn Valley. About 1520, there were about 50000 miners working in the mines, of which 10000 were in Schwaz alone. Power-political interests of the Hapsburg dynasty met with economic interest of foreign investors (Fugger) at the silver mines of Schwaz.

The particular social position of the miners appeared above all in legal respects. As early as the Middle Ages, the particular working and production conditions had led to individual, regionally different codifications of general mining law. The interest of the landlords and liege lords brought the miners privileges which no other class of that time – except for nobility and clergy – owned. In many districts, miners got exemption from taxes, and in the parish churches of Schwaz and Rattenberg they were allowed liturgical places of honour in the miners' nave.

Pit bank and man engine, 19th century (M, D)
The shaft is divided into a hoisting compartment and a ladder compartment. The filled ore skips are set down on the pit bank at the upper end of the hoisting department and then discharged into the wagons. The ladder compartment is divided into platforms with ladders for the miners descending into or ascending from the mine. In 1833, Georg Dörell developed the man engine, two wooden beams with foot boards and handles, moving in opposite direction. By changing beams, the miner could either reach the working spot or come out to daylight.

After the end of the Thirty Years' War, mining was in a desolate state. Where any mining activities were still carried on, the struggle for survival began. The war-time demand for iron and non-ferrous metals had dropped off; the prices fell. Technical innovation couldn't be expected at that time.

Though several attempts to develop new techniques of drainage, mechanical hoisting etc. had been made at the end of the 17th century (among others, the names of Gottfried Wilhelm Leibniz and Christian Huygens are to be mentioned here), their practical usefulness mostly fell short of the theoretical expectations.

The introduction of the blasting techniques and the use of steam engines brought about new advances in mining. This progress was continued by the introduction of the steel cable (Wilhelm August Julius Albert, 1834), of the track railways for haulage and of the electrical mining locomotive (1882). However, it must be kept in mind that work at the mine did not yet correspond to the requirements of a new era. Child labour in English mines still concerned Parliament in 1844.

During the second half of the 19th century, there was a rapid rise of technical achievements in mining. A few examples: double shafts – one for hoisting and one for ventilation; brick and concrete lining; introduction of metal roof support; the development of safety lamps; the use of electric energy and compressed-air techniques; the cutting and stripping methods and many others.

Information on the Exhibition

The Mining Department is one of the largest collections of the Deutsches Museum and is divided into 3 sections: Mining engineering in the proper sense with sections like shaft sinking, shaft hoisting, mine safety etc.; the mines with displays on the mining of ore, salt and coal; and a third section with mining machinery, ore preparation and coal treatment. The arrangement of the mines is very complicated, so that there is no guided tour indicated in the map. It is accessible from the spiral staircase leading down from the Surface Mining section. Unfortunately, because of the stairs, a visit with wheelchairs or prams is not possible. The tour, following the guide-line, takes about 45 minutes. Because of guided visits, the entrance may be closed twice a day for about an hour.

Shaft Sinking

In order to run a mine, it is necessary at first to make the deposit accessible from the surface. This is achieved either by horizontal *galleries* or by vertical *shafts.*

Exceptionally, even inclined shafts are laid out. There are winding, ventilation, man and material shafts. One of the oldest devices of its kind is the trepan device, Kind-Chaudron type, of 1914. Though shaft sinking is nowadays done with bigger and modern machinery, the proven jack-hammers and blasting operations are still required in many cases. In

Manual shaft sinking, about 1925 (M)
In solid rock, compressed-air hammer drills are used to sink the shaft bottom. The broken material (as well as the miners) are lifted to the surface in skips. Steam-operated sinking pumps provide for shaft drainage.

Ore transport by barges in the Ernst August tunnel (adit) of the Upper Harz iron ore mines, in a depth of 364 m, 1835–1892 (M)
With the penetration of underground mining into greater depths, the problem of water drainage increased. The solution was found in drainage by adits which were advanced from valley cuts towards the ore lodes. The Ernst August adit with its length of 26 km was the longest drainage adit of that time and was also used for ore transport by barges hand-pulled along a rope put up under the back of the gallery.

Pit bottom with skip winder and electric car decking device, 1925 (R)
The pit bottom is called the transloading place of the mined ore from haulage to hoisting. A decking device pushes the filled cars into the hoisting cage, and thereby the empty cars out of the cage to the opposite side of the pit bottom. The scene shown here is a reproduction of the former Klenze shaft in the coal mine of Hausham, at a depth of 750 m.

order to ensure stability and to avoid water inflow, shafts are lined with cast-iron rings (tubbings), masonry or concrete. Successful shaft boring presupposes water drainage. The model of a Thomson water-raising device is an example of early mechanization.

Shaft Hoisting

Winding (of material) and (man) *haulage* were strenuous and time-consuming in the early periods of mining. First steps towards mechanization and – simultaneously – humanization were taken in the 15th century, with water-power used as source of energy. The invention of the *reversible wheel* for material hoisting and – considerably later – of the *man engine* for men hoisting eased the miner's work.

The level of hoisting techniques around 1925 is demonstrated by the reconstruction of a pit bottom in 720 m depth, taken from the Klenze shaft of the Upper Bavarian coal mine of Hausham. At several levels, the mine cage takes in the filled cars pushed into the cage one-by-one by a decking device. Simultaneously, an empty car is pushed out of the cage at the opposite side.

Mine illumination; naked-light lamps; safety lamps
The earliest lights used in mines were pine torches. Small earthen vessels for the burning of vegetable and animal oils and fats followed, and locally different lamp shapes developed in the course of time. New materials like bronze, brass and iron were used for them, but their luminosity remained insufficient and the risk of firedamp explosions increased with the spreading of mining activities. In 1815, Sir Humphry Davy and George Stephenson created the first handy safety lamp, of which many improved versions followed. The most common type of mine lamps used today is the electric storage-battery light attached to the miner's helmet.

Mine surveying with the miner's compass and the graduated arc (M)
From the early 17th until the 19th century, the most important means of mine surveying were the hanging compass and the graduated arc. Both instruments were hung on a taut cord going from a point of known height (altitude) and position to another point, the position of which has to be measured. This is how the term *hanging compass* originated.

Working with mallets and iron chisels in an iron ore mine (R)
The strain of mining work before the invention of modern methods appears in a scene showing a miner driving a tunnel with mallet and chisel. Historic documents prove that the rate of advance in solid rock was about 10 m per man per year.

Ore Mining, Mine Surveying, Mine Safety

Walking past a number of mining tools, used by miners in prehistoric and modern times, and several different *models of ore mines* of the 19th century, the visitor reaches a section which gives a survey of historic extraction and tunneling methods.

Ore extraction by *fire-setting* is demonstrated here, as well as a *water-raising device* of the 16th century. Ore *transportation* by *barges* was a transport type especially common in the Harz mines, where drainage adits – like the Ernst August adit near Clausthal, reconstructed here – were the prerequisites.

The winning of galena, black jack, copper pyrite with feldspar and quartz as dike rock is shown by a scene illustrating overhead stoping in steep seams.

The subsequent items explain the work of the *mine surveyor* (surveying engineer), mine *ventilation* and *drainage* and the evolution of *rescue and resuscitation devices* as well as of *miners' lamps*.

Salt Mining

This section begins with the reconstruction of a natural and of an artificially contained *salt spring* and with the model of the well house of Bad Reichenhall.

An insight into *spraying pumps* and *sumpworks* explains how salt can be released from underground beds by means of water and pumped to the surface as brine with a salt content of 26%. During the 18th century, however, salt was also mined by *room-and-pillar work* at Wieliczka near Cracow. The very pure rock salt found there was marketed in blocks or barrels without further processing.

Through a reconstructed *extraction chamber of a potash mine of the Southern Harz,* of about 1925, the way leads to a film projection room designed like a tunnel of the Hattorf potash mine.

Coal Mining

The section of *coal mines* begins with a display on pitch coal extraction in Upper Bavaria around the turn of the century. Coal production had started there in the 16th century and ended in 1971. The seams, 70 cm thick, were mined by hand. The roof support was made from wooden props. *Pit ponies* pulled eight to ten mine carts to the pit bottom. The explanation of mining techniques about 1955 starts with an engine room

Blast-hole drilling in potassium salt room-work, 1925 (R)
In 1861, shortly after Justus von Liebig had discovered the value of potash salts for agricultural fertilization, the development of the potash industry started. Where the salt deposits are level, the extraction method is room-work, which leaves quadrate pillars to support the rock mass. The extraction method still prevailing today in German salt mines is drilling and blasting.

Trolley mine locomotive by Siemens & Halske, Berlin, 1883 (O)
The first trolley locomotive for haulage was put into service in 1882, in the colliery of
Zaukeroda near Dresden. Only one year later, in September 1883, the trolley locomotive of 7,5 kW capacity – now on display in the Deutsches Museum – was set in operation in the hard coal mine of Cons. Paulus Hohenzollern at Beuthen in Upper Silesia.
The tramming distance was 750 m. The trains consisted of 15 wagons, each of a capacity of 55 kg. Thus haulage was increased to 50 tons of coal per hour.

for *blindshaft hoisting,* i.e. hoisting in a shaft connecting the single levels, but not reaching to the surface.
Compressed air is the dominant form of drive used for the subsequent
rotary percussive drilling of blast holes in tunnel-driving as well as in the
presentation of *overhead shovel loader.*
Another scene illustrates coal extraction in *steep seams,* i.e. stepwise by
pneumatic picks. The subsequent *road on a lower level* with flexible steel
arch support primarily gives an idea of the difficult working conditions
in *thin coal seams.* In addition to a storage-battery locomotive, a tipping
device for the backfilling of a worked-out face and a blindshaft loading
station can be seen there. In a *flat seam,* coal is precut by a compressed-
air coal cutter, breaks down because of the rock pressure, is shovelled
onto a retarding disk conveyor and slips down to the pit bottom.
The beginning of modern extraction methods is demonstrated at a flat
coal seam of 2 m in thickness. A *coal plough,* i.e. a gliding machine fitted
with picks, is pulled to and fro along the coal face by electric winches
and cuts off some 8 to 10 cm during each operation. The coal above

then breaks down by its own weight and rock pressure. Owing to its ploughshare shape, the coal plough slides the broken coal onto a *double-chain conveyor* which passes it on to a conveyor belt. Both conveyor and plough are pressed against the coal front by compressed-air cylinders. The roof support consists of flexible *steel props* with wedge locks. At the rear part of the face is a *hydraulic support.* The coal mine ends with a display on *pneumatic stowing.* Small-sized refuse (dead rock) is blown through a pipe into the worked-out fields. Roof-fall-exploitation is shown near the hydraulic support; this method, however, is used only in great depths, where no damage due to mining may be expected.

Modern Mining

In the last 30 years, mining has developed into a high tech branch of the economy. In many areas today, extraction and processing are fully automated. In order to put the large and heavy machines needed for this work into operation, it was necessary to enlarge the traffic and transportation routes – the roadways. With this enlargement, the miners received a working environment that was brighter, clearer and safer, and that had little in common with the narrow, dark underground workings of earlier times. The introduction of modern technology into mining increased the productivity per man and shift by 3 to 4 times.

Roadway drivage with a roadheading machine, 1981 (O)
Roadways form the traffic and transportation routes underground, and are driven either by blasting or by machine. Roadway drivage with a roadheading machine protects the mountain because unnecessary loosening is avoided.

Baum jig for coal (M, P)
Test jig by Schüchtermann & Kremer-Baum AG, 1952. Raw coal still has a considerable content of rock material which has to be separated from it. Water is used for separation and set into vertical motion by a pulsing air stream. The lighter material, i.e. coal, is thus lifted and brought to an overflow, whereas the heavy rock material sinks down to the bottom of the jig where it flows to a separate reject gate.

Extraction and Haulage

In this room, the evolution of rotary, churn, percussion and hammer drills, of pick hammers, pit props, mine carts, cutting machines and rams can be followed. One of the highlights of this exhibition is one of the first electric trolley locomotives set into practical operation in 1883. Various models of shaft hoisting devices and extraction methods complete the displays.

Ore Dressing

The products obtained by mining are raw materials. They have to be separated from dead rock by classification and sorting in order to be ready for further metallurgical processing or for use as energy supply (coal). The Ore Treatment section illustrates the evolution of implements and plants, showing such items as the basin of a gold washer or a centrifuge for the mining of salt, other original models which can be set into motion and dioramas.

Coal Treatment

In the room dedicated to *coal treatment,* the theme of coal as an energy source and raw material is dealt with in its manifold variations. The possible use of hard coal and lignite, from the production of brown coal briquettes to coal gasification, fluid-bed firing and up to the most recent type of flue gas desulphurization, is explained here.

W. Kretzler

Metallurgy

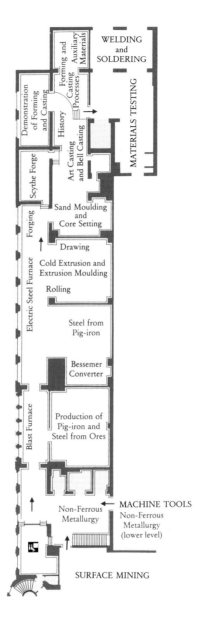

The great importance of metals in the history of civilization is reflected by the names given to entire historic eras in accordance with the metals mainly used then, e.g. Bronze Age, Iron Age. The utilization of metals is unrivalled in its significance for cultural development. Thus the improvement of letterpress printing by Johannes Gutenberg of Mainz, achieved after the year 1400, was made possible only by mass production of cast printing letters made of alloys of tin and zinc with a low melting point.

The first known metals were probably gold and copper, occurring in pure form; they were worked into jewelry and decorative items (some finds are about 7000 years old). The production of larger metal parts from gold or copper was possible only after the invention of pottery, which made fireproof crucibles for melting and casting available.

The beginnings of metal extraction from ores are unknown to us. The oldest traces of smelting processes date back to 6000 years ago. The Egyptians reduced malachite from the Sinai Mountain to copper, using shaft furnaces of about 1 m in height and charcoal. Copper was the first metal used by man to a large extent. By simultaneous melting of oxidic tin or zinc ores, the first tin bronzes were produced some 5000 years ago, and the first brass production took place about 4000 years ago. The first extraction of iron from ores, about 4000 years ago, is ascribed to the Hittites in Asia Minor. The historic extraction methods were based upon experience; the recipes were often carefully kept secrets and passed on from generation to generation.

The ore had to be transformed in a way unintelligible to man. Since it was possible to produce only relatively low temperatures up to 1100 °C, metallurgy was limited to metals occurring in solid form, like gold, silver, copper and mercury, and easily reducible oxides of the elements copper, lead, antimony and iron.

The evolution of analytic chemistry, about 200 years ago, and of physical chemistry, about 100 years ago, was the basis for a scientific approach in metallurgy. Towards the end of the 19th century, the distinction between iron and steel metallurgy and non-ferrous metallurgy, familiar in our times, was introduced. The iron and steel industry, producing larger quantities, required a highly differentiated professional training.

Today, there are two widely differing ore-extraction principles: pyrometallurgy works with high temperatures, and hydrometallurgy uses chemical solution and precipitation processes at low temperatures (up to about 300 °C). The link between these two processes is fusion electrolysis, used for aluminium production, for example. Pyrometallurgical and hydrometallurgical processes can be distinguished in metal extraction and refining just as with ore enrichment.

Whereas the production of iron will probably remain a field reserved exclusively for pyrometallurgy (the metal is mostly extracted in liquid form), the non-ferrous metallurgy increasingly gives room to hydrometallurgy (solution of the metals by acids or lyes with subsequent recovery by wet chemical or wet electrolytic processes).

Information on the Exhibition

The department of metallurgy is divided into the following sections: non-ferrous metallurgy, iron and steel metallurgy, forming methods and finally forming and casting.

The non-ferrous metallurgy section begins in the basement, as a continuation of the guide-line through the departments of mining, ore dressing and coal treatment. On the ground floor, a film projection room gives a general introduction to the iron and steel metallurgy section.

In its first room, the iron and steel metallurgy section presents the production of pig-iron and sponge iron, in the second room, steel production from pig-iron and scraps, and in the third room, forming processes.

The forming and casting section shows fundamental historic and present-day methods; twice a day, presentations by the Museum's staff illustrate casting practice.

Non-ferrous Metallurgy

The extracting of non-ferrous metals from the raw materials generally takes place in two steps: reduction to the raw material, and its refining to a purity degree of 99%, mostly even 99,9% or more.

Heat, chemical or electric energy is needed for these steps. Preparatory metallurgical processes used for sulphur-bearing ores are enrichment, roasting (oxidising or sulphating) and sintering.

Metallurgy is continued on the ground floor with a display on the extraction methods in use at the time of Agricola (16th century) in a parting, refining and smelting room.

The Freiberg assaying furnace or Plattner's furnace (19th century) and some samples illustrate the methods used for the determination of noble metal contents in minerals.

Sectional models of electrolytic cells demonstrate the production of aluminium and magnesium.

A graduated bank shows the various forms in which the products of metallurgical plants are marketed.

Roasting, 16th century (Di)
The metals bound to sulphur in pyritiferous ores require an additional preparatory process to enrichment: roasting. In the 16th century, the comminuted ore was heated in heaps and sheds to a temperature beneath the melting point. The uncontrolled escape of calcination gases with their content of sulphur dioxide seriously damaged the surrounding vegetation.

Metallurgy of the 16th century: parting room (R)
The lightened silver, i.e. the gold-bearing raw silver obtained by cupellation, was separated into pure silver and gold by the nitric acid process, i.e. by *quartation,* developed at Goslar in 1493. Silver was dissolved into silver nitrate by the nitric acid (aqua fortis); a fine gold mud remained and was melted in the crucible.

Iron and Steel Metallurgy

The transformation of iron from ore to semi-finished steel products is explained in its historic evolution and in the following production steps: extraction of pig-iron, steel production and forming. Frequent fundamental terms such as iron, ferrous products and steel are explained here:

Iron is the name of the element Fe and of the working material with a degree of purity between 99,8 and 99,9% Fe; ferrous products are all metal alloys, the average iron percentage weight of which is higher than that of all other elements;

steel includes all ferrous products which are generally suitable for hot forming; steel has a maximum carbon content of about 2% (except for some steels with rich chrome contents);

pig-iron and cast-iron have a carbon content of over 2% approximately; they can be formed only by casting.

Production of Pig-Iron and Iron Sponge

Historical displays of bloomery fires and the evolution of furnaces lead to the blast furnace processes and their products.

The extraction of liquid pig-iron from ores takes place in the blast furnace by *reduction* (separation of oxygen from iron) with coke. In the steel works, the liquid pig-iron is refined to steel by means of oxygen (decrease of carbon and other unwanted admixtures to defined percentages). The product of direct reduction is iron sponge in solid form, from which steel is melted in electric steel plants. The dominant manufacturing sequence, blast furnace – oxygen blowing steel works – continuous casting, is completed by the secondary line, direct reduction – electric steel plant – continuous casting.

Production of Steel from Pig-Iron and Scraps
Refining hearths and puddling works produce steel in a pasty form, called *wrought iron.*
Steel in liquid state, called *ingot steel,* is the product of the Bessemer, Martin-Siemens, Thomas and crucible steel processes.
The distinction between wrought iron and ingot steel become obsolete with the disappearance of puddling works (early 20th century). Today steel is produced by electric or oxygen steel-making plants.

Forming

Modern classification of forming processes is based upon the active strains in the deformation zone (forming under compressive, tensile and compressive, tensile conditions, by bending and under shearing conditions). In this room, forging, rolling and drawing prevail.

Forging has the longest tradition. In the beginnings, the blacksmiths were also miners, charcoal burners and melters. Opendie or drop forging, using hammers or presses, was done.

Rolling is the dominant forming process today; over 90% of the world's entire raw steel production undergo plastic deformation by hot-rolls.

Bloomery fire of the Siegerland, La Tène period, after 500 B.C. (Di)
Since 500 B.C., in order to extract forgeable iron and steel from rich manganiferous iron ores, the Celts used numerous bloomery fires with natural drought on the heights and slopes of the Siegerland. In shaft furnaces of about 1,7 m height, alternating layers of charcoal and comminuted ore were charged on a charcoal fire. The daily output was about 25 kg of bloomery iron and steel.

Bessemer converter, 1874 (O)
In 1855, Henry Bessemer
(1813–1898) was awarded a patent
for his process which blows air into
liquid pig-iron and thus converts it to
steel. This was the beginning of large-
scale steel production. The converter
on display here worked for 30 years.
The charge weight was 6,5 tons.
Blowing took 14 minutes, the complete melting process 25 minutes.
After 20 to 24 melting operations, the
bottom had to be replaced.

Blast furnace and hot blast stove, 1951 (M)
The main product of the blast furnace is pig-iron extracted from the ores by refining
and melting. The sectional model shows the construction type of a blast furnace and of
a hot blast stove, the flow chart in the shaft visualizes the processes. Two to five hot
blast stoves are connected with each blast furnace and preheat the combustion air for
the ore reduction and melting processes to about 1200 °C.

Scythe forge from the Black Forest, of about 1800 (O)
The many steps of scythe manufacture are illustrated by samples. The hammer is of the tail hammer type, belonging to the chop hammers, just like front hammers and tilt hammers. The turning arbor of the hammer, mostly driven by an undershot water wheel, was fitted with cams depressing the hammer end with a reinforcement ring.

Drawing has a long history in wire production. The most common products of modern drawing are wires, bars of round or profiled cross-section and pipes.

Moulding and Casting

Casting produces geometrically designed parts with defined properties. Besides forging, casting probably is the most ancient production method (known for more than 5000 years) which reached a high standard of quality very early.

Today the manifold moulding and casting techniques are called archetypes.
F. Frisch

Welding and Soldering

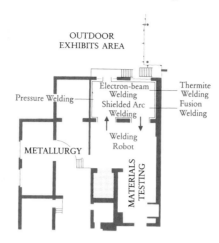

Welding and soldering belong to jointing techniques, thus to the few rare production techniques particularly subject to the law of rapid change. They can look back to a long historic evolution, while their importance is still growing today. The origins of jointing techniques date back to the Stone Age.

About 6000 years ago, the Egyptians already used forge welding in meteoric iron processing. About 3400 B.C., lead welding was first practised in Mesopotamia in the production of pipes and receptacles and then brought to perfection by the Romans who manufactured lead pipes of standardized formats. This process fell into oblivion and was rediscovered only in the 13th century.

It can be proved that the art of soldering is at least 5200 years old, probably even older, and preserved up to our times. Around the year 1580 B.C., an important invention for soldering and casting techniques came from Egypt: the blast apparatus. Thus the melting and soldering processes could be simplified and accelerated.

The earliest example of cast welding is the so-called repair casting process, used after 1500 B.C. for the repair of bronze items in Europe, which reached its culmination in the 9th century. Cold-press welding was first practised in Ireland, around the year 800 B.C., in gold and silver sheet processing, but the first written mention of this process by Andreas Libavius only goes back to 1597 A.D.

Early masterpieces of welding techniques which deserve to be mentioned are forge welding of platinum-gold alloys (500 B.C. to 500 A.D.), the welding of steel strips of different carbon contents into damascene blades (300 A.D.) and the production of enormous guns with barrels of 5 m in length from welded iron bars (15th century).

After the middle of the 19th century, soldering and welding developed in an impressive way. Autogenous welding with a hydrogen-air mixture was invented by E. Desbassayns de Richemont in 1838, with an oxy-acetlyene flame by Edmond Fouché in 1901.

Cast welding of cast-iron was first practised in Belgium (1860). Resistance welding goes back to Elihu Thomson (1867) who also introduced the upset welding process. In 1885, the arc welding method was practised by Nicolas von Benardos, and in 1899, thermite welding by Hans Goldschmidt.

Whereas the welding activities were mainly focused on gas welding until 1910, arc welding developed after the introduction of alternating current and three-phase current.

In 1930, inert gas shielded arc welding was invented, and submersed welding ten years later. After the end of the Second World War, big and complicated machine bodywork, which so far had been cast from gray iron, were mostly manufactured by electric welding. The weight of machinery could be reduced, rigidity and bending stiffness, however, increased. In machine tool manufacturing, the so-called "light construction" had been introduced fifteen years earlier.

From 1950 to 1970, more special welding techniques were developed: friction welding, plasma welding and laser-beam welding.

Information on the Exhibition

During the past eighty years, several hundred welding processes have been developed, of which about fifty are of major importance now. A small selection of the most important processes and devices is on display here.

Soldering

Soldering is a method used for the joining of metal working materials by means of a molten binder, the *solder*, and flux, protective gases or vacuum conditions if necessary.

Soldering makes it possible to join different, even non-metallic working materials, keeping the required heat energy and the distortion of the parts to be jointed low. Further, soldering allows secured jointing of completely different parts and – in many cases – automatization of the work. Disadvantages of soldering are, among others, little strength of soft solder joints, increased corrosion risk, drop of solidity with high temperatures and unwanted flux inclusions.

The items on display in the *soldering* section are presented to the visitors in a big showcase.

Welding

Welding is the jointing of metallic work materials under heat or pressure, or heat and pressure, with or without addition of a working material of the same type, with equal or nearly equal melting point. Fusion welding and pressure welding are distinguished by the pasty or molten state of the weld.

In fusion welding, a flame of fuel gas and oxygen or an electric arc is used to heat the area of the joint and melt the weld metal. The joint is obtained by the flow of the molten substance, without pressure.

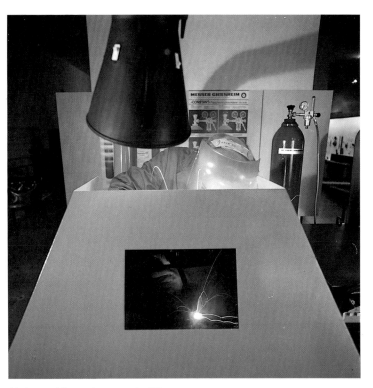

Modern welding equipment, 1985 (O)
During the guided visits, shielded arc welding by the TIG and MIG-MAG welding processes is demonstrated. Through a transparent pane, the arc may be safely observed.

In pressure welding, the joint is obtained under pressure, or under pressure and electric heat, mostly without additional weld. In this section, the visitor can study the function and characteristics of both welding processes by means of various items, partly in working condition. Welded workpieces on the boards show the different types of welded seams.

Flame-cutting

In autogenous flame-cutting, the iron content of the steel is burnt to iron oxide and subsequently blown away from the cut gap by the pressure of the oxygen jet.

Cuttable by flame-cutting are all unalloyed and low-alloy steel types, whereas high-alloy steel types, grey cast-iron and non-ferrous metals can be separated only by special thermal processes.

In the Deutsches Museum, flame-cutting is demonstrated by means of a hand-operated flame-cutter in working condition.

K. Allwang

Materials Testing

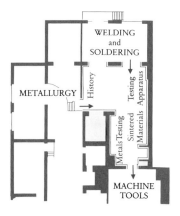

The fields of materials testing are the testing and improvement of new materials, defect detecting in metallurgy, the investigation into cases of damage and fundamental research in the theoretical science of the strength of materials. In accordance with the properties to be determined or with the methods applied, a distinction is made between destructive and non-destructive tests.

Materials testing has been known since man started shaping tools from stones, about 100000 years ago. About 2300 years ago, it was given scientific principles by Archimedes, the Greek mathematician and scientist, who referred to the properties of materials in order to verify the purity of a gold crown. The next known experiments date back to the 15th and 16th century and are therefore nearly 1800 years younger: Leonardo da Vinci's wire strength test and Galileo Galilei's bending test of unilaterally clamped beams.

In the context of further investigation into this field, the following names occur: Robert Hooke, who formulated the law of force and deformation in 1678; Charles Augustin de Coulomb, who gave in 1776 the correct formula for bending stress; A. Duleua, who determined the modulus of elasticity of wrought iron in 1812; and Louis-Marie-Henri Navier, who – nine years later – established the general equations of the elasticity theory.

About 1850, Johann Ludwig Werder constructed a materials testing machine, and in 1856 August Wöhler started fatigue tests in order to determine the behaviour of working materials under continuous stresses and vibrations. He himself designed the necessary apparatus. In 1871, the *Königlich Mechanisch-Technische Versuchsanstalt,* a forerunner of the *Bundesanstalt für Materialprüfung* of today, was founded in Berlin, and in 1900 Georg Chapry carried out the first notched bar impact bending test. In the same year, Johan August Brinell presented a process of hardness testing, named after him, at the Paris World's Fair. The hardness testing method by S.P. Rockwell was developed in 1908, the one by Vickers-Armstrong Ltd. in 1925.

About 1930, S. Sokolow and O. Mühlhäuser introduced testing by ultra-sonics, and the first practical apparatus for x-ray testing appeared on the market.

Information on the Exhibition

In accordance with the importance of metallic materials testing, a considerable number of testing apparatus, samples and displays are shown here. One part of the exhibit is of particular interest from the historical point of view, e.g. the tensile fatigue testing machine by August Wöhler, of 1860; another part includes machines presently used in industrial plants, e.g. the universal testing machine UEDE 40, of 1974. Except for some historic items, all testing machines are still in working condition and can be demonstrated, if there is a sufficient number of interested visitors.

K. Allwang

Tensile fatigue testing machine by August Wöhler, 1860 (O)
This machine is one of four originals by August Wöhler in possession of the Deutsches Museum. By means of these machines, Wöhler carried out the tests preceding the formulation of his laws on the endurance of materials.

Machine Tools

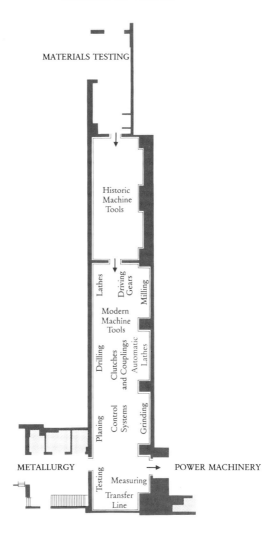

MATERIALS TESTING

Historic Machine Tools

Lathes

Driving Gears

Milling

Modern Machine Tools

Drilling

Clutches and Couplings

Automatic Lathes

Planing

Control Systems

Grinding

METALLURGY

POWER MACHINERY

Testing

Measuring

Transfer Line

Large-scale production of utility articles and consumer goods seems a matter of course in our times. Only a small percentage of the world's population knows that all necessary goods must first be manufactured, using in some way – directly or indirectly – tools and machine tools. There has been a long period of evolution, from the work of aboriginal man done with his bare hand, to the first implements shaped to fit into his hand, and finally to what we call today *tools*.

In the beginning, things found in nature were shaped and improved according to the purpose they served; only much later in history, compound devices followed and became the forerunners of machines. Probably the first machine tool – a drilling device set in rotary motion by a fiddle bow – was constructed about 6000 years ago. Lathes and other simple machines followed and were gradually improved over several thousand years.

During expeditions of conquest, migrations of nations, voyages of discovery and trade activities, experiences were exchanged to some extent. This is why it is impossible to indicate today when and where all the machine elements invented up to the middle ages first turned up in the individual machine tools. Not until about 1500 A.D. are we informed more exactly, by means of technical drawings, of new achievements completing and improving machine tools.

In most history books, the steam engine, invented around 1700 and improved several times in the same year, is considered to have been fundamental to the industrial revolution of the 19th century and to the evolution of industrial society. However, a closer examination of the historic evolution of the new power engine shows that only part of the revolutionary changes in production methods and social structures of the past century were accelerated by the construction and utilization of steam engines. A share of at least equal importance in the change and in the abandoning of manual production methods, as well as in social life, has to be ascribed to machine tools.

It was only by fundamental improvement of drilling machines and lathes as well as by the invention of new machine tools in the second half of the 19th century that it became possible to achieve the precision necessary for the further evolution of the steam engine and to produce interchangeable machine parts in large numbers. In our century, the whole field of machine tool manufacture experienced two revolutionary innovations:

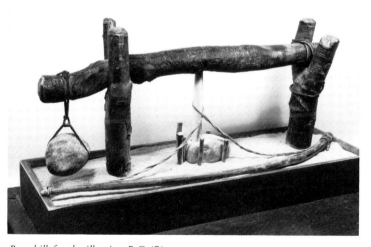

Bow drill, fourth millennium B. C. (R)
During the Neolithic period, in the 4th millennium B.C., an astonishing number of improved drilling operations can be recognized from findings. About the turn of the century, after the study of individual findings and drilling tests, Robert Forrer designed and tested a device which corresponds to the main features of the present construction. It consists of two wooden posts and of a stone-weighted crossbeam which keeps the bone drill fixed and produces the necessary drill pressure. A fiddle-bow provides the drive.

View of the Historic Machine Tools Section
In the front, the oldest lathe preserved in Germany (about 1810) can be seen next to a screw press (1855); behind: a surface lathe (1830).

1. The group drive with its innumerable belts, exclusively used until about 1930, disappeared with the introduction of single drive. Gradually, every single machine was equipped with its own electric motor, later on with a hydraulic or pneumatic motor.

2. In 1950, NC machine tools with numerical – mainly punched-tape operated – control were introduced to the market in the United States. After 1955, they rapidly spread in Europe. With this control system, a change in machine tool manufacture set in, replacing more and more men in machine operation and direct control of the production steps. All types of machine tools, such as single purpose, multi-purpose and special-purpose machines, transfer lines and machining centres, were taken over by electric control. It is not yet foreseeable, which machine construction types will successfully use microprocessors for operations control.

Information on the Exhibition

In this section, the machine tools are grouped exclusively by the type of drive used: *Historic* machines have one main line shaft in common and are set in operation by a back gear. *Modern* machines have a separate drive assembly.

Historic Machine Tools

Point of departure is the replica of an Egyptian relief of the fourth millennium B.C. It shows a drill set in rotary motion by a fiddle-bow. Around this central point, the groups of turning, planing, milling machines and machines used for gear production, all of the past century, are arranged. Most of the machines are connected to the main line shaft by a back gear and thus in working condition. Four dioramas illustrate the evolution of lathes and drills over a period of more than a thousand years.

Modern Machine Tools

Modern machine tools are distinguished by a rigid, vibration-free construction, high dimensional stability and power; qualities which – together with the introduction of carbide and ceramic tips – made possible a two-hundredfold increase of cutting rates during the past hundred years. Because of the limited space available and because of the problem of weight only a modest selection of the manifold recent cutting and non-cutting machine tools can be shown here. The same aspect has also determined the selection of bits, chucking tools, gear mechanisms, coupling and clutch types and control systems.

Whereas interested visitors can study the functions of the machine elements "driving gears" and "couplings" by playing with them, it is not allowed to manipulate the precious machinery.

K. Allwang

View of the Modern Machine Tools Section
In the front, there are several pumps with mechanical and hydraulic drive; at left, in the rear, a recent upright radial drill. Along part of the central passageway and the wall opposite, lathes of different construction types are arranged. The rear end is formed by milling and planing machines with mechanical and numerical control (which do not appear clearly on the picture).

Power Machinery

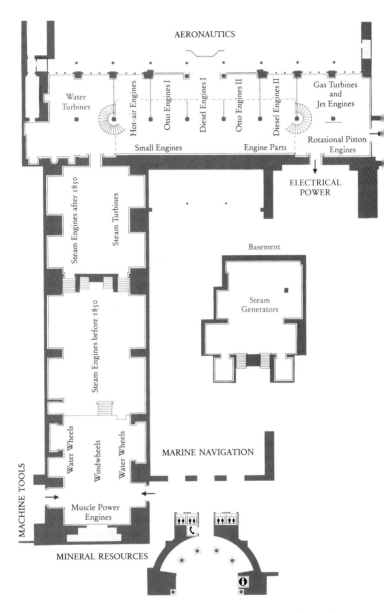

Water Turbines

Hot-air Engines

Otto Engines I

Diesel Engines I

Otto Engines II

Diesel Engines II

Gas Turbines and Jet Engines

Small Engines

Engine Parts

Rotational Piston Engines

ELECTRICAL POWER

Steam Engines after 1850

Steam Turbines

Basement

Steam Generators

Steam Engines before 1850

Water Wheels

Windwheels

Water Wheels

MARINE NAVIGATION

MACHINE TOOLS

Muscle Power Engines

MINERAL RESOURCES

Power Engines convert various forms of energy to mechanical energy, so that it can be used for technical purposes, normally in the form of rotary motion.

Our modern life is inconceivable without power engines. Just think of the enormous turbines in the power stations which produce electric current by means of generators; of the jet engines which enable modern aircraft to bridge even the longest distances in a minimum of time; or of the engines making the work in industrial and manufacturing plants, in agriculture and in private households easier. And finally, who would want to be without the car – despite environmental pollution and other disadvantages – which is also driven by a power engine, the internal combustion engine? The number of 450 million automotive vehicles – that is the figure 1984 statistics gave for worldwide circulation – is self-explanatory. It is, however, easily forgotten that muscle power of man and animals was the most important form of energy for thousands of years. Muscle power transported the goods, on land and sea, drove machine tools and other machinery; mining and agriculture practically depended entirely upon it. The labour for the muscle power engine, unworthy of man and sustained by slaves and bondmen over long periods, is still present in our modern idiom of "working at the old treadmill".

Utilization of water power was the first step away from the treadmill. Without regard to the scoop wheels, first mentions of water wheels, which drove corn mills in Rome and in Asia, date back to the first century B.C. They spread very sluggishly – muscle power was very cheap at that time – and it took another millennium until they were introduced into manufacturing work and mills. On a large scale, water power has only been used in our century, in turbines. The second step away from the treadmill was made when man started to utilize wind power. In the Orient, this began approximately in the 7th century, and increasingly from the 11th century onward, in the Mediterranean area and at the coasts of Central Europe. Most of the machines driven by wind power were corn mills and water scoops. After the turn of the century, high-speed wind turbines, built in accordance with aerodynamic principles, were added to the low-speed wind wheels; in our times, further development of wind turbines is being encouraged with a view to their use in large wind-driven power plants.

About 250 years ago, the moment was reached when the rapidly growing energy demand could no longer be met by muscle, water or wind power. Moreover, water and wind power were not always available everywhere. Industrial plants designed to work by water power had only a limited choice of sites. Rather often, they had to install their plants near suitable water courses, far away from inhabited districts, and to transport their products to the consumers on bad roads. If the entire technological evolution was not to come to a standstill, it was necessary to discover new sources of energy and to develop new machines for their utilization.

Such a machine – or better: *the* machine of the 18th century – is the steam engine, which had a big share in the industrial revolution. The decisive step in steam engine construction was the invention of the condensor by James Watt in 1769. After this date, rapid progress towards machines of increasing capacity was made.

Compared to the piston steam engine, the steam turbine brought an improvement in the efficiency and of power per unit; the first successful steam turbines were developed in the eighties of the 19th century. Due to greater efficiency, the steam turbines have now completely replaced the piston steam engines.

The steam engine clearly favoured large-scale industrial plants, and its spreading prompted small manufacturers and craftsmen to demand a power engine suitable for their purposes. The hot-air engine, internal combustion engine and electromotor were developed not least to meet their requirements, and led to the common drive types of today, fitted to individual purposes.

Information on the Exhibition

As far as possible, this section shows closed groups of different machine types, arranged in the chronological order of their evolution.

Muscle Power Engines

The wedge, lever, pulley, shaft and wheel are simple devices which make possible a more efficient use of muscle power. Several such devices are combined in muscle power engines. The effects of such a combination can be demonstrated by the central exhibit of the *muscle power* section, a gin-driven mangle from a dye house of 1838 vintage. Around this exhibit, the typical representatives of muscle power engines are arranged in groups, partly as originals, partly as dioramas: *cage wheels, treadwheels* and *gins.*

Hydraulic Power Engines

Under this heading, the groups of *waterwheels, water column machines* and *water turbines* are on display. Because of the structural limitations, these groups had to be housed separately. Thus on your tour you will find the *water turbines* beyond the *steam power engines.*

Ox treadwheel, of about 1600 (Di)
Up until the early 19th century, such treadwheels drove corn mills in the Po basin. They were used because the fall of the Po river was not sufficient for the driving of water wheels.

Corn mill with wooden spoons, of about 1870 (O) This mill comes from Rumania. Spoon wheels are particularly suitable for small water quantities with high heads. This is why they were used mainly in mountain regions.

The first machines capable of transforming the power of flowing water into rotary motion were the *undershot waterwheels*. As *scoop wheels,* they have been constructed, nearly unchanged, for several thousand years. Even today, such waterwheels still operate on the Regnitz in Central Franconia. A model of a Franconian *scoop wheel* can be seen next to the entrance of the department.

Artificial water flow and constructive measures made it possible to increase the efficiency of *waterwheels.* This is exemplified by an *overshot wheel,* a *breast wheel* and a *waterwheel with spoons,* all three fitted in wall niches.

The *water column engines* form the transition – not only by their position – to the *piston steam engines.* Instead of steam, pressurized water drives the piston of the former to and fro in a cylinder. The dominant exhibit of this group is the *brine raising machine* constructed by Georg von Reichenbach in 1817.

Wind-driven Engines

The utilization of wind power started with ship's sail more than 5 000 years ago. The evolution of wind wheels can be traced back to the 7th century A.D. Initially, they were installed in a fixed position, oriented to the prevailing wind direction. Advanced techniques of construction allowed the wheels to always turn to the wind direction. Around the *high-speed wind wheel* of 1905, standing in the middle of the room, a series of models documents the essential evolutionary phases of wind wheels.

Steam Power Engines

In the following room, some steps below, the evolution of the steam engine up to about 1860 is shown. Models of the *steam pump,* which didn't have a piston and was developed by Thomas Savery in 1698, and of the *atmospheric steam engine* first built by Thomas Newcomen in 1711, make clear: the widespread belief that James Watt is the inventor

of the steam engine cannot be true. It is true, however, that the *double-acting industrial steam engine* with rotary motion, constructed by J. Watt in the 1780s, brought a decisive change in the world of labour. This room is dominated by an accurate reconstruction of the last-mentioned engine, a *beam steam engine* of 1813 placed on a masonry base, and by a *valve steam engine* by the Sulzer brothers, of 1865 vintage.

About the mid-nineteenth century, the steam engine had become common in everyday life. New methods of engineering, such as the accurate registration of thermodynamic processes, determined its further development. *Multiple expansion engines* made a more efficient use of steam pressure, and *high-speed engines* were used to drive electric generators directly.

At the dawn of the 20th century, the development of *piston steam engines* was practically completed when the internal combustion engines, electromotors and steam turbines started superseding them.

In the last room of the "historic" power engines hall, there are "perfected" piston steam engines and exhibits representing the *constant-pressure turbines* and *reaction turbines,* developed in the 1880s by Carl de Laval and by Charles Parsons respectively.

Water Turbines

The most efficient water power engines are the water turbines. They transform water power to driving energy with nearly no loss. The most important types in use today are *Pelton, Francis* and *Kaplan turbines.*

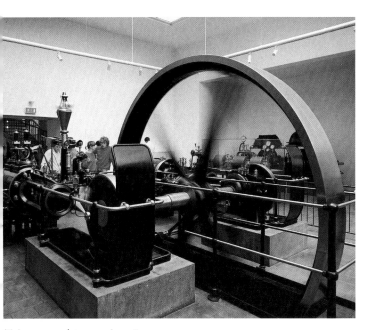

Twin compound steam engine, 1899
In this compound engine, the steam is used twice for work output: first, in the high-pressure cylinder, and, subsequently, in the low-pressure cylinder, which is of larger dimensions because of the steam's larger volume therein.

Pelton turbines are used for small water quantities and high falls. With these types, the fall is often more than 1 000 m in height. For medium falls, ranging from 20 to about 600 m in height, Francis turbines are used, and Kaplan turbines for small heights of fall up to 80 m and high flow rates.

The tour first leads you to the historic turbines and then to functional models and various running wheels which will familiarize you with the modern water turbines.

Runner of a Pelton turbine, 1930 (O)
Pelton turbines are especially suitable for use on water heads of 300 m or more. This runner operated in the power plant, Vermunt, of the Vorarlberger Illwerke AG from 1931 to 1952. With a fall of 700 m, a water flow of 4 m³/s and a turning rate of 500 m⁻¹, it produced 24.3 MW (33 000 PS).

Hot-air Engines

One result of the various attempts to find a suitable power engine for craftsmen is the *hot-air engine.* A decisive contribution to its development was made by John Ericsson, in the middle of the 19th century. Besides the steam engine, it is the earliest *heat engine;* compared to the steam engine, it had the advantage of working without a steam boiler, thus the severe and costly regulations for installation, operation and maintenance were not applicable.

Different engines of the open and the closed type, including a *Stirling engine* of 1953, show the development in the field of these engines.

Internal Combustion Engines

The combustion engine, too, resulted from the endeavour to offer a suitable power engine to craftsmen and trade.

In 1860, Jean Lenoir built the first useable *gas engine.* Seven years later, it was outdone by the much more efficient *atmospheric gas engine* con-

The first Diesel engine,
1897 (O)
In 1892, Rudolf Diesel started experiments with his engine. Only his third engine brought the desired success. The engine on display here was completed in 1897. It is considered to be the first Diesel engine.

structed by Nikolaus August Otto and Eugen Langen. Gas engine production was abandoned in 1876, when Otto started series production of his four-stroke engine which became the example for all later combustion engines.

The various classification terms used for engine types, such as petrol and diesel engine, fractional-horsepower and high-power engine, two-stroke and four-stroke engine or automobile engine and aero-engine, are often confusing to the lay mind. In principle, however, they all are much the same. First, the fuel-air mixture must be brought into a cylinder. There it is compressed and then ignited. The energy set free by the subsequent explosive combustion drives the piston.

It is common use to divide the engines roughly into *Otto engines, diesel engines* and *rotary piston engines;* thus they are grouped accordingly in this exhibition area.

Gas Turbines and Jet Engines

With both engine types, precompressed air is heated in combustion chambers. Then this air streams through a turbine. The turbine shaft is connected with an air compressor, in gas turbines also with the group to be driven, e.g. with a generator, a pump or the rotor blades of a helicopter. In a *jet engine,* the turbine only drives the compressor and a few auxiliary aggregates. The desired effect, i.e. the propulsion of an aircraft without propellers, is achieved by the recoil effect of the combustion gases streaming out of a propelling nozzle. The development of the gas turbine, which made only slow progress until the fourties of our century, was accelerated by the rapid wartime development of jet engines.

Gas turbines and jet turbines, the most recent types of power engines, form the end of the Power Machinery department which covers about 2 000 m² (square meters).

E. Rödl

Jet turbine engine Jumo 004 B, of 1944 (O)
The development of the 004 jet engine started in 1939. When the Jumo 004 B went into production, at the end of 1943, this marked the beginning of large-scale series production of jet engines.

Electric Power

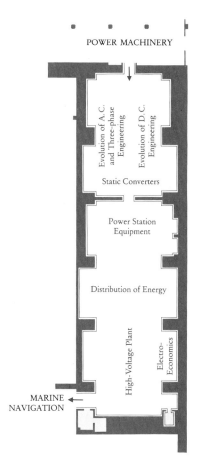

POWER MACHINERY

Evolution of A.C. and Three-phase Engineering

Evolution of D.C. Engineering

Static Converters

Power Station Equipment

Distribution of Energy

High-Voltage Plant

Electro-Economics

MARINE NAVIGATION

Electric power is generated almost exclusively by mechanically driven generators, i.e. by conversion of mechanical energy. The basic principle of this conversion was established by Michael Faraday in 1831, when he discovered the phenomena of electromagnetic induction.

In 1832, using steel magnets to produce the magnetic field, Hypolite Pixii built the first electric induction generator. Generators were improved during the following years; they were used to supply current for arc lamps and electroplating equipment, but it was not common yet to transmit electrical energy for driving purposes. The dynamo-electrical principle, discovered in 1866 almost simultaneously by Alfred Varley, Werner von Siemens and Charles Wheatstone, initiated heavy current engineering and – together with advances like laminating the armature, perfecting the collector, armature and field coils as well as improving the cooling system – led to the construction of powerful machinery.

After the development of practical incandescent bulbs by Joseph Wilson Swan and Thomas Alva Edison, the first power stations were built around 1880. They were situated in the centre of the district and supplied direct current. Later on, alternating current power stations and three-phase power stations were added. Since transformation of voltage was easier with these types, they could be placed outside the consumers' centres.

In addition to lighting technology, electric drive gained increasing importance. The 1400 V direct-current transmission from Miesbach to Munich over a distance of 57 km in 1882 and the 15 000 V three-phase current transmission Lauffen-Frankfurt over 175 km in 1891, two large-scale experiments initiated by Oskar von Miller, proved that electric energy can be transmitted economically even over long distances and distributed by power stations in convenient places.

The need to supply larger districts and to transmit growing quantities of energy led to increased transmission voltages and to greater capacity requirements for transformers and switching plants. The power output of generators grew from a few kilowatts (kVA) to over 1000 megawatts (MVA), and the transmission voltage from a few hundred to several hundred thousand volts.

With the connection of individual network sections in order to meet the demand of electrical energy in large areas, the economic – and also the ecological – aspect of electrical power engineering, i.e. electro-economics, has developed into an independent field which created a coherent network from the North Cape to Sicily in the UCPTE (Union pour la Coordination de la Production et de Transport d'Electricité) international grid system, even before the political unification of western

The path of current from the generator to the consumer (Di)
A diorama of 1953 shows a landscape of the Alpine foothills with the different types of power stations and demonstrates the path of electric current, passing through substations and networks of different voltage and ending at the consumer's plug in private households or agriculture.

Europe. This grid is designed for up to about 200 000 MW in parallel operation and for the exchange of electrical energy free of national administration, customs duties and import restrictions.

Information on the Exhibition

The section of Electrical Power mainly deals with the production and distribution of electrical energy as well as with its conversion to useful effects at the consumer's end – in accordance with the three main fields of electrical machinery industry, electric systems engineering and high-tension engineering. This division is reflected by two rooms arranged in 1953:

1. The first room illustrates the historic beginnings and further development of electric machinery: at the left, direct-current engineering, at the right, alternating current and three-phase engineering.

2. The second room deals with electric systems engineering with its main fields, power stations and networks, showing – among others – generators, switching equipment and protective devices. High-tension engineering is explained by means of a demonstrable high-voltage plant as well as by equipment such as transformers, cables, overhead lines and switches. Finally, the field of electro-economics – updated to the latest figures in 1986 – is dealt with.

These are the individual sections with their main objects:

Direct Current Engineering
First dynamo by Werner von Siemens, 1866 (O).

Alternating and Three-phase Current Engineering
Electric generator by Hypolite Pixii, 1832/33 (O).

First dynamo by Werner von Siemens, 1866 (O)
In 1866, Werner von Siemens discovered that the residual magnetization in the iron core of the electromagnet of a generator is sufficient for the induction of an initially low voltage in the rotating armature. The resulting current can be utilized for the intensification of magnetization in the field electromagnet to saturation. This self-excitation is called the dynamo-electrical principle. Werner von Siemens was the first to discover its significance for the generation of electrical energy.

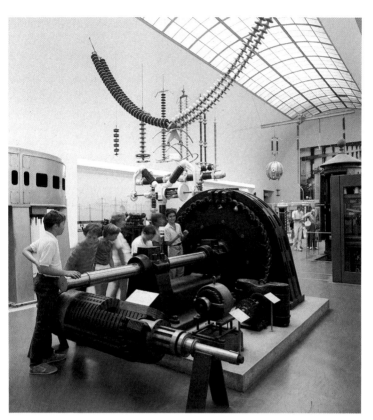

Generation and distribution of electrical energy
In the front, a very early turborotor (by BBC, 1902); behind, the generator of the
world's first three-phase transmission from Lauffen to Frankfurt (Oerlikon claw-pole
type generator, 1891). Clearly visible are also the insulator strings for overhead-
lines, in particular the suspension chain of the world's first 735 kV transmission
(Canada, 1965).

Ring transformer by Otto Titus Blathy, Max Déri and Carl Ziper-
nowsky, 1889 (O).
First three-phase generator by August Haselwander, 1887 (O).
First three-phase motor with squirrel-cage by Michael Dolivo-Dobro-
wolski, 1889 (O).

Static Converters
First mercury arc rectifier for high voltage direct-current transmission,
Brown Boverie & Cie, 1939 (O).

Power Station Equipment
Generator of the power transmission Lauffen-Frankfurt, 1891 (O).
Large diameter multi-pole 3000 kVA generator with a Kaplan turbine,
1953 (O).

High-Voltage Plant
Besides the planetarium, the presentation by the Museum's staff which
takes place here three times a day is the main attraction for the visitors

High-voltage plant, 1952 and 1975 (O, P)
Tracking discharges and the protective function of a Faraday cage at potentials up to 300 000 Volt; measurement of voltage by a sphere gap; electric field; lightning striking model houses; splitting of wood and the vaporization of wire with an impulse generator using voltages of up to a million.

of the Museum and intends to familiarize the public with power engineering, with A.C. voltages of 50 Hertz and with impulse voltages. Experiments with A.C. potentials up to 300 000 V (electric arc, screening/shielding etc.) and with A.C. current of up to 1000 Ampere (power effect) are followed by others with impulse voltages simulating lightning strokes and reaching their crest voltage of 800 000 V in two millionths of a second. On models of houses and church steeples, the effectiveness of grounding measures in lightning storms is simulated.

Electro-economics
Twelve boards show tables, diagrams and texts belonging to the following fields: generation of power from primary energy and replenishable sources, power distribution, electricity tariffs, environmental protection and many others.

F. Heilbronner

Suggestions for the continuation of the tour
Now you may either turn left around the corner, go up the ramp and pass the snack bar to the Hydraulic Engineering department, or turn to the right and visit the *Marine Navigation* department (p. 115) first.

Hydraulic Engineering

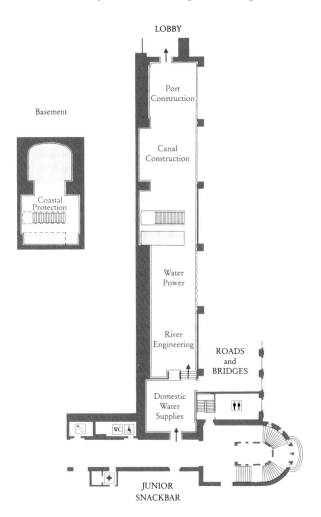

Hydraulic engineering – the earliest field of civil engineering – played a decisive role in the development of the first civilizations in Egypt, Mesopotamia, India and China.

Vigorous intervention by man in the natural circulation of water is necessary in order to gain farmland and to protect it against flood damage, to irrigate fertile soil, to provide public water supply and to dispose of sewage, to utilize water power, to make rivers navigable, to construct new waterways and to provide the transfer of goods.

Information on the Exhibition

The exhibition is accessible directly from the entrance hall, by the right stairs leading to the Snackbar.

Domestic Water Supplies

After 1850 and since the beginning of the industrial era, qualitative water management has acquired special importance. Only a little water is really consumed; the major part is only used temporarily and then returned to the natural waters. Unfortunately, water is almost without exception polluted during use: so water becomes waste water.

In the Federal Republic of Germany, of about 7,5 billion cubic meters needed for private households, industry and trade (in addition to the cooling water for power stations), about 5,5 billion cubic meters are delivered by public water supply companies in 20000 plants today (1987).

The cycle of domestic water supply consists of the following five steps shown in a model of 6,50 m in length: water catchment, water treatment, water storage and distribution, water consumption, sewage purification.

High-pressure sluice valve, 1912 (O)
Gate valves are seals in pipelines; they are used to hold and regulate large quantities of water at high pressure in dammed reservoirs and in power stations. The picture shows a flat slide valve of the Moehnetal reservoir in Westphalia. The ball valves represent another type of valve construction (at the right).

River Engineering

River engineering serves river regulation, protection of the banks, ground-water regulation and flood protection. All measures taken are preceded by examination of water-level and water-flow, evaporation, fluctuations of the ground-water level etc. Scale models of water flow are often used in this field. River beds are fixed and deepened and the banks protected by construction work. Embankments protect the land along the banks against flood. Dams – mostly equipped with movable weirs – regulate the water flow.

Water Power

For thousands of years wheels have been driven by water power. Since the introduction of dynamos, water has also been utilized for the generation of electricity. Water is retained and stored in the courses of rivers, in reservoirs and in barrages. According to the quantities of water and the height of fall different kinds of turbines are used.

Coastal Protection

This section is housed in the basement and mainly deals with the measures taken at the coasts of the North Sea; the flat land there is particularly jeopardized by strong tides.
Dykes are built in order to preserve cultivated soil and to gain new land. The drainage of the dyked coastal lowlands is effected by dyke locks or by pumping stations. Tidal barrages protect river mouths against storm floods. Prediction of tides is therefore an important task.

Canal Construction

Since early times, natural shipping lanes have been extended by canals. The development of canal construction came to a first high point when the first navigable canal in the history of man was built in Egypt about 1900 B.C. Especially since the 17th century, a network of interlinked waterways has been created. Up until the construction of the first summit canal with barrage locks, the Stecknitz Canal, in the 14th century, ships were pulled up inclined surfaces in order to scale differences in height. Today ship lifts work efficiently and without loss of water.
Open canals are still used in water supply systems where large quantities of water are needed.

Port Construction

In former times, harbours were situated inside the towns, mostly as inland harbours on big rivers, according to their importance. Loading and unloading of the ships was done by hand. Nowadays the size of ships and the number of handling procedures require a multitude of large installations with different characteristics for various goods and handling operations. Compared to the seaports, the inland harbours are of less importance now.

F. Heilbronner

Carriages and Bicycles

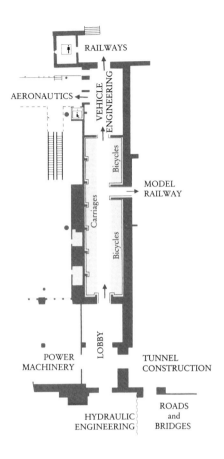

For thousands of years, travel and transport of goods off the waterways was very arduous. The prehistoric invention of the wheel became significant for land transport only when the use of horse-drawn vehicles and carriages was made possible by an expanding network of roads in the Roman Empire. Ox, donkey and horse served as draught-animals. In the Middle Ages, the improvement of the harness and the introduction of the horseshoe led to a substantial increase of their performance. When the Roman roads fell into decay, land travel became so strenuous that even princes, kings and emperors preferred travelling on horseback. The transport of heavy loads had to wait until the beginning of winter which made the use of sledges possible.

The spring-suspended carriage appeared only in modern times. Its construction was developed to perfection in the 19th century. It was widespread in the form of the mail-coach and omnibus, but also as means of individual traffic. It did feeder service for the railroads, and was used as cab until 1925. During the thirties, it was finally superseded by the automobile.

Travelling coach, about 1810 (O), and Landauer, about 1825 (O)

Man uses the major part of his muscle power for locomotion. With the same expenditure of energy, the bicycle increases his reach fourfold. In its present form, it supplanted the *Ordinary* bicycle, a fast but very dangerous sporting device. The break-neck falls, head first, of the high riders were the consequence of the rapidly growing diameter of the front wheel in the *velocipedes*. The velocipede riders did no longer propel themselves along by paddling their feet against the ground, like the hobby-horse riders before 1860, but drove their vehicle by means of pedal cranks.

The bicycle gained popularity only with the *low wheel.* Though its price then was equivalent to half a year's wages of a labourer – the same applies to a motor-car today – it was bought by millions. Still before the turn of the century, special construction types were added: the *ladies' bicycle,* the *racing bicycle,* the *tandem* and *folding cycles* for army use. Bicycle engineering gave an impetus to the whole field of vehicle construction. The steel tube frame, ball-bearings, wire spokes and – in 1888 – pneumatic tyres were first tested on the bicycle. More than the coach, it became the forerunner of the automobile.

Information on the Exhibition

The most important vehicles without an engine – *vehicles driven by muscle power, carriages* and *bicycles* – are on display in front of the Railways Hall. Six carriages of the 19th century illustrate the heyday and end of the era of horse-drawn carriages. The victory of the single-track bicycle over the multi-track three-wheeled or four-wheeled vehicles driven by muscle power is visualized by a comparison of these vehicle types. Particularly interesting is the evolution from the wooden dandy-horse to the pedigree racing bicycle. *H. Straßl*

Vehicle Engineering

Physics is the basic science for all machines, thus also for the vehicles, the behaviour and characteristics of which are determined by the laws of mechanics in particular.

The aim of *vehicle engineering* is the application of these fundamentals in accordance to the individual requirements. Since all vehicles of land transport are based upon the same – or, at least, very similar – conditions, vehicle engineering is a universal discipline. So the wheel, for instance, as a connecting link between the vehicle and the roadway, is an essential constituent of most of the land transport vehicles. It carries the vehicle, transmits the forces for steering in the curves and also serves propulsion and braking in many cases. All these requirements have to be met in the bicycle, in automobiles, in railborne vehicles, even in the aircraft rolling on the runway. Conventional vehicle engineering remains applicable also in new types of traffic systems, such as the magnetic levitation trains, for instance. Engineers even speak of the "magnetic wheel".

One of the main fields of vehicle engineering is the integration of the wheel into the vehicle. Spring suspension types are necessary not only for reasons of comfort: without a spring suspension, an equal distribution of the load on the wheels and their adhesion to the ground would not be guaranteed, and they would not be able to fulfil their task safely. The suspension also transforms the vehicle into an vibrating body, which makes measures of vibration-damping necessary. Moreover, a flexible power transmission between the driving unit in the vehicle and the driven wheels is required. Manifold solutions for these problems are possible. The improvements in road stability for automotive vehicles and higher speeds in railborne traffic result – not least – from the perfection of vehicle engineering in this area.

Due to the change in human awareness of energy problems, aerodynamics again have been given more attention in vehicle design. True streamline shapes are hardly possible because of the limited length of the vehicles. The influences resulting from the surroundings often cause the streaming conditions around the moving vehicle or beneath the vehicle floor to be more complex than in aviation.

Though vehicle engineering operates within a framework of defined fundamental physical rules, it is still far from dealing with the complete range of possibilities. Computer-aided design and the simulation of technical processes by high-speed computer systems have disclosed new dimensions for further development.

Information on the Exhibition

Because of the significance of vehicle engineering for land transport, this room of the exhibition forms the transition from the *Carriages and Bicycles* section to the *Railways Hall* and to the *Exhibition of Motor Vehicles*.

Shaft with universal joints (D)
In vehicle engineering, shafts with universal joints serve the transmission of rotary motion if angular displacement arises between the axles. With simple universal joints, the rotary motion at the driven part has a varying velocity ratio. This is why "constant velocity joints" are used in motor vehicles with frontwheel drive.

The exhibition gives a survey of the general physical fundamentals of vehicle engineering and explains the acting forces of inertia, the forces of air currents and the effects produced by uneven road surfaces. The peculiarities relevant to wheeled vehicles are described on the long wall of the exhibition room. By means of exhibits, pictures and graphs, the problems inherent to the wheel bearing, to steering as well as to wheel-driving systems and brake systems are explained in detail. Noteworthy experiments on springs, on adhesion to the road under influence of transverse forces and on tracking can be seen. A small area is dedicated to the levitation technology and its similarity to conventional vehicle engineering.

L. Schletzbaum

Suggestions for the continuation of the tour
Leaving the *Vehicle Engineering* exhibition, you now enter the *Railways Hall* (p. 99) dominated by the locomotives. However, we would suggest going downstairs by the escalators right in front of you and continuing your tour in the *Motor Vehicles* Hall.

Motor Vehicles and Motorcycles

The history of the motor-car is closely linked to the evolution of individual traffic about the turn of the century. Millions of cyclists experienced daily to what degree the freedom of movement was increased by owning a private vehicle. They could reach every point of the country without depending on railways and in half the time of a horse carriage. The range of action, however, was restricted by the limited muscle power of man.

As a matter of fact, man became *mobile* only by the automobile. The prerequisite for this was a small, light power source with low fuel consumption. Neither the steam engine nor the electromotor met these requirements. The internal combustion engine prevailed because petrol is the fuel with the highest energy output. Of course, the low-noise steam carriages and the electromobiles without exhaust gas production were much more popular with the city population than the annoying early motor-cars, but the racing trophies helped the petrol cars over-

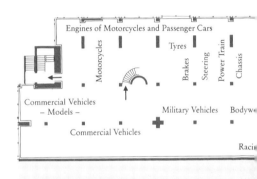

come their competitors. For the development of motor vehicles, the motor-car competitions played an outstanding role. Less than ten years after Carl Benz had constructed his motor-car in 1886 and Gottlieb Daimler had motorized a coach, races already took place in France.

The best automobiles were constructed for competitions, e.g. the famous *Mercedes* of 1901. Its 35 hp engine did not fit under the rear seat any more, as it had in the motor carriages of the 19th century. The automobiles emerged into the 20th century with front engines. Wilhelm Maybach, the designer of the Mercedes car, had created the model for the motor-car of the future.

Hundreds of automobile factories were set up at that time, most of them by extension of a machinery or bicycle production plant; in rarer cases, they were newly founded.

The first manufacturer of production cars was Benz of Mannheim, the most important Henry Ford of Detroit, USA. Of his T model 15 million cars were built, from 1913 onwards in assembly-line production. In the

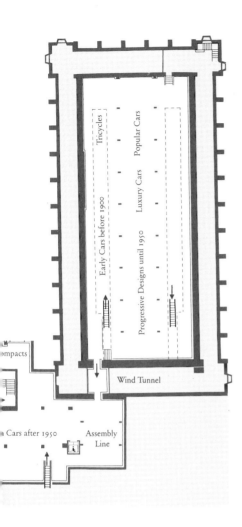

Tricycles

Popular Cars

Luxury Cars

Early Cars before 1900

Progressive Designs until 1950

Compacts

Wind Tunnel

Cars after 1950

Assembly Line

United States, the "Motorcar for Everyone" already competed with the railways while in Europe the First World War seriously affected the spreading of the passenger car. Motorcycles and commercial vehicles were in demand then. Smaller car manufacturers had no chance in the post-war period any more. They either stopped production or joined larger companies, like Daimler-Benz, Opel-GM, Auto-Union etc. The motorcycle manufacturers were luckier, because the motorcycle had become the "automobile of the ordinary man". The true *people's car* (Volkswagen) still was to come.

Though automobiles with self-supporting body, front drive or rear engine were lighter and consumed less fuel, frame construction and standard drive (front engine, rear-wheel drive) predominated in the thirties, especially in deluxe cars. Since these limousines and cabriolets were mobile "visiting cards" rather than means of locomotion, their weight and fuel consumption were of no importance. In order to look more aerodynamic, the cars got streamlined bodies as the latest fashion hit. Truly streamlined cars, however, hardly existed before the Second World War.

During the Second World War, the horse was definitely superseded by the motor vehicle; the American *jeep* and the military version of the *Volkswagen* fully acquired its cross-country mobility and reliability. The long and severe trial benefitted the post-war *Beetle* which became the car with the world's highest production figure. Its competitors took on more or less sporting airs. They continuously grew flatter, broader and faster. Registration figures jumped, but so did the accident rates. In 1972, ten thousand car passengers died in the Federal Republic of Germany. One car generation later, in 1985, the figure of car passengers killed in car accidents had sunk by half – thanks to safety belts and crush zones.

Mass motorization made the passenger car a common commodity. The compact middle class car superseded the sub-compact as well as the "battleship". Light construction and streamlined body design have been used for the reduction of fuel consumption since the days of the energy crisis. Motors with improved environmental compatibility ensure that the pleasure of driving will not be lost, for there is no way of doing without the motor-car today.

Information on the Exhibition

The *Department of Motor Vehicles,* newly arranged and considerably enlarged for the centennial of the automobile in 1986, can be reached either by escalators from the the *Railways Hall* or from the *Aeronautics Department.*

It is divided into two halls with a total surface of 2 200 m², connected by a ramp. Visitors who are mainly interested in motor-car engineering first go to Hall II, beneath the *Aeronautics Hall,* while oldtimer fans prefer Hall I in the basement, beneath the *Railways.*

Benz motor car, 1886 (O)
The first developable motor vehicle with a petrol engine

Adler Diplomat with wood-gas producing plant, 1938 (O)
Because of the wartime shortage of fuels, this Adler limousine was adapted to wood-gas. The gas producer at the car's rear had to be filled with about 18 kg of wood every 25 miles and allowed a speed of up to 45 miles per hour.

Passenger Cars until 1950

In the basement of the Railways Hall, there is an exhibition of 40 passenger cars, each of which represents a noteworthy step in the evolution of automobiles until 1950. The juxtaposition of *steam carriages, electric cars* and *vehicles with petrol engines* at the beginning of the tour through the Automobiles Department corresponds to the situation around the turn of the century.

The most ancient and most precious car is the *Benz tricycle* of 1886. Its inventor donated it to the Deutsches Museum only twenty years after its first drive. Since that time, it has stood here, at the beginning of a series of automobiles which grew more and more powerful and faster, but also heavier and increasingly environment-polluting.

An illustrated timeline represents the development of the motor vehicle

Audi Alpensieger, 1914 (O)
With this car, August Horch won the 1914 Austrian Alpine Trial.

Horch drophead coupé, 1939 (O)
The price of the elegant Horch 853 A was not less than that of a representative house in the suburbs then. The stars of the movies and sports scene preferred this model even to the Mercedes cars, the SS type of which (of 1932, behind), however, cost about twice as much.

in the history of civilization. It deals with the effects on society and encourages the visitors to evaluate the original cars from this aspect. The comparison of vehicles similar to motorbikes with popular small cars by *Wanderer, Hanomag, Opel* etc. and with motorized coaches with chauffeur, followed by *Mercedes, Bugatti, Minerva, Horch* luxury cars, illustrates the social and income differences during the first half of the 20th century. The progress achieved in vehicle engineering during this period can be seen from the *Lancia-Lambda, Citroen 11 CV, Opel Olympia, DKW F7* and *Tatra 87.* They were more spacious than the small cars, but also lighter and more economical than the luxury cars. Every year they became more compact in shape. The running boards, exposed headlamps and mudguards disappeared. For aerodynamic reasons, windscreen design adopted more and more inclined and swept-back lines. This development is shown by models in the passage leading to Hall II and illustrated by original cars of the fifties and sixties, such as the *Borgward Hansa, Citroen DS, NSU Ro 80* e. g.

Car Production

During the boom of motorization, *assembly line production of private cars* was increasingly automatized including the introduction of mounting devices and robots. The joining of body and chassis of a modern *BMW 325 ix* as well as the fitting of the rear door by a robot can be commanded by activating a press-button in Hall II. Thus visitors can observe a process taking place thousands of times per day in modern car production and get an idea of the expenditure necessary for an output of one car per minute.

Racing Cars, Competition Vehicles

Passing from the Aeronautics Hall to the automobiles in the basement, the visitor immediately sees cars which have a striking affinity with aircraft types. The *Rumpler "tear-drop" car,* the *Silver Arrows* by Mercedes and Auto-Union, the BMW and Porsche racing cars are the result of the same guiding principles that are applied to the construction of propeller aircraft: low air resistance, small weight – therefore light construction – and powerful engines. These speed-cars became more and more different from the cars in everyday life. Only with the introduction of the rally sport did passenger car types similar to cars built in large numbers, such as the *Audi Quattro,* turn up again on the racing scene.

Auto-Union, 1936 (O) Grand-Prix racing car with a 16-cylinder compressor motor, a power of 380 kW (510 hp) and a maximum speed of 210 miles per hour

Commercial Vehicles

The first trucks and *omnibuses* with petrol engines appeared about the turn of the century. They spread rapidly and became an important factor of economic life. For a long time now, in the western industrial countries, their share in the total traffic volume has exceeded that of the railways. In addition to 33 models, there are only six original vehicles on display because of the limited space available: the most ancient is a *Büssing truck* of 1903, the largest one the *M. A. N. omnibus of 1965*, the bodywork of which is absent so that a view into the floor assembly of lattice frame construction is possible. In the off-road vehicles, the military vehicles form the substantial part. Their design varies from a heavy *BMW motorcycle with side car* to a *Volkswagen floating off-road vehicle*.

Automative Engineering

In Hall II, visitors with a special interest in car technology find sectioned constructional parts, arranged in the groups of *engines, chassis* and *bodywork,* used in historic and modern automobiles. The demand for higher efficiency and more safety made them more and more functional and reliable. From a series illustrating the development of engines the technical progress can be seen very clearly.

Rumpler "teardrop" car, 1921 (O), at the left
The aeroplane designer Edmund Rumpler was the first to shape a series limousine according to aerodynamic principles. The shape was similar to a falling drop of water; its favourable drag coefficient $c_D = 0{,}28$ was equalled again only in the most recent car types.

Robots in car production, 1986 (O, P), at the right
The main attraction of the "car production" section of the exhibition is the demonstration of a robot used for the fully automatic fitting of the doors into passenger cars.

Motorcycles

At the foot of the spiral staircase to the Aeronautics Hall, the visitor is attracted to two important motorcycles: a *Daimler-Maybach of 1885* and a *Hildebrand & Wolfmüller of 1894,* the world's first motorcycle to enter series production. They stand at the beginning of a series consisting of 35 motor bicycles and tricycles, many of which were produced in larger numbers than the automobiles of their time.

H. Straßl

Motorcycle by Daimler-Maybach, 1885 (O)
In order to test their newly-made petrol motor, Daimler and his designer, Maybach, used a wooden bicycle with supporting wheels on the sides. Although it was not developed further, it can be considered the first motorcycle in the world.

Passenger car chassis types, from Rolls Royce (of 1922) up to the Volkswagen
Before the self-supporting bodywork was invented, all automobiles had a more or
less heavy frame on which the most different types of body construction were
mounted. Today chassis frames are only found in commercial vehicles.

Magirus mobile turntable ladder, of 1934 (O)
Mobile fire-escape of 30 m lifting height. Maximum speed: 34 miles per hour

Suggestions for the continuation of the tour
After the visit of the motorcycles exhibition, you now can either go up the
winding staircase around the earliest motorcycles, continue with the visit of the
aeroplanes (p. 180) and enter the *Railways Hall* (p. 99) from the corner with
the jet aircraft types, or you return to the first room, go upstairs by the escalator and visit the *Railways* department from there.

Railways

Ground floor

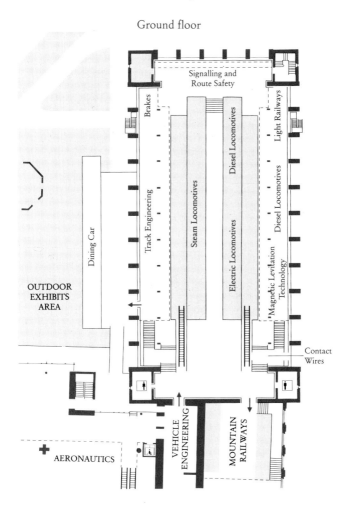

The field of railway traffic in the widest sense comprises all track-guided means of transportation with which the vehicle and the track form a unit.

The beginnings of railway traffic go back to the track-guided mine wagons of the Middle Ages, though the appearance of railways according to the modern definition coincides only with the beginning of the industrial revolution in England, in the 18th century. There the early horse-drawn railway vehicles were used for the transport of coal from the mines to canals and navigable rivers.

They originated as a supplement to the existing infrastructure and as an accompanying phenomenon to industrialization. Thus the situation in England was completely different from that on the Continent with its scattered economic areas which formed separate regions and had no

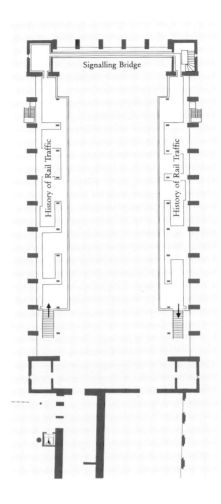

communications network in the proper sense. There the railways initiated the industrial revolution only several decades later.

The final success of the new transportation system was made possible by two essential inventions of the new age: first, the possibility of producing cheap cast-iron on a more or less large-scale industrial level by means of mineral coal instead of charcoal, a new technique which started in the English town of Coalbrookdale in the mid-eighteenth century and made it possible to replace the wooden rails, used until then for the railroads, by durable iron tracks.

Second, James Watt invented the double-acting low-pressure steam engine in 1782. The most important "side-effect" of this machine was the production of a rotary motion – an enormous improvement in comparison with the common Newcomen type steam engine of that time, which produced a to-and-fro motion and was therefore suitable only for the direct driving of piston pumps.

Based upon Watt's machine, Richard Trevithick built the world's first steam locomotive in 1804: however, it was not a success, because it was too heavy for the weak cast-iron rails of that time. Only a few years later, William Hedley had a much greater success with his locomotive named *Puffing Billy*, and in 1825, when the Stockton and Darlington Railway was opened, the locomotive had become a serious rival of the horse in the field of propulsion.

In 1830, the railway line from Liverpool to Manchester was opened, and the news of the "miracle" and its success quickly spread over the borders and engendered a "Railway Mania" which helped to establish a series of new routes.

In May 1835, the first steam-operated railway ran in Belgium; in December of the same year, the first public railway in Germany linked Nürnberg and Fürth. They were followed by railways in France, Austria, the Netherlands and Italy.

Most of the material needed for the construction and operation of these railways had to be bought from England which had an enormous lead in the field of machine-building. It was not until 1841 that the first German locomotive manufacturers built their plants: Kessler in Karlsruhe, Maffei in Munich and Borsig in Berlin.

By 1855, more than 8000 kilometers of railway tracks were laid in Germany, and in this initial phase, the gigantic demand for railway material

Steam engine "Puffing Billy", 1814 (R, P)
The "Puffing Billy" locomotive served coal haulage on a colliery railway near Newcastle in the north of England. It proved so satisfactory in operation that it remained in service for nearly 50 years.

brought an enormous boom, especially of the developing iron and machine-building industries. After the different railways had grown into one network, economic life in general profited from it by the development of new markets. Intensive exploitation of raw materials, such as iron and coal, the creation of the factory system as a new form of production, and the development of capital as a factor of production opened the door for the industrial age.

However, this also changed the experiential world for each individual. The dimensions of time and space shrunk. Compared to the mail-coach, travelling times were suddenly cut to a third or a fourth. Man became mobile. In the commuter-belt of the towns, the place of residence and the place of work no longer had to be next to each other. During the last third of the 19th century, a change took place in human self-understanding also. In the era of industrialization the individual became more and more alienated from his work, and the wish for free-time grew. The term "leisure time" emerged. A variety of small excursion railways developed in the regions, and rack railways and cable railways in the mountains.

Before the beginning of the First World War, the German rail network comprised more than 60 000 kilometers of main-line and secondary railways, for which over 25 000 locomotives were available. The effects of the war were severe for the railways. The prerogative of railway opera-

View of the Railways Hall: steam locomotive S 3/6, 1912 (O) and diesel locomotive V 140, 1935 (O)
In the vast Railways Hall, 14 original vehicles are on display: the dominant items are steam, electric and diesel locomotives as examples of more than 100 years of railway and railcar history. At left, next to the Bavarian express locomotive of the S 3/6 type, there is the world's first large diesel-hydraulic locomotive, which starts an evolutional series leading up to the latest diesel locomotives of the Deutsche Bundesbahn.

tion, which had been owned by the German Lands, such as Prussia, Bavaria, Saxony etc., passed over to the German Reich on the 1st April, 1920 – the *Deutsche Reichsbahn* was founded.

Reparations and inflation after the war depressed the German economy and also the transport system. In 1928, about 3000 locomotives were no longer running, either because there was no use for them or because they were damaged. The recovery of the economy, started during the Weimar period, only took effect later on.

In the early thirties, automobiles and aircraft began to create a situation of competition with the railways. This was just the beginning, and the reaction to the competition of that time is still of concern today: to make travelling faster, more comfortable and more attractive. From May 1933 onwards, the diesel driven train *Fliegender Hamburger* ran between Berlin and Hamburg. In 1936, Cologne, Frankfurt, Leipzig, Nuremberg, Stuttgart and Munich were connected in the fast railway network. Steam locomotives with streamlining were used for heavy long-distance trains.

For the last time, during the Second World War, the railways of all sides played the great strategic role they had always had during the wars since the mid-nineteenth century. Their big loading capacity, however, was misused for the deportation of millions of people – for transportation to mass extermination.

At the end of the war, in May 1945, the major part of the German rail network was destroyed. The remaining network was divided. The railways of the part of Germany under Soviet occupation kept the name *Deutsche Reichsbahn;* for the railways of the other zones, the designation *Deutsche Bundesbahn* was introduced in 1949.

During the following years, despite the German economic miracle, the newly founded *Deutsche Bundesbahn* experienced a run into the deficit. Reconstruction work had to be financed by the railways alone, whereas motorcars and trucks were clearly favoured as traffic carriers. The networks of roads, motorways and waterways were extended and their quality standards improved.

The increasing deficits of the railways led to the policy of "shrinking to a profitable size". The reduction of carrying capacity, however, only further increased the trend towards shifting railway transports to other traffic carrier systems.

Present plans are for a concentration of railway traffic on a network of main-lines with high carrying capacity, whereas the service in the distribution area is left to bus, truck and individual traffic in as far as structural policy allows. Long-term planning of the Bundesbahn backs the construction of new high-speed lines and the development of long-distance lines with heavy traffic loads. In 1991, the newly laid lines Hannover–Würzburg and Mannheim–Stuttgart will be completed and considerably reduce the travelling times.

Information on the Exhibition

The Railways Hall mainly shows items illustrating vehicle engineering, such as steam, diesel and electric locomotives, as well as displays dealing with the railway system and routing.

Smaller sections deal with the subjects of magnetic levitation technology, light railways and brakes. On the raised gallery of the hall, models and pictures give a survey of the history of railways.

Railway Vehicles

At the entrance to the exhibition hall, the *Puffing Billy* locomotive (R, P), one of the first operational steam engines, can be seen in dominant position. The middle gangway is flanked by the first locomotive manufactured by the Krauss company (O) and the 1000th locomotive of the Maffei company (O). The presumably best-known express locomotive of the Deutsche Länderbahnen, the Bavarian S 3/6 (O, P) of 1912 vintage, forms the end of this series. This locomotive pulled such famous trains as the *Rheingold Express* and was in service until 1957.

Opposite the steam locomotives, there are several prominent vehicles from the history of electric locomotives. At the beginning of this series, one of the most precious items on display in this exhibition, the world's first electric locomotive by Werner Siemens, of 1879 (O), can be seen. On the main track, next to it, stands Germany's first locomotive for single-phase alternating-current (O). The current system used for this

The first electric locomotive, of 1879 (O)
The world's first electric locomotive by Werner Siemens was put into service in 1879, at the great Berlin Exhibition of Trade, where it presented an alternative for the future under the slogan "railway without steam and without horses". Locomotives constructed according to this new technique soon became the keenest rivals of steam locomotives and made railways the environmentally safe means of transport that they are today.

"LAG 1" electric locomotive for local railways, of 1905 (O)
Nowadays European railways are mainly operated by electric power. A very important step forward was the utilization of high-voltage single-phase alternating current for the propulsion of railways. The first locomotive which proved satisfactory with this electric system was the "LAG 1", built in 1905 for the Munich Localbahn Aktiengesellschaft. The single-phase AC system was widely adopted by European railways.

locomotive is the most frequent in Central Europe's railways today. This locomotive of 1905 is followed by the first electric standard gauge locomotive for three-phase current (O), of 1899, and an electric express locomotive of the *E 16* class (O) of the Deutsche Reichsbahn, built in 1927.

The end of the track displays the *V 140* (O) diesel locomotive, the first large locomotive with hydrodynamical power transmission. It was built in 1935 and marks the beginning of a technical evolution which is illustrated up to the latest diesel engines of the Deutsche Bundesbahn. The driving unit of a modern diesel locomotive class *216* (O) with motor, gears and cardan shafts can be seen below the nearby gallery.

Close to it stands one of the most recent items of the exhibition, a prototype illustrating the magnetic levitation technology (O), of 1971. The first experiments in this field date back to the thirties. A test train with the latest generation of vehicles is running on trial in the Emsland at this time (1987).

Signalling and Route Safety

The end of the exhibition hall gives a survey of signalling techniques; it starts with early mechanical signals and signal boxes, then leads to the electromechanical signalling techniques and finally to modern light signals and panel-operated signal boxes.

Tracks and Rails

An insight into track engineering is offered under the left gallery, next to the exit to the outdoor exhibits area; different forms of tracks are shown there, along with equipment and machinery for repair and renewal of the rails. The most impressive exhibit is a tamping machine (O, P) for compacting the ballast under the sleepers.

The History of Railways

On both galleries of the hall, a survey on the history of railways is given, from the beginnings up to modern high-speed traffic. The main events of early railway construction, the history of travelling by railway, but also the technical evolution from the steam locomotive to modern electric trains are commented upon there.

The exhibition comprises a variety of models and interesting documents illustrating the history of railways. It offers information to technology enthusiasts as well as to visitors interested in historical details. The route through this section starts at the left side.

Mountain Railways

A separate section, housed in an anteroom to the main Railways Hall, offers an insight into the development and technology of mountain railways.

The limited friction between wheels and rails makes conventional railways suitable only for gradients up to about 7 percent. Considerably steeper gradients, however, can be overcome by means of cogwheels in

Prototype of the magnetic levitation vehicle, 1971 (O)
The world's first magnetic levitation system, the "Principle Vehicle" of 1971, ranks among the most recent exhibits of the Railways Hall. Magnetic levitation trains advance without mechanical contact of the vehicles with the track and allow far higher speeds than the wheel-on-rail system of conventional railways.

the locomotive and racks laid between the rails. Rack railways scale gradients of up to 25 percent. Special constructions like that of the Swiss *Pilatus railway* even cope with gradients of up to 48 percent. Another technical alternative for climbing steep gradients is the rope-and-pulley type rail car, where the car runs on the rails and is pulled up by a rope, the whole system being powered by a stationary engine.

Nowadays, the most common mountain railways are suspension cableways, which can be built at considerably lower cost.

The main exhibits of this section are a railcar of the Pilatus railway (O), of 1900, and a rack steam locomotive (O) of a Yugoslav railway, built in 1908. In addition to them, an electric cogwheel driving unit of the *Zugspitz railway* (O) and interesting constructional parts of aerial cableways can be seen.

Model Railway

The model railway layout on the scale of 1:87 has a total rail length of 240 m. It is installed on a surface area of 40 m² and demonstrates express traffic, goods transport and the particularly interesting splitting of goods trains on a hump. Interesting comparisons are made between a light railway and a rack railway, both climbing the same mountain.

L. Schletzbaum

Tunnel Construction

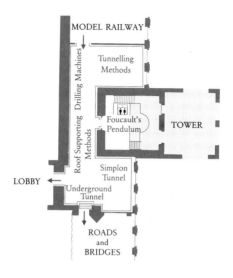

Tunnels as they are shown here are subterranean parts of permanent traffic routes which – opposed to galleries – come to the surface at both ends. Only in solid rock, the excavated spaces don't require any support. In *friable* or *soft* rock types, they must be secured by temporary supports, such as timbering or steel arches, and permanently by masonry (roof arches and abutments).

After the introduction of the railways, the number of tunnels had already increased at such a rate that they soon ceased to be regarded as a kind of wonderwork; during the 20th century, however, their number grew even more because of road traffic. As early as the first decades of the 19th century, four construction methods had been developed for modern tunnelling practice, each of which was distinguished by the procedure of excavation, of timbering and of masonry sequence:

1. the German system was developed as early as 1803 for the construction of the Tronquoy tunnel on the St. Quentin canal, imitated in 1837 for the Königsdorf tunnel, the first German railway tunnel, of the Aachen-Cologne line, and almost exclusively applied in Germany for a long period;

2. the Belgian or underpinning system, first used for the construction of the Charleroy Canal in Belgium, in 1828;

3. the Austrian system, first used in 1837 for the construction of the Oberau tunnel on the Leipzig-Dresden line; it was then improved during the great through-cuts through the Austrian Alps;

4. the English system, first applied in 1834 for the construction of the Kilsby tunnel of the London-Birmingham line.

Timber propping reduces the space of working and impedes the use of big machines; this is why special methods were developed very early for tunnelling in water-bearing or soft strata and in argillaceous layers where the risk of collapse is high (the freezing method, grouting of the subsoil by injection of chemicals are such special methods). Such a special method is the shield driving method, which was already used for the construction of the tunnel under the Thames in London (1821–1841), where serious difficulties had to be overcome: eleven times water broke in.

This method in particular, which uses concrete rings for the roof support, has been improved continuously and is being used for the construction of the Munich underground. This type of tunnel driving is done by means of fully mechanized equipment now.

Only after 1850, drilling machines were used for breaking off the rock and made the strenuous hand-work underground easier: in 1860, John Cockerill constructed the first pneumatic rock drilling machine for the Mont Cenis tunnel; in 1876, Alfred Brandt constructed a hydraulic rotary drilling machine for the hard granite of the Pfaffenberg tunnel of the St. Gotthard line; and in 1879, Werner von Siemens constructed an electric percussion drilling machine. Modern rotary percussion drills work at a speed of 3000 strokes per minute.

Information on the Exhibition

The exhibition shows models and full-size displays illustrating the tunnelling methods as well as important drilling machines and tools by means of originals; the visitor can compare the various methods of roof support in exhibits of natural size.

F. Heilbronner

Simplon tunnel, 1898–1905 (R)
The first tunnel mentioned in history was built for a water pipe (of about 1 km in length), on the island of Samos, around 522 B.C. The construction of the first Alpine tunnel through the Semmering (1430 m) lasted seven years (1848–1854); for the Simplon tunnel, the world's longest tunnel up to then, a period of five and a half years had been scheduled. Because of the extraordinarily high rock temperatures (55 °C), a system of two tunnels, 17 m apart, was planned for the first time in history in order to ensure better ventilation. This new communication line from western Switzerland to Upper Italy was opened on the 1st June, 1906. From 1912 to 1922, the second tunnel was finished. An additional model (scale 1:30) represents the driving of the tunnel.

Roads and Bridges

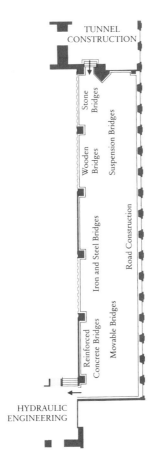

From the historic point of view, every improvement of traffic routes always had two causes: first, a central political power, and, second, an increase of trade. From the 18th century onward, the construction of roads, bridges and canals was increasingly based on practical experience, as well as on scientific findings.

About 6 000 years ago, when the wheel and wheeled vehicles were invented in Asia Minor, the paths had to be improved by stones or transverse logs (log roads). The earliest road networks (Amber Route, Silk Road, Tea and Salt Routes) weren't built roadways in the modern sense with the necessary bridges, but trails which were adjusted to the conditions changing with time; beginning and end, mountain passes and the best river crossings were the only fixed points. There, the first settlements developed; they became towns later on.

History shows that important networks of constructed roads can be created only by a state with central administration: the Persian Royal Roads, Roman roads, Inca roads, Napoleonic roads, motorways, highways. The fall of the Roman Empire was accompanied by the decay of the roads. A few new earth roads were built around 800 by order of Charlemagne. Around 1300 a certain activity in road construction set in; paved streets, made of broken stone and gravel, are found in Cologne and in Paris.

After the introduction of *Roman Law* in Germany (1496), everybody had to provide the maintenance of the streets along his estate; this requirement was valid also for the main roads. As the road toll was raised by the landlord and the peasants had the burden of maintenance, the roads were repaired very little, and the coachmen simply drove where it was best possible, often far away from the original way. Regulations ruled the type of road repair work to be done by the bondmen; probably the earliest such regulation is the *Jülich-Bergische Polizeiordnung*, of 1554.

In France, where soon a central power prevailed, the minister Maximilien Sully started the first activities of road construction in the 17th century; the destructive effect of water was minimized by several layers of stones. A scientific approach to several methods began with the foundation of the "Ecole des Ponts et Chaussées" and its first director, Pierre M. J. Trésaguet (1775).

In England, too, road construction was exemplary; John Loudon MacAdam, general surveyor of road construction (1816), set great value on a waterproof crown, to the profile of which he added 7 to 8 cm in the middle, whereas Thomas Telford particularly worked on the durability of the grounding layer from 1803 onward.

Paved streets prevailed in the cities; paved roads were rare. In order to eliminate the noise of iron-wheeled horse-drawn vehicles, wooden pavements were first intruduced in St. Petersburg about 1850. Small paving stones, however, were cheaper and spread from Stade after 1885. Concrete paving stones were first used in Bergamo in 1928; in 1936, the first test section for heavy traffic was built near Neuß on the Rhine. Small granite stones are preferred for heavily strained surfaces, such as motorway access points, roads with steep gradients etc.

No machine is more typical for road construction than the road roller. At first, it was indispensable for the compaction of the ground and for surfacing; it is still in use today, but more for smoothing the road surface. Before it was introduced, road surfaces were compacted by means of heavy tappets in arduous handwork, or else this work was left to the iron wheels of the coaches.

From 1840 onward, horse-drawn road rollers prevailed, and after 1865 steam rollers were put to use. In our times, diesel road rollers prevail; their use spread from England in 1902.

With the increasing number of fast horse-driven carriages and the introduction of automobiles after 1900, the dust nuisance on the roads made of gravel and broken stone became intolerable. Tourism in Monaco, for instance, would have broken down completely, had the physician Ernest Guglielminetti from the Valais not introduced surface tarring there in 1902; his example was soon copied elsewhere. In the United States, road dust was first fought by spraying Californian petroleum which encouraged the cementation of dust particles by its asphaltic contents.

In order to keep the surface dustfree and durable for motor traffic, it was also sprayed with bitumen and crushed stone; however, it proved more satisfactory to work a layer of stone screenings into the surface by rolling, using bitumen or tar as binder. This presupposed a strong substructure, adequate to the fast motorized road traffic of today with its share of heavy trucks. The following techniques were therefore adopted in road construction: building of gravel sub-base from stone screenings and gravel; additional compaction by bituminous binders; concrete surfacing in cities and on motorways; the first tar concrete pavement on the Avus of Berlin in 1929; the application of asphaltic concrete surfacing on the motorway near Darmstadt in 1934/35.

Bridges

A systematic classification of bridges can be introduced in accordance with many different criteria:

Fixed bridges

1. by the traffic system they carry or the goods they conduct: highway bridges, railway bridges, aqueducts;
2. by the material used: timber bridges, stone bridges (of masonry, concrete or reinforced concrete), steel bridges (riveted, screwed, welded), aluminium bridges;
3. by the type of construction: plain-webbed construction type, truss type;
4. by the type of superstructure: beam bridges, arched bridges, suspension bridges;
5. by the design of the main girders: straight or curved main girders;

6. by the position of the traffic route: track or roadway on the top (deck bridge for roads) or below (through bridge for railways);
7. by the number of decks: single deck or double deck bridges;
8. by the purpose: permanent bridges, temporary bridges, work bridges, emergency bridges;
9. by static aspects: independent main girders and planking, combined main girders and roadway girders, main girders elastically coupled with the roadway;
10. by the angle between their longitudinal and latitudinal axes: straight and askew bridges.

Movable bridges

1. by the material used: timber, steel etc.;
2. by the type of movability: mostly lift bridges, swing bridges, bascule bridges; rarer types are pontoon bridges, suspension ferries, rolling bridges and draw bridges.

Information on the Exhibition

The themes of this exhibition, which covers about 680 m², reach from the primitive routes and natural trunk bridges to the modern motorways with their bridge construction types.
The bridges dominate the view of the exhibition. The visitor can follow the evolution of bridge construction and look more deeply into different types of construction and explanatory texts.
The bridges are grouped according to the material used.

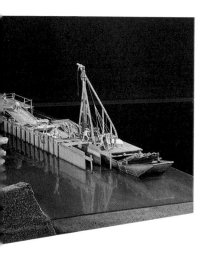

Seine bridge near Neuilly, 1768–1774 (M)
Bridge engineering is indebted to French engineers who published studies on the theory of arch construction and structural mechanics – a period which began with Jean Rodolphe Perronet (1708–1794). The Seine bridge of Neuilly (Paris) was considered his boldest and most beautiful work. It was demolished in 1939 for reasons of traffic improvement. The series of models shows three phases of the construction work for this stone bridge with five arches, each with a span of 40 m and a width of 15 m: the laying of the footing courses in dammed-in building pits with drainage; the vaulting technique, by the example of an arch with centers; and an end pier with abutment work on the river bank.

Stone Bridges

Primitive peoples developed a variety of construction methods for wooden bridges. Stone slabs could bridge only small spans. Arch construction, suitable for large spans, was perfected by the Romans. Much of their knowledge was lost during the Middle Ages. One of the first scientific approaches dates back to the 15th century in Italy, the Quattrocento. Leon Battista Alberti had studied the wide field of architecture in 1451/52; based upon the theory of dome construction, he developed the arch and stone bridge construction: *"Its parts are the following: the retaining walls on the banks, the piers, the arch and the roadway"*.

In the 18th century, with the development of civil engineering science, masterpieces of stone bridges were constructed in France: the ratio of arch rise to span was reduced, compared to the Roman bridges, thanks to the more accurate calculation of stability possible then.

Wooden Bridges

The earliest wooden bridges known are beams supported by piles. The Romans already knew the principle of the arched truss bridge. In the Middle Ages only simple beam bridges were built. Construction of suspension bridges and trussed bridges started in the Renaissance. In the 19th century, trusses for long spans were developed for railway bridges.

Iron and Steel Bridges, Suspension Bridges, Movable Bridges

The first cast-iron bridge was built in England (Coalbrookdale) in 1775. The introduction of wrought iron about 1850 created the possibility of bridging ever increasing spans due to the development of new truss systems. In recent times plain beam bridges have been built of high quality steel with welded joints. The suspension bridges of the 18th century were built as chain bridges. The widest spans are reached today, by means of the wire cable, first used in 1815. Wherever they disturb ship traffic, bridges must be movable. According to the situation, they are constructed as bascule bridges, lift bridges or swing bridges. A special form is the suspension ferry.

Concrete and Reinforced Concrete Bridges

The introduction of cement caused the revival of the concrete-pouring construction technique already used by the Romans. An ideal construction material resulted from the combination of concrete with steel. In 1875 the first reinforced concrete bridge was built in France. Since 1928 a method using prestressed concrete has been adopted.

Roads

The roads exhibition is arranged along the window side, so that the historic development nearly corresponds to that of bridge construction. The display is much more concise, because it does not show exhibits in full size, but almost exclusively models and pictures: chronology begins with the early history of man and thus with the history of paths, ways, roads and streets.   *F. Heilbronner*

Marine Navigation

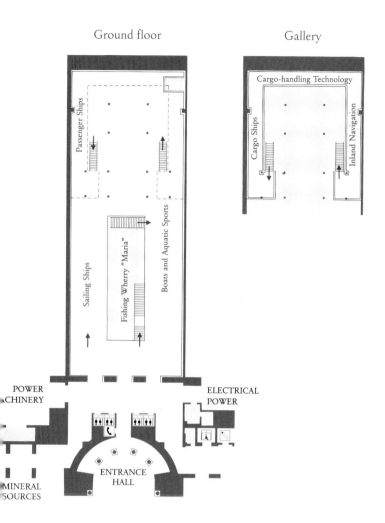

Ground floor

Gallery

Passenger Ships

Sailing Ships

Fishing Wherry "Maria"

Boats and Aquatic Sports

Cargo-handling Technology

Cargo Ships

Inland Navigation

POWER
MACHINERY

ELECTRICAL
POWER

ENTRANCE
HALL

MINERAL
SOURCES

Shipping doesn't appear in headlines any longer. It is expected to do its service in worldwide traffic and to operate reliably. Petrol, grains and ores, products and essential commodities are to be transported at the cheapest possible rate. The requirements of highest speed and of fast passenger traffic are meanwhile much better met by other means of transport.

The role of marine navigation in history was to make the Earth accessible to the nations, to make communication, trade – and wars – between the continents possible. The sailing ship, the steam engine and the container are milestones in its development. However, navigation was effective not only on the oceans; waterways were also important for inland traffic, under the primitive traffic conditions of former times. The rivers, the "waterways with inherent driving power", could be uti-

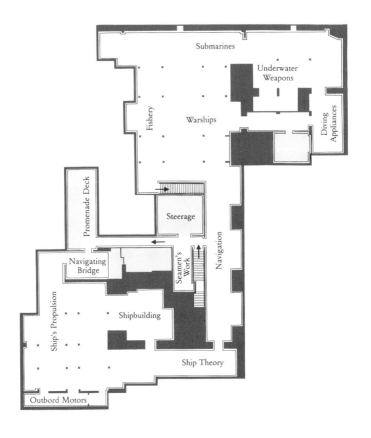

lized like conveyor belts. Eventually, even the digging of canals was rewarding: they allowed the profitable use of the physical properties of water, the smooth and yielding surface which made the moving of vehicles easier than on land.

In order to move about on water, i.e. for the construction of a suitable vessel, man first had to use the materials available in his environment: reed and grasses, a tree, its bark, hides. According to his skill and experience, he made floating bodies of manifold shapes: rafts by bundling together floating materials or inflated skins, dugout canoes by hollowing out trunks, and finally boats by covering frames or joining planks together. Only the last mentioned construction type was capable of development and offered the opportunity of building ships of growing dimensions thanks to sophisticated joining techniques. Wood as the sole suitable construction material for this purpose soon grew scarce in seafaring nations. This led to a destructive exploitation of forests, the ruinous effects of which are early examples of permanent ecological damage caused by man. The introduction of iron and steel brought no essential change in the structural shipbuilding technique, but abolished the limitation in size inherent in the construction of wooden ships. Extensive mechanization of the assembly process took place in the shipbuilding yards. Electric welding, brought in under wartime conditions, made sectional construction methods and thus shorter times of construction possible.

For propelling and steering his vessel, man may first have used his hands, later on paddles made of flat pieces of wood. A more efficient use of muscle power was achieved by the lever action of the oar.

Favourable winds were always welcome to ease the rower's job. Foliage and – later on – latticework and weavings were put up to catch the wind. In northern Europe, sails were used crosswise to the ship's direction, in the Mediterranean area also lengthwise. The struggle to build ships of larger size and good manoeuvrability led to the combining of both types into the three-masted sailing ship – "just in time" for the voyages of discovery of the 15th and 16th century. It allowed Europeans to develop merchandise traffic with the newly opened regions and to advance the creation of colonial empires. Sailing ships, which take the propelling energy from the environment, i.e., wind as fuel, were the

Fishing wherry "Maria", 1880 (O)
One of the last preserved sailing ships of this type. In the 19th century, wherries were widespread on the Lower Elbe, used either for freight transport or for fishing.

prerequisite for long voyages to unexplored regions. Only nuclear-powered ships have succeeded in circumnavigating the earth without refuelling – with considerably higher expenditure. The spread of canvas as a means of propulsion disappeared from the oceans just at the moment when it turned up in a new application field and became the object of detailed scientific study: in the lift of an air-foil.

The steam engine proved the new driving force in shipping. Developed from a cumbersome pump drive for mines in a relatively short period of time, it offered a double advantage: first, independence from wind conditions, so voyage planning became possible; second, undreamed of increase in performance, but not yet comfortable places of work for stokers and coal trimmers. The piston steam engine brought a decisive change for merchant vessels and warships.

The steam turbine then overcame the structural limitations of the piston steam engine, and with the diesel engine the combustion of the fuel was shifted into the engine itself; thus no expensive boiler plant was required any more. The big marine diesel engine has become the most common and economical power engine and is now frequently remote-controlled from the navigating bridge, without engine room staff.

The great advantage of the engines, i.e. the consistent availability of their power, could be utilized for the making up of time-tables only as soon as the ratio of engine capacity to ship's speed became known. The many centuries of experience with sailing ships were useless for this task. A theory of the ship, applicable to the practice, had to be found in order to enable the engineers to find the right construction type for ships of increasing size and speed and to harmonize the engine, screw and hull with each other.

Wherever the highest speed was at stake, as for instance with the transatlantic luxury liners, the aircraft soon proved superior. The rapidly rising fuel prices, however, also obliged freight ship traffic not only to speed up the sea steaming times, but also the transshipment of goods in the harbours and to shorten lay times. The introduction of the container allowed the mechanization of time-consuming loading and stevedoring work, which so far had to by carried out by hand, and the improvement of junctions with the existing traffic systems.

It seems a matter of course that shipping traffic operations nowadays take advantage of modern technology, such as radio, radar and satellite navigation. In former times, navigation often had to rely upon its own inventions for the determination of the ship's position and course at sea. The construction of an accurate chronometer for longitude determination or the gyro-compass are examples of this.

Throughout history, shipping traffic, maritime commerce and sea power have also implied the existence of weapons and suitable protection against them. For a long time, there was little change in the technology of ships, regardless of whether the freight area and the armature were fitted into the same ship or separately to special merchant vessels and to warships. The introduction of steel and the development of special steel types for guns and armour, made possible by new methods of steel manufacture and processing, led to the development of an independent technology of arms. The lead storage battery and the electro-

Steam tug "Renzo" from Venice, 1932 (O)
One of the many tug-boats which towed barges or lighters on inland waterways or tugged larger ships in harbours. Her engine plant (small picture) – consisting of a coal-fired, later oil-fired boiler and a two-cylinder compound engine – and the fuel bunker filled nearly the whole shiproom.

motor, which also served as dynamo, provided the submarine with an air-independent propulsion system.

Together with the torpedo, the submarine became a new weapon in sea warfare. Its use during two world wars resulted in the mass production of transport vessels, the development of detecting methods and the aircraft. Technology in the service of destruction brings death and inexpressible suffering to millions of people.

The Marine Navigation Department is housed on the ground floor, behind the entrance hall. After the destruction during the war, it was re-arranged on two levels (ground floor and basement), and reorganized and completed after fire damage in 1983. The exhibition comprises individual self-contained topics on the history of naval technology. We suggest the following tour:

The Evolution of the Sailing Ship

A series of models along the left side of the ground floor exhibition explains the advance in utilization and mastery of wind power for long distance voyages.

The cog of the Hanseatic League, caravels and three-masted ships, like the *Peter von Danzig,* are milestones in this development. These ships, the largest technical devices at the beginning of modern times, opened up far-away continents and already showed all essential features of the future sailing ship types.

Early Steam Ships

This section illustrates a fundamental change in 19th century technology: by means of the steam engine, man frees himself from dependence upon wind power and muscle power.

"Kaiser Wilhelm II",
1903 (M)
The cutaway model shows the coal bunkers and, above, the sumptuous dining room of the First Class. In order to give this room light and height, four decks were cut out. A deluxe hotel travelling on the seas.

Liquefied-gas tanker, 1985 (M)
Liquefied-gas tankers transport natural gas, the volume of which is reduced to 1/600th for transportation by means of liquefaction. Such LNG tankers with their costly technological equipment are considered the top quality cargo vessels.

The competition between sailing ships and steam vessels, which advanced the technical evolution of sailing ships, is shown by means of models and graphs. The two largest originals of the collection, the wherry *Maria* and the steam tug-boat *Renzo*, represent the characteristics of both eras: the traditional rigging, consisting of simple individual parts, has been substituted by an immense engine plant hidden in the ship's hull.

Passenger Ships

The designs of *passenger ships* built in the first half of the 20th century were to demonstrate the high technical standards and the national prestige of the leading seafaring nations. Three models illustrate the changes in the architecture of the ships' exterior; two wooden figures show the overdone decoration typical for saloons of the imperial era.

The Ship as a Means of Transport

The most important task of modern shipping is the subject of the display on the newly installed gallery. A few series of models explain the various types of transport vessels developed for the manifold transport requirements of industrial society. The *technology of cargo handling,* too, had to keep up with the tempo of our time. The container linked shipping, road and railway traffic in one traffic system. *Inland navigation* has been an indispensable means of transport since pre-industrial times, before other means of mass transport came into use.

Boats and Water Sports (Aquatics)

Man made his first trips on the water by means of rafts and boats. Industrial society revived the various types of boats used for work by the primitive tribes and changed them into sport equipment. Thus, fighting with the winds and waves has become a leisure-time adventure. Several originals, ranging from the raft to the gondola, represent the constructional principles of these individual water vehicle types with their great variety of regional forms. The racing shells and the racing jolly show the craftsmanship of the shipbuilders whose skill can be decisive in sports competition.

Wheelhouse of the freighter "Adolph Woermann", 1922 (O, R)
It was reconstructed in 1986 and houses the steering column and the compass; moreover, a self-steering gear linked with a gyro-compass as well as telegraphs for the transmission of orders to the engine room staff.

The Ship as Living Space

From the staircase leading from the open side of the wherry *Maria* down to the basement, the visitor gets a view into the simple lodgings of fishermen and the confinement of the steerage (R) in which emigrants were housed during their journey into an uncertain future; it contrasts with the spacious promenade deck (R) of a passenger ship. During their scarce spare time aboard, seamen made fancywork from ropes, models and bottled ships on display opposite the "steerage".

Navigating Bridge

The navigating bridge is the centre where the equipment for navigation and communication is concentrated. In the reconstructed wheel house of a cargo ship (of 1922), the effects of steering gear operations are demonstrated at varying speeds of the ship.

Mechanical Ship Drives

The *mechanical ship drives* consist of the power engine and power transmission to the propelling element, such as the *paddle wheel* or the *screw propeller*. The first *steam engines* with their small number of revolutions harmonized with the equally slow paddle wheels (original of a *twin-cylinder steam engine* with oscillating cylinders, of 1857). Because of the higher performance and numbers of revolutions of screw propulsion, vibration problems arose with the enormous *steam piston engines* in the flexible hull of the ship and required detailed study of machine dynamics (demonstration of mass balancing). The *steam turbine* with its smoother running was economical only when tuning of turbine and propeller became possible by the construction of suitable gears. However, the steam turbine was soon rivalled by the combustion engine. Today the diesel engine in particular has developed into the most economical and most common power engine.

Ship Theory

It is the task of ship theory to study the flow around the ship and the propeller, and to supply fundamentals for ship design. Even today, the technique of model experiments is widely used in this field (demonstration of the cavitation experiment and of the model tank).

Shipbuilding

Until the mid-nineteenth century, *shipbuilding* was determined by the tradition of craftsmanship in wooden shipbuilding. We show a collection of typical wood working implements, next to cross-sections of boats and ships and to a diorama of a shipbuilding yard for wooden ships. Steel shipbuilding got a strong impetus from the introduction of autogenous cutting and of electric welding. Section building allowed extensive pre-fabrication of large panels in the sheds. Together with mechanization and – later on – automation of working cycles, it has considerably cut down the construction time for ships (diorama of a steel shipbuilding yard).

Navigation

It is the task of *navigation* to fix a safe and economical course for a ship and to keep to it. In the beginnings of seafaring, this was possible only in

Yard for the construction of wooden ships, around 1830 (Di)
The work of the shipwright may be followed up through the constructional phases of different ships: laying down the keel, the erection of the frames, the launch. The ship's construction takes place on the soft river bank, without machinery and work-halls.

the protection and sight of the coast. The registration of conspicuous details of the coastline in manuals went on for a long time. A simple but important auxiliary means of coastal navigation is the *plumb-line* for the measurement of water depth. Around the 14th century, the *magnetic compass* came into use for the determination of the cardinal points. Together with the log, a device for the measurement of the ship's speed relative to the water – not above the ground –, it made a nearly accurate recording of the covered distance possible. We show a few selected magnetic compasses and the first *gyro-compass* by Herrmann Anschütz. With gyro-compasses, the rotation of the Earth is used for the definition of the true north. Fixing the ship's position on the high seas was achieved in a more accurate way by astronomical navigation, which eliminated the influence of winds and currents. As soon as the course of the stars and their position in the sky were known, the latitude of the ship's position could be fixed by means of *angle measuring equipment,* such as the sextants. The determination of the longitude, for which it is necessary to have the accurate local time, gave stimulus to the development of a precision chronometer in the 18th century.

Electromagnetic waves penetrate clouds and fog. As early as the turn of the century, attemps were made to "signal" distant objects to an observer using such waves. Christian Hülsmeyer's *telemobiloscope* (1904) may be considered a forerunner of the radar which, however, was developed only during the Second World War. Wireless position finding and – in recent times – satellite navigation allow accurate position fixing even with bad weather.

"U1" submarine, 1906 (O)
The engine room houses two electromotors for unterwater moving and two petrol engines for propulsion on the water surface in the narrow pressure hull of circular shape.

Rescue cruiser of the "Theodor Heuss" class, 1960 (O)
Rescue cruisers assist people in emergencies at sea. For this purpose, they are equipped with the most modern ship technology. Length: 23.2 m. Capacity: 1290 kw, 3 propeller, 20 kn (37 km/h).

Fishing

Fishery provides a substantial part of the world's food. In the basement, below the stern of the wherry *Maria,* we show the evolution and intensification of fishing methods and the appropriate vessels (original of a fishermen's dugout from the Lake of Starnberg and of a Portuguese dory). Increasing industrialization of fishery led to the decrease of fishing stock. International treaties are expected to prevent overfishing.

Warships

In the section on warships, opposite the reconstructed gun deck of a frigate of about 1690, we show a developmental series of sailing warships which takes up the theme of the development of the sailing ship. The armament of the Navy of Imperial Germany and of the German Reich as well as the technical development of their ships are illustrated by models and graphs. The originals of this section are: a functional model of Wilhelm Bauer's submersible (1852), the submarine *U1* (1906), which was brought to the Museum in 1923, and a two man submarine of the Second World War.

Diving Appliances

Civil diving technology, serving oceanic research, is displayed by the bathysphere (R) of Auguste and Jacques Piccard which reached a diving depth of 10916 m.   *J. Broelmann*

Suggestions for the continuation of the tour
The tour of the ground floor ends here. Up the main staircase, you go past the restaurant and arrive at the first floor. There, going around the corner at the right, you will find a room with a display on the *History of the Deutsches Museum* (p. 126), which you should have seen before entering the *Hall of Fame.* You also can continue your tour in the *Aeronautics* department (p. 180), the historical section of which is situated on the first floor.

History of the Deutsches Museum
(in preparation)

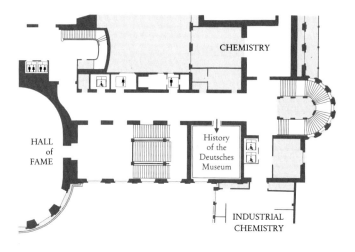

In the 18th century, when French craftsmanship was the best in the world, a museum of arts and crafts, the *Conservatoire des Arts et Métiers*, was founded in Paris. Later, when England took over the lead in industrial competition, the first museum of technology was set up in London – the *South Kensington Museum*, named *Science Museum* today. About 1880, a young engineer from Munich, Oskar von Miller, visited both institutions. The historic items from the fields of handicrafts, natural science and technology captivated and inspired him. However, he regretted that they were so "dead", so immobile and directed only to experts. From that moment, Oskar von Miller cherished the idea of setting up a museum of technology in Germany, preferably in Munich. But this should be a truly "vivid" museum of natural science and technology, a kind of a technological "playground" for ordinary people, amusing and educational at the same time.

For two decades, Miller did not achieve any progress. Then Germany took a leading position among the industrial nations. In the young empire, a broad technical knowledge became an important economic factor. In 1903, Oskar von Miller brought the association *Museum of Masterpieces of Natural Science and Technology* into existence. Only three years later, the foundation-stone for an ample museum building was laid on an island of the Isar. Simultaneously, the extensive temporary collections were made accessible to the public in two unoccupied public buildings.

The construction of the museum, only made possible by private gifts, was continued – despite enormous difficulties – even during the First World War, and was received with enthusiasm by all social classes. In order to express this fact, the museum was given the name *Deutsches Museum.* From the very beginning, the approximately 40 departments, which opened in 1925, documented continuously the international development of science and technology.

The development of a completely new exhibition system enabling the visitor himself to set in motion defined processes and to repeat them until he really understood them – "comprehension by grasping" – did not satisfy the museum's founder. During the worst economic crisis of modern times, he had another building constructed – the Library building. Here the – perhaps superficial – impressions of the "show collections" could be deepened by reading and listening. In 1932, Oskar von Miller opened the comprehensive technical library to the public. The Congress building with its lecture halls was finished in 1935, after the death of Oskar von Miller.

The National Socialists criticised the Deutsches Museum as out of date and planned a *House of German Technology*, intended to correspond to the spirit of the time, on the opposite bank of the Isar. The Second World War prevented its construction. Air raids destroyed 80 percent of the buildings of the Deutsches Museum and about 20 percent of the exhibits; the most important ones had been evacuated before. The inventory of books remained intact. After the 1945 collapse the Museum had to be almost entirely rebuilt. The companies traditionally linked to the Deutsches Museum contributed the construction material and made the necessary workers available. In 1947, the Congress building was re-opened and used for commercial purposes by the Museum in order to earn money for the reconstruction of the exhibits. In 1948, the Physics department was the first section to be re-opened.

Though the reconstruction was finished at the end of 1960, the Deutsches Museum will never be completed. Its task is to show the development of natural science and technology from the latest historical viewpoint and from that of the most recent discoveries. This is why the catalogue of the exhibition topics and the way of their presentation are subject to continuous change. In recent years, among others, the following halls have been inaugurated: the ample Aeronautics and Astronautics Hall (in 1984), the re-arranged Railways Hall and the Power Machinery Hall (both in 1985), the Motor Vehicles Hall with doubled dimensions as well as the Marine Navigation Hall (both in 1986).

With the increasing part played by technology in daily life in the 1950s and 1960s, our relation to technology has changed. Technology is no longer considered exclusively as a purely material base of civilization, but increasingly as an integral part of cultural life whose effects should be studied. This idea led to the foundation of the *Research Institute for the History of Natural Science and Technology.*

The history of technology as the history of civilization – this is the way of thinking that the Deutsches Museum wants to inspire in its visitors, especially in its young visitors. During the educational boom of the 1970s, when 1000 school classes per month came to the Deutsches Museum, assistance for teachers became a necessity. Since 1976, teachers and instructors can attend continuation courses at the *Kerschensteiner Kolleg* in the Deutsches Museum.

Z. Hlava

Hall of Fame

In the Hall of Fame, great German scientists and inventors are honoured with busts, reliefs and paintings. In the *Amtlicher Führer (Official Guide),* first edition 1925 (still in Oskar von Miller's lifetime), the appropriate text reads: *"Here the point was to make a thankful commemoration of outstanding scientists, engineers and industrialists and to create a Hall of Fame worthy of the achievements of these intellectual heroes and their infinitely beneficial effects for mankind".*

Ernst Abbe	23.01.1840 – 14.01.1905 Physicist, social politician	Bust
Georg Agricola	24.03.1494 – 21.11.1554 Humanist, physician, mineralogist	Bust
Albertus Magnus	1193 (?) – 15.11.1280 Scientist, theologian	Relief
Adolf von Baeyer	31.10.1835 – 20.08.1917 Chemist	Bust
Carl Benz	25.11.1844 – 04.04.1929 Engineer, entrepreneur	Relief
August Borsig	23.06.1804 – 06.07.1854 Locomotive designer, industrialist	Relief
Carl Bosch	27.08.1874 – 26.04.1940 Chemist	Bust
Robert Bunsen	31.03.1811 – 16.08.1899 Chemist	Painting
Rudolf Clausius	02.01.1822 – 24.08.1888 Physicist	Bust
Nicolaus Copernicus	19.02.1473 – 25.05.1543 Astronomer	Relief
Gottlieb Daimler	17.03.1834 – 06.03.1900 Engineer, machinist, entrepreneur	Relief
Rudolf Diesel	18.03.1858 – 29.09.1913 Engineer, machinist	Relief
Albert Einstein	14.03.1879 – 18.04.1955 Physicist	Bust
Joseph von Fraunhofer	06.03.1787 – 07.06.1826 Physicist, optician	Painting
Karl Friedrich Gauß	30.04.1777 – 23.02.1855 Mathematician, astronomer	Painting
Otto von Guericke	20.11.1602 – 11.05.1686 Engineer, physicist	Painting
Johannes Gutenberg	1395 to 1400 – Febr. 1468 Inventor of letterpress printing	Relief
Fritz Haber	09.12.1868 – 29.01.1934 Chemist	Bust
Otto Hahn	08.03.1879 – 28.07.1968 Chemist	Bust

Friedrich Harkort	22.02. 1793 – 06.03. 1880	Bust
	Industrialist, politician	
Hermann von Helmholtz	31.08. 1821 – 08.09. 1894	Bust
	Physiologist, physicist, mathematician	
Heinrich Hertz	22.02. 1857 – 01.01. 1894	Bust
	Physicist	
Hugo Junkers	03.02. 1859 – 03.02. 1935	Bust
	Aircraft designer, entrepreneur	
Johannes Kepler	27.12. 1571 – 15.11. 1630	Relief
	Astronomer, mathematician	
Alfred Krupp	26.04. 1812 – 14.07. 1887	Relief
	Engineer, industrialist	
Gottfried Wilhelm Leibniz	01.07. 1646 – 14.11. 1716	Painting
	Polymath (scientist), philosopher	
Justus von Liebig	12.05. 1803 – 18.04. 1873	Bust
	Chemist	
Otto Lilienthal	23.05. 1848 – 10.08. 1896	Bust
	Engineer, aeronautical pioneer	
Carl von Linde	11.06. 1842 – 16.11. 1934	Bust
	Engineer, industrialist	
Wilhelm Maybach	09.02. 1846 – 29.12. 1929	Relief
	Engineer, entrepreneur	
Julius Robert Mayer	25.11. 1814 – 20.03. 1878	Bust
	Physician, physicist	
Georg Simon Ohm	16.03. 1789 – 07.07. 1854	Bust
	Physicist	
Nikolaus August Otto	10.06. 1832 – 26.01. 1891	Relief
	Machinist, entrepreneur	
Max Planck	23.04. 1858 – 04.10. 1947	Bust
	Physicist	
Wilhelm Conrad Röntgen	27.03. 1854 – 10.02. 1923	Bust
	Physicist	
Ferdinand Schichau	30.01. 1814 – 23.01. 1896	Relief
	Ship designer, entrepreneur	
Werner von Siemens	13.12. 1816 – 06.12. 1892	Relief
	Engineer, industrialist	
Friedrich Wöhler	31.07. 1800 – 23.09. 1882	Bust
	Chemist	

The ceiling shows a fresco painting of Prometheus. Two reliefs, one above each portal, symbolize the Study of Nature and Technology by Daedalus and Icarus, and by a wise man initiating his disciples in the world of celestial bodies.

Georg Friedrich Brander
Joseph von Fraunhofer

Between the Hall of Fame and the Physics Exhibition, there are two exhibition rooms showing scientific instruments of two famous instrument makers of Germany.

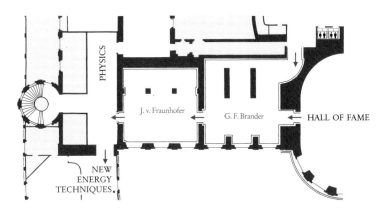

Georg Friedrich Brander (1713–1783), Scientific Instrument Maker

The first room houses the collection of Georg Friedrich Brander. In the 18th century, he was the best known manufacturer of scientific instruments in Germany. His workshop was in Augsburg. As a founding member of the Academy of Science of the Electorate of Bavaria, he became the main supplier of scientific instruments to the Munich Academy founded in 1759. Among his clients were numerous universities and observatories. In the southern German-speaking area he mainly supplied the important Benedictine abbeys reputed to be the spiritual carriers of the Enlightenment.

He first made a name for himself by the construction of the first reflecting telescope in Germany, later by the micrometers on glass plates first manufactured by him with high precision. These glass micrometers, fitted into telescopes and microscopes, made considerably more accurate measuring possible.

G. F. Brander's workshop – similar to those of his renowned contemporaries in London and Paris – offered the entire range of scientific instruments known at that time. The main source of income of the workshop was the sale of instruments for geodesy, i.e. of telescopic alidades, surveyor's boards, optical distance meters, and theodolites. Upon request, Brander even made large astronomical instruments. His quadrant, a masterpiece of that time, was installed in the Court Gardens of Munich, in 1761, for the observation of the transit of Venus through the solar disk. The result of these measurements was a correction of the geographical position of Munich. Brander also manufactured instruments for physics and meteorology. His divided-glass micrometers possibly paved the way for the discovery of diffraction grating by Joseph von Fraunhofer.

The collection shown here comprises about 140 of Brander's instruments. Of an 18th-century manufacturer, it is therefore one of the most comprehensive collections and gives an excellent survey of the art of scientific instrument-making in the 18th century.

Joseph von Fraunhofer (1787–1826), Optician and Astronomer

The next room shows instruments manufactured by Joseph von Fraunhofer, Georg von Reichenbach (1772–1826) and Joseph Liebherr (1767–1840), thus illustrating the beginnings of the renowned Munich school of scientific instrument-making of the 19th century.

As a consequence of the *Napoleonic Wars* and the concomitant demand for maps, official surveying of Bavaria started in 1801. One year later, in 1802, G. von Reichenbach and J. Liebherr founded an institute of mathematics and precision mechanics in order to manufacture the required surveying instruments. In 1804, Joseph von Utzschneider joined the institute as financier, and in 1806, Joseph von Fraunhofer as optician. In 1809, a separate optical instrument-making institute under

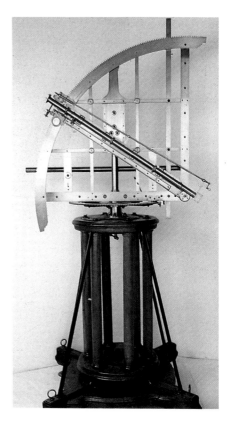

Azimuth quadrant by G. F. Brander (O)
This instrument was made in 1760/61 for the Academy of Science of the Bavarian Electorate and intended for the observation of the transit of Venus through the solar disk on June 6, 1761. In the 18th century, Brander was the most important instrument-maker in Germany. In his Augsburg workshop, he manufactured a variety of scientific instruments for astronomy, geodesy and physics. The observation of the transit of Venus through the solar disk served, first, the determination of the exact local time differences between distinct observational places and thus of their longitudes, second, the indirect calculation of the diameter of the earth's orbit around the sun.

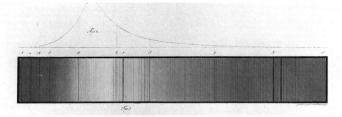

Solar spectrum, drawn by von Fraunhofer, 1814 (O)
Solar spectrum, showing dark lines (discovered by Joseph von Fraunhofer presumably in 1814); above is a curve indicating the intensity of the light. This drawing was made and coloured by von Fraunhofer himself.

the supervision of Fraunhofer and Utzschneider was founded. Both the Reichenbach and the Fraunhofer institutes gained worldwide fame by their scientific instruments. They laid the foundation of scientific instrument-making in Germany. Numerous students came forth from these institutes and spread the acquired knowledge and craftsmanship by their own workshops.

Fraunhofer's outstanding achievements were: the production of pure optical glass; the development of new methods of calculation for objectives; and the introduction of new manufacturing processes. This made the manufacture of achromatic lens telescopes with objective diameters of up to about 40 cm possible for the first time. For about 75 years, this instrument type supplanted the astronomical reflecting telescopes. The planet *Neptune* was discovered by means of Fraunhofer's instruments (by Johann Gottfried Galle, in 1846) and the finite distance of various fixed stars from the Earth (stellar parallax) was measured for the first time (by Friedrich Wilhelm Bessel, in 1838). Most of the important observatories of the 19th century were equipped with Fraunhofer's instruments.

Fraunhofer's success in the production of suitable optical glass was based upon his discovery of the dark absorption lines in the solar spectrum. These lines bear his name now. Not until 1886 was his method of glassmaking improved by Otto Schott, Ernst Abbe and Carl Zeiss. Moreover, Fraunhofer found out that glass measuring devices with very close parallel lines (glass micrometers, gratings) also diffract white light into a spectrum by interference. This was decisive evidence in favour of the wave theory of light, contested at that time.

The collection of instruments by Fraunhofer and Reichenbach on display here comprises the most important ones: the prism spectrograph, heliometer, Galle refractor and astronomical universal theodolite are outstanding masterpieces. In addition to them, Fraunhofer's pendulum grinding machine, then a revolution in the manufacture of optical lenses, can also be seen here.

A. Brachner

New Energy Techniques

PHYSICS

The Nature of Energy

Additional Energy Sources

The Main Energy Sources

Energy Saving

Energy from Uranium

For thousands of years, the muscle power of man and of his animals was the only available energy source. The Middle Ages added the utilization of flowing water and of the wind. Since the 17th century, heated steam has gained outstanding importance as a means of energy transfer in ever-improving machinery.

The burning of wood alone soon proved insufficient to meet the rising power demand of modern civilization; however, the burning of fossil fuels such as coal or petrol, and the increasing use of uranium in recent times influence the environment to such a degree that since the energy cost crisis in 1973, efforts have had to be made to save energy through increasing efficiency of production methods or the additional use of replenishable sources.

In daily life, the concepts of work and power are often used unclearly. *Energy, heat* and *work* are quantities of the same kind. They are measured in units of equal value according to the International System of Measurement: *1 joule = 1 watt second = 1 newton metre.* Many energy carriers are burnt when used. In order to obtain comparable values for the energy contents of different energy sources, reference is made to the calorific value of hard coal as *29,3 megajoule per kilogramme.* Thus, *1 coal equivalent = 29,3 megajoule.*

When energy is expended, heat is released or work is done, and the required amount of time during which this happens is taken into account, we speak of power; the appropriate unit being the *watt.* Electric power is usually measured in *kilowatts* (kW).

The description of work as a fundamental value of mechanics, which has to be expended wherever forces are to be overcome, goes back to Jean Victor Poncelet who in 1829 was the first to use the term "work" for the product of force multiplied by distance.

Information on the Exhibition

In the Deutsches Museum, many separate sections of the exhibition departments deal with aspects of the technology of energy: an area of about 2 000 m² is dedicated to exhaustible *sources of primary energy,* such as coal, mineral oil and natural gas, and another two departments with 800 m² to regenerative sources of primary energy, such as water or wind. *Secondary energy,* i. e. improved primary energy, illustrated by the themes of Steam Engines, Electrical Power Engineering, Coal Treatment and Oil Refining occupies another 2 000 m².

If the study is extended to the forms of energy directly used by man, such as industrial heating or mechanical work, i.e. to usable energy, it may be said that including the departments of Metallurgy and Industrial Chemistry as well as the vast departments of Motor Vehicles (Automobiles and Motorcycles), Railways, Aeronautics and Marine Navigation more than half of the Deutsches Museum is dedicated to energy.

Because of the separately housed displays, the department of New Energy Techniques gives a survey of the fundamentals in an area of about 600 m², enlarged by the subject of *nuclear energy.* The utilization of this exhaustible source of primary energy has not yet been dealt with in the Deutsches Museum in a way corresponding to its importance.

The route is about 100 m long and includes the following five sections with their main exhibits:

The Nature of Energy

Energy is one of the basic necessities of life and of technology. It appears in six different physical forms: heat, mechanical energy, nuclear energy, chemical energy, electricity and radiation. During technical processes these forms are changed from one to another in numerous ways. The final result of such energy conversion chains is heat.

The Main Energy Sources

The nuclear fusion processes in the sun supply nearly all the energy for the Earth. Non-replenishable energy sources like coal or crude oil are forms of stored solar energy. However, even the water flowing through the turbine uses energy from the cycle of evaporation and precipitation caused by the sun.

By pictures, tables and a few original objects the importance of the main energy sources is illustrated. These find their place in different sections of the Deutsches Museum, such as Mining, Mineral Oil and Natural Gas, and Water Turbines. In addition, the processing of energy within our industrial society is shown by means of four diagrams.

Entrance area of the "New Energy Techniques" exhibition
The exhibition was opened in December 1983. The entrance area supplies information on the nature of energy; the subsequent globe shows the geographic distribution of the main energy sources – coal, mineral oil, natural gas, water power and uranium – on the Earth. The sun dial hanging above (on which slides on solar activities are projected) indicates the fact that in the end all energy comes from the sun, except for nuclear energy which is won from uranium. In the rear, there is an air lock on the way to the reconstructed nuclear plants of a nuclear power station; it is preceded by a whole-body contamination monitor. At the right, in the background, stands a sectioned "Helioman", a concentrating collector for solar farms; in the cylinder focal line, thermo-oil as a means of energy transport is pumped to a heat exchanger.

Air lock (R) of a reactor and whole-body contamination monitor, 1977 (O, P)
Nuclear fission produces heat, radiation and waste. In order to protect the environment, the nuclear fuel in the reactor core is surrounded by several safety barriers. The air lock allows staff members to move in and out of the nuclear plants, through the steel safety container and the outer reinforced concrete walls: the low pressure prevents the escape of radioactive material from the reactor. For the protection of staff working in nuclear plants, controlled areas are established at the air locks. After leaving them, staff members are checked for radioactive contamination by monitors. The whole-body monitor separately measures the head, chest, hands, legs and feet and thus makes a quick localization of contamination possible.

Pressure vessel and fuel element of a pressurized water reactor, 1978 (R)
The blue Cerenkov radiation is visible in the water of the pressure vessel of the reactor.
On the right stands a piece of steel cut out to allow a view of the cross section. Above
the concentric concrete shield (biological shield) is to be seen. This heat source of
today's standard atomic power plant of 1300 megawatt capacity is made up of 193 fuel
elements each with 236 fuel rods 4 meters long.

Energy from Uranium

Since the discovery of nuclear fission in 1938 uranium has been used as
an energy source.
Within the cross-section of a life-size reactor the barriers around the
radioactive uranium are explained; the processing of the uranium from
ore to fuel elements and – after its use in the reactor – its transport to
the reprocessing plant and final storage is shown. Problems of safety,
environment and monitoring are also dealt with here.

The New Energy Source: To Save Energy

Much energy can be saved by building insulation. But other processing
methods, too, such as new operational methods for power plants, like
waste heat use, on-site power plants (cogenerators), the optimization of
the national grid and the use of environmental heat bring about a more
efficient use of fuels.

Additional Energy Sources

As a consequence of the price increase of fossil fuels since 1973, the use of natural energy sources has again gained in importance. Nature supplies nearly inexhaustible reserves which, however, because of the low concentration and inconsistent supply, can only be exploited with a considerable expenditure on concentration and storage. This is why currently solar energy, wind energy, biomass energy, tidal and geothermal energy can only be *additional* and not *alternative* sources of energy to the main energy sources like coal, mineral oil, natural gas and nuclear energy.

F. Heilbronner

Heat pump, 1982 (O, P)
The radiator (left) gives off more energy than the amount of electrical energy that is supplied to the driving motor of the compressor (on top); the difference is taken from the environment (below, at right). The heat pump is nothing more than the cooling element in the refrigerator; the only difference being that the main feature is the heat-supplying liquefier (left) and not so much the heat-absorbing evaporator (right). The working fluid – called refrigerant in the refrigerator – is a liquid boiling at a low temperature (about 10 °C). In the form of vapour, it is compressed by the compressor (on top) and thus heated. In the subsequent heat exchanger the vapour is condensed by chilling (liquefier) and leaves as a liquid that sinks down to the throttle valve (below). There, another chilling by reduction of pressure takes place. The liquefied working fluid then reaches the evaporator, absorbs heat from the environment and can boil again using this heat; the resulting vapour is then compressed in the compressor, and the cycle starts again. The heat pump contributes to energy saving particularly if the compressor is not driven electrically, but by a gas motor; two energy flow diagrams illustrate this fact.

Physics

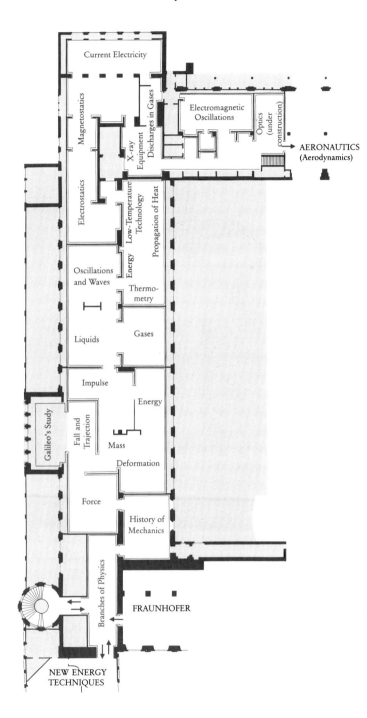

Current Electricity

Magnetostatics

Electrostatics

X-ray Equipment

Discharges in Gases

Electromagnetic Oscillations

Optics (under construction)

→ AERONAUTICS (Aerodynamics)

Low-Temperature Technology

Energy

Propagation of Heat

Oscillations and Waves

Thermo-metry

Liquids

Gases

Impulse

Energy

Fall and Trajectory

Mass

Galileo's Study

Deformation

Force

History of Mechanics

Branches of Physics

FRAUNHOFER

NEW ENERGY TECHNIQUES

Physics is a science that is basic to the whole field of technology. It investigates the regularities apparent in inanimate nature by means of theoretical study and experiment. It is an exact science, that is to say it expresses these relationships in mathematic formulas using precisely defined symbols.

The arrangement of the exhibition follows the path of historic development which separated the different fields according to the human senses. *Mechanics* deals with the movements of bodies, especially under the action of external forces. An important branch of mechanics is the *theory of oscillations,* which has become an element of all other branches of physics, e.g. of *optics.* Simple laws of *mechanics* and *optics* were already known in Greek Antiquity, but substantial progress began only around 1600.

A *theory of heat* developed around 1700 with the construction of the first thermometers. Electrical phenomena, however, do not correspond directly to a single human sense perception. Their scientific study began in the 18th century.

Philosophical speculation about the *structure of matter,* atoms and molecules can be traced back to Greek Antiquity. Experimental insight, however, was obtained only by research in the 19th century. At the beginning of the 20th century, a field of knowledge that dealt with parts of atoms, i.e. with the elementary particles, developed and became the basis of the whole of physical science.

The historic evolution of the individual branches, however, was quite different and will be described in detail on the following pages.

Early mechanical aids: wheel, winch with pulley block, piston pump for wells (O)
By means of such aids, man has tried to make life easier, at least since the time of recorded history.

Information on the Exhibition

Visitors entering the department through an introductory room will see the subsequent sections more or less obligatorily along the guide-line, until they reach the optics section where they have to cross the Aeronautics department (aerodynamics section) in order to get to the exhibition of atomic and nuclear physics and the study of elementary particles.

Introductory Room

The exhibition of the branches of physics is preceded by an introductory room with fundamental experiments; here the visitor is given a survey of all branches of physics and thus an idea of the themes that are explained along the guide-line of about 200 m in length. Passing through this room, he will easily understand the didactic intention of the entire department, i.e. the opportunity of making experiments oneself.

Mechanics of Solids

The needs of daily work soon caused man to take advantage of physical principles, even though he had no clear comprehension of them. Simple levers and the inclined plane were the oldest tools of man. Screws used as driving mechanisms, and pulleys, were added only in Greek Antiquity. The belief in man being able to "outwit" nature (which is the ori-

Galileo's study (R)
About 1609, from experiments on the inclined plane, Galileo discovered the law of falling bodies and thus created the first physical theory.

Momentum transfer by elastic spheres hit by central impact; a demonstration set up in the Physics department. The impulse (momentum) is a physical quantity which is conserved in any kind of force-free motion.

gin of the word "mechanics" in Greek) persisted for a long time. One of the discoveries that heralded the modern era was that although it is possible with a machine to lift a heavy load with a small force, the distance covered by the force must be correspondingly increased, so that the work done is the same as if the load had been lifted directly. This was a discovery which was extended to the general law known as the "principle of the conservation of energy" (19th century) which has gained fundamental importance for the whole field of physics and technology.

A decisive part in the evolution of mechanics towards mathematical science was played by Galileo (early 17th century). In 1687, Isaac Newton introduced a comprehensive scientific system of mechanics which widely influenced the European civilization of the 18th and 19th centuries. This theory became a model for all other endeavours to accumulate scientific knowledge of nature. Thus mathematics became the fundamental discipline of physics.

The theory of the simple mechanics of solids starts from the supposition that the atoms are rigidly connected to each other. In the following rooms of this section mechanical terms and their relationships are explained by means of simple experiments. The basic quantities are: mass, length, time. All other quantities, e.g. force, work, energy, are combinations of these.

Mechanics of Liquids and Gases

The fundamental laws which form the basis of mechanics of liquids and gases at rest (hydrostatics) were partly known in Antiquity. About 250 B.C. Archimedes drew important conclusions from the phenomenon of buoyancy, and in the first century A.D. Hero of Alexandria introduced the concept of atmospheric pressure into the explanation of his devices. But in this field, too, there was no further advancement until

Exhaust pump and Magdeburg hemispheres by Otto von Guericke, 1663 (O)
By means of his exhaust pumps, Guericke showed that it was possible to produce spaces of at least rarefied air. Thus he defeated the opinion that "nature fears the vacuum" (horror vacui).

modern times. Molecules of liquids, as compared with those of solid bodies, can more freely change their position relative to one another. This explains why they flow easily and why they take the shape of their containing vessel. However, the compression of liquids is almost impossible since their molecules are so close together. The molecules of a gas, on the contrary, are almost completely independent as they move around in their enclosure. They can therefore be compressed easily, as compared with solids and liquids. The production of extremely rarefied gases has attained special importance in the form of vacuum technology. The magnitude of the atmospheric pressure can be demonstrated in a particularly interesting demonstration.

Hydrodynamics deals with flowing liquids and gases. Research in this field is essential for all activities in which flowing substances play some part, especially in shipbuilding and aircraft construction.

Oscillations and Waves

The first oscillation ever studied in detail was that of the pendulum (Galileo, 1609). Wave propagation on the surface of water, as well as acoustic waves, were described precisely by Newton (1687). However, it was not until the 18th century that a basis for a deeper understanding of these phenomena was created.

Oscillations are periodic movements in which states of rest and states of movement continually alternate, as with the clock pendulum. If oscillations can spread in their surrounding medium, the formation of waves, e.g. of water waves, is the result. It is a special property of waves that intersecting wave formations can either amplify or extinguish each other. This phenomenon is called interference. Oscillation theory first gained great importance in mechanics. It applied, for example, to the whole field of acoustics, since sound waves are nothing else but propagating waves of compressed and rarefied air.

The wave theory subsequently became an essential element of other branches of physics. Just think of electric oscillations and of the propagation of electromagnetic waves. The same applies to optics, since light can be described as an electromagnetic wave.

Heat

In the course of the 18th century it was recognized that, as regards heat, two different ideas are to be distinguished: temperature and the quantity of heat. Bodies having the same temperature can nevertheless contain different quantities of heat.

For a long time it was generally thought that heat was a substance which penetrated bodies. Only after the beginning of the 19th century did the idea gain acceptance that what was then called heat was the random motion of molecules. Thereupon it became possible to associate heat with the law of conservation of mechanical energy. This led to the general "principle of conservation of energy" first enunciated by Julius Robert Mayer in 1842: *"Energy cannot be generated, but only converted from one form to another".*

A great impulse to fundamental physics resulted from later developments in the study of heat. Problems arose in connection with radiation; their solution by Max Planck (1900) led to the quantum theory.

Electricity

The first precise experiments in this field were carried out by Henry Cavendish (around 1771) and Charles Augustin de Coulomb (1785). They demonstrated that the force acting between two electric charges is very similar to the force of attraction between two masses, described by Newton's law of gravitation.

Especially important, however, is current electricity. We all know that electric current flows through metallic cables. The *frog's leg experiments* carried out by Luigi Galvani (1786) initiated detailed investigation into the phenomena of current electricity. In 1820 Christian Oersted discovered the magnetic field of electric current. By accurate measurement, Georg Simon Ohm found the basic relationships between voltage,

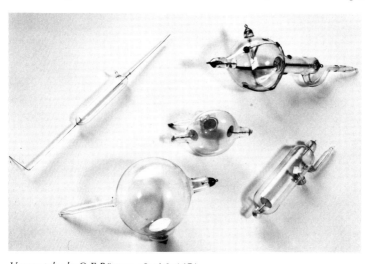

Vacuum tubes by C. F. Röntgen, 1895/1896 (O)
Using these tubes, Röntgen discovered the radiation called x-rays. It made substantial progress in medicine possible.

Hertz's apparatus (O)
In the years 1867–1889 Heinrich Hertz proved the existence of free electromagnetic radiation, thus confirming the theoretical system elaborated by J. C. Maxwell and laying the foundation for electrical wireless communication.

current and resistance. The discovery made by Michael Faraday of the fact that the movement of a magnet relative to a conducting circuit produces an electric current (law of induction, 1831) revealed another link between electric and magnetic processes.

James Clerk Maxwell summarized the concepts of his time and widened them; the result was an admirable theoretical system of electrodynamics (after 1856) that comprised electric and magnetic phenomena. This theory was the basis for extensive conclusions. It anticipated the existence of electromagnetic waves, discovered by Heinrich Hertz in 1887–89. Today these are familiar to us in the form of radio and television. Experiments on electrical discharges in gases (beginning about 1869) supplied a key to one of the most profound secrets of nature – the structure of the atom.   *A. Brachner*

Optics (opening in November 1989)

Optical phenomena occur everywhere in nature. The rainbow, the refraction of light in water, the flickering of the stars in the nocturnal sky or the irridescent play of colours caused by a thin oil film on a water surface have always fascinated man.

This section is in the planning phase at present. Scheduled are three groups of exhibits:

The first group begins with a short historic survey of man's discovery of optical phenomena from Antiquity to the present time. The following *panopticum* comprises the most important optical phenomena and their corresponding phenomena in nature.

The next group of exhibits deals with the human eye and vision. The function of the eye, defective vision, the methods of defining nature and degree of sight defects and their correction by vision aids. Included in the vision group are also displays on optical illusions and colour television.

The third group deals with optical instruments, beginning with optical media like glass, crystals etc. as well as with the optical components manufactured from them. They are followed by different groups of optical instruments, the earliest and most important ones – microscope and telescope – occupying the largest space, according to their importance. The instruments are intended not only to show chronological sequence and technological development, but also their effects on human life, e.g. the place of the miscroscope in medicine.   *M. Seeberger*

Atomic, Nuclear and Particle Physics

Towards the end of the 19th century numerous experiments in many fields of physics led to the conclusion that matter must consist of invisibly small structural elements. In 1911 Ernest Rutherford developed a model of the atom based on the structure of our planetary system. In 1913 Niels Bohr improved this model by introducing quantum conditions: he admitted only exactly defined orbits for the electrons revolving around the nucleus.

The evolution of quantum mechanics (1926) transformed the previous concepts of these orbits into the electron cloud. It is known now that even the nucleus has a compound structure, i.e. it consists of particles of positive charge and neutral particles of about the same mass, called respectively protons and neutrons. The forces which keep together protons and neutrons in the nucleus are much stronger than the electric forces binding the electrons to the nucleus. The technology of nuclear energy deals with the release of these nuclear forces in order to set free large amounts of energy.

S. Hladky

Historical instruments used in atomic and nuclear physics (O)
Left: a betaspectrometer used by Otto Hahn and Lise Meitner about 1915. *Right front:* Otto von Baeyer's betaspectrometer from about 1920. *Right:* an instrument used by Otto Hahn to separate radiothorium from the mother substance, about 1906.

Telecommunications

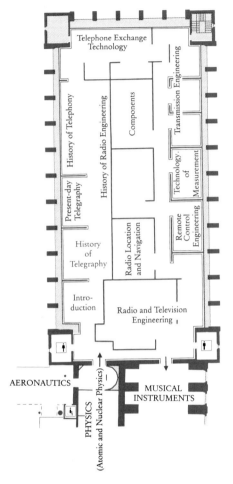

Telephone Exchange Technology

Transmission Engineering

History of Telephony

History of Radio Engineering

Components

Technology of Measurement

Present-day Telegraphy

Radio Location and Navigation

Remote Control Engineering

History of Telegraphy

Introduction

Radio and Television Engineering

AERONAUTICS

MUSICAL INSTRUMENTS

PHYSICS (Atomic and Nuclear Physics)

The wish to transmit messages without material transportation, by acoustic or optical signals, is old. Drums, fire signals and – as late as in the 19th century – optical telegraphs were used for this purpose. They remained makeshifts – mainly reserved for military and political affairs. An exchange of information on a large scale, serving also commercial and private needs, would not have been possible with these methods.

The breakthrough was only achieved by new findings on electric and magnetic phenomena and their increased study and use since the beginning of the past century. Based upon them, electrical communication engineering with its classical branches – telegraphy, telephony and radio engineering – could develop.

Electrical communication engineering deals with the transformation, transmission, distribution, storage and processing of information. It takes advantage of the possibilities resulting from the electrical signals travelling at the velocity of light.

The messages may have the form of letters, figures, symbols or measured values, of sound oscillations or values of brightness and colours. Their conversion to electric signals is the condition for their transmission over electric cables or – in wireless communication – by means of electromagnetic waves. The transmission over lightwave conductors (optical fibre communication) adopted at the end of the 1970s requires an additional conversion of electrical to optical signals and vice versa. The routing, i.e. the translation of addresses, as well as the storage and processing of the message takes place, above all, by means of electric and magnetic effects. The re-conversion of the electric signals to the original form of the message is the final phase.

The electrical output necessary for these purposes ranges from a billionth of a watt in satellite receivers to several megawatts in broadcasting transmitters and radar impulses. The frequencies used cover the whole range from zero (direct current) up to many gigahertz (10^9 Hz). For carrier purposes in lightwave conductors even frequencies in the visible range, i.e. hundreds of thousands of gigahertz.

Information on the Exhibition

This department was opened on May 7th, 1968, covering an area of 1500 m². By means of original apparatus, models and demonstrations, visitors are given some idea of the problems encountered in electrical communication engineering and of the solutions found.

It is preceded by an introductory room in which the nature of a message in the sense of telecommunications is explained and some problems of technical reliability are dealt with. Above all, however, the intention here is to give a survey of the arrangement of the individual sections within the department and of the themes dealt with there. On yellow boards at the beginning of each new topic, a survey of the display is given by an introductory text. The eight sections with technical and functional displays on present-day technology, beginning with telephone exchange technology, are preceded by three sections (telegraphy, telephony, and radio engineering) with mainly historic exhibits.

Telegraphy

Electric telegraphy was the first practical application of electricity at the beginning of the 19th century. Only a few decades later the development of telegraphs, cables, lines and relays had created the basic elements for worldwide telegraphic communication. The result was the enormous growth of classical telegraphy which was temporarily checked, however, by increasing use of the telephone about the end of the century. The history of modern telegraphy begins in the early thirties with the introduction of the teleprinter, which is always ready for operation, is suitable for switching networks, and does not require trained telegraph operators. Today the teleprinter copes with the major part of communications traffic, using automatic switching equipment and special transmission techniques. In addition to the teleprinter, other terminals, such as analog recorders, picture telegraphs and facsimile

Telegraph by C. F. Gauß and W. Weber, 1833–1838 (R)
The instruments – originally made for studies of Earth magnetism – were linked by an
uninsulated line between the two institutes of the two professors in Göttingen, situated
about 1000 m apart. In the centre of the photograph, the transmitter (a bar magnet
with induction coil) can be seen; in front of it, there is the receiver (at left, the magne-
tometer; at right, the observation telescope). Based upon agreed combinations of mag-
netometer deflections to the right or to the left, the transmission of messages thus
became possible (about 9 symbols per minute). The equipment consists of replicas of
the apparatus reconstructed by W. Weber in 1873 for the World's Fair of Vienna. In the
background, there are telegraphs and additional exhibits from the history of radio
engineering.

machines are used and also data communication units and data terminals.

Numerous original objects, beginning with the electrochemical telegraph of 1809/11 by Samuel Thomas von Soemmering and the first
printing telegraph of 1836 by Carl August von Steinheil, show the development of classical telegraphy: there are pointer telegraphs, Morse
apparatus, synchronous telegraphs and – last – a Siemens high-speed
telegraph with a telegraphic speed of 2000 characters per minute.

The basic functions of a teleprinter can be studied on enlarged models.
Its operation in modern telegraphic networks with subscriber-con-
trolled trunking scheme and measures for faultless operation over radio
circuits are visualized by illustrated diagrams. The equipment of message storage exchanges and devices protecting stored data, as well as

analog recorders, facsimile machines and picture telegraphs complete the display of modern telegraphy.

Telephony

In the beginning, electrical transmission was possible only for telegraph signals, but in 1876 speech transmission by means of electric current was achieved for the first time in a practical way. Thus electric telephony came into existence.

The necessary equipment at both ends of a connection was much easier to handle than the complicated telegraph devices and could be handed over to the communication partners themselves. In order to take full advantage of the telephone, it was necessary to abandon the fixed communication between two distant stations. Central switching equipment had to be developed, so that every subscriber could be connected with every other subscriber. This task was assumed first by manual exchanges. Only a few years later, in the early nineties, the first automatic dial exchanges went into service. Density and extension of telephone networks rapidly grew with the number of subscribers. The range of telephone calls, however, was limited to a few hundred kilometers, as long as no amplifying element existed for voice frequencies, while the relay had been available for telegraphic transmission from the beginning.

The amplifier tube, which overcame this problem and subsequently also revolutionized other fields, brought in a new era in telephony, along with amplifiers and equipment for the multiplexing of cable and radio channels.

In this section, the development of subscriber's sets can be followed up. The display starts with the microphone and the telephone by Philipp Johann Reis and Alexander Graham Bell's telephone, partly in the form of sectioned models, then leads to early table and wall telephone sets and to a modern coin-box telephone. Telephone exchange equipment

Prepayment telephone coin-boxes of the past and present (O)
About 1900, with the telephone coin box for manual exchange (left), it was possible only to reach the operator by insertion of the coins, whereas since 1977, the telephone coin-box at the right can be used also for direct international dialling (worldwide).

shown in the historic group only comprises manual exchanges, of which several examples can be seen. They range from a pyramidal switchboard for five terminals to a switchboard for up to 20000 jacks.

Radio Engineering

Just before the turn of the century, another system of communication, namely radio, was added to those using lines; its chief importance then was that it met the need for communication with ships. The successful transmission of Morse signals by radio was performed in 1896 by Guglielmo Marconi, using an ingenious combination of Hertz's arrangement for generating high-frequency oscillations, Alexander Popov's antenna and Edouard Branly's coherer.

The prerequisites for far-reaching radio communication were created in 1898 when Karl Ferdinand Braun successfully used his coupled transmitter for increasing radiated power, and, in addition, an increase of the spark sequence was made possible by the quenched-spark transmitter invented by Max Wien in 1908.

The latter made a clear distinction of transmitted signals from atmospheric disturbances possible. This caused an enormous increase in radio station coverage. Two types of transmitters for undamped oscillations, namely the arc transmitter developed by Valdemar Poulsen after 1902 and the machine transmitter, also paved the way for wireless telephony. The latter transmitter had been developed during the same years by Reginald Aubrey Fessenden together with Ernst Frederich Werner Alexanderson. At the receiver end, the insensitive coherers – the response of which varied within wide limits – had long been substituted by other detectors.

A substantial change, however, was not achieved until the introduction of electric amplification which offered the opportunity of controlling a local source of power by the low energy received from a distant transmitter. The amplifier valve served this task. In radio engineering, it soon supplanted all other types of detectors.

After Alexander Meißner had developed the feedback circuit for the generation of high-frequency oscillations by means of the amplifier tube in 1913, and the production of tubes for higher power at high frequencies had become possible, the spark transmitters, arc transmitters and machine transmitters were pushed more and more to the background. The valve dominated the field of radio engineering.

In this section, the development of radio engineering is shown by numerous transmitting and receiving devices, beginning with a display demonstrating the working principle of G. Marconi's transmitting and receiving arrangement. Among these devices, which include shock excitation type spark transmitters, quenched-spark and arc transmitters, the first valve transmitter by A. Meißner, by which speech transmission was achieved from Berlin to Nauen in 1913, deserves special attention. A display of the influence exerted by the amplifier tube on the further evolution of telecommunications leads from the historic, mainly application-oriented part of the department to the technical part organized according to function.

Automatic local, national and international exchange, 1968 (O)
Three rack assemblies show the telephone exchange technology commonly used by
the Deutsche Bundespost in 1968; it is characterized by the selectors and couplings
working by means of mechanical contacts. In trunk dialling, electronic components,
too, were used for the control, translation and routing already then. Since 1982, telephone exchanges with electronic dialling systems have been built.

Switching Technology

Switching technology creates the possibility for every subscriber of a
communication system to set up connections with any other subscriber.
In this field, automation began even before the turn of our century.
The growing traffic of communication creates problems at the intersec-
tions of the networks where the connections between individual subscribers are made. The former manual exchanges are now replaced by
automatic local, national and international exchanges. Charge-metering is effected automatically, partly by time and partly by distance
metering. Similar equipment is used in telegraphy and in data communication networks.
In this section, the main problems of exchange technology and their
solution by means of automatic equipment are explained, using telephony as an example. The visitor is first introduced to the hierarchy and
subdivision of telephone networks. He is then given an idea of the
equipment used in exchange centres by operational racks of automatic
local, national and international exchange. Activating several illuminated diagrams, he can inform himself on the processes occurring in setting up a connection as well as on charge-metering. The functions of the
most important switching devices which can be remote-controlled by
the subscriber may be studied on models in working condition. Private
exchange technology is represented by an illuminated diagram illustrat-

ing its special possibilities, as well as by a private branch exchange with or without through-dialling.

Transmission Technology

Transmission technology provides the means and techniques by which distances between subscribers of a commercial network are bridged. Cable and radio systems complement one another. The necessity of anti-interference devices and of economical operation, e.g. by multiplexing of communication channels, is also explained here.

Digital signal conditioning, for time-division multiplex transmission in particular, is growing more and more important. The optical fibre as a wideband means of transmission with little attenuation has grown out of the experimental phase. Since the late seventies, it has been used in communication networks.

The introductory part of the section emphasizes the importance of modulation for the adaptation of the signals to the transmission channel and for the multiplexing of transmission channels. After a fundamental explanation of the frequency-division and time-division multiplex method, group translation into other frequency bands as well as the time-sharing interlocked processing of signals are dealt with in detail. A separate niche of the exhibition is dedicated to the structure and application of various cables and cable fittings. The importance of pupinisation, amplification and regeneration for increasing ranges is explained.

Wireless transmission of information and the resulting problems are referred to by means of various types of mobile radio equipment, assemblies, high-power radio stations and commercial receiving apparatus. A display of the propagation of waves and of antennas leads to directional radio, with a demonstration of the directivity of parabolic antennas.

Satellite communication is represented by a model of the Earth Station Raisting and by a demonstration of the receiving conditions with synchronous and orbiting satellites.

Components

Telecommunication equipment consists of individual components, mainly resistors, capacitors and inductors. The performance of such equipment depends on the characteristics of the components and on their combined effect. By the invention of amplifying elements, such as the valve and the transistor, the possibilities of telecommunications grew substantially over the course of time. The same is true for new technologies with highly integrated components and very fast signal processing, in particular for the integrated circuits of microelectronics. The components are already interconnected during their production, connecting hundreds of thousands of transistors, capacitors and conductor arrangements into processors or storage units on the surface of a crystal chip of a few square millimeters.

Typical circuit diagrams from various fields of communication engineering indicate the multiple application possibilities of the individual component types. The different types of construction are illustrated by

Five components for high-power transmitters (O)
Shown in the transmission technology section (from right to left): glass-metal-ceramic type transmitter valve for medium-wave and short-wave, 1968; water-cooled variometer for the frequency tuning of a 600 kW radio station, 1966; four-chamber klystron (transmitting tube of a 11 kW television transmitter), 1968; high-frequency aerial feeder for medium-wave and long-wave transmitters of up to 2000 kW, 1969; cavity resonator of a power amplifier for 2,5 kW UHF colour television transmitters, 1967.

characteristic examples, their application and function explained by a series of demonstrations.

Technology of Measurement

The science of measurement provides important data for the development, production and continuous supervision of components, equipment and systems. Measurements are also necessary for detecting faults and for acquiring new knowledge. In communication engineering, ranges of power and of frequencies have to be understood; moreover, magnetic, optical and acoustic quantities have to be determined in addition to electric values.

Numerous demonstrations first introduce common methods of measuring the voltage, frequency, resistence, capacitance and impedance. Subsequently, the visitor can experiment with special measuring techniques of communication engineering, such as reflection, phase-angle, level and attenuation measurement, or carry out a selective voltage measurement. There are also devices for the measurement of non-linear distortions and for filters and cores by the sweep frequency method, all installed in working condition.

Information Processing

Here a particularly interesting exhibit is the reconstruction of the world's first programmed computing machine – the Z 3 – which was completed in 1941 by Konrad Zuse, the German pioneer in the field of programmed computers.

A separate exhibition on *Computer Science and Automation – Microelectronics* is in the preparation phase (see p. 273); the opening is scheduled for May 1988.

Remote Control Engineering

Remote control engineering provides the technological means for remote supervision and control of equipment. It has to cope with tasks ranging from remote control of a simple switch to the monitoring of spacecraft. Special procedures have been developed so that information can be transmitted safely and faultlessly. This is achieved by storage in special units at the ends of the connection, followed by encoding, error-checking and decoding.

In the form of three typical examples from the fields of water supply, railway operation and power supply, the principles and the mode of operation of remote-control equipment are illustrated. From the control desks, the visitor may activate – partly using original devices – the remote-controlled plants simulated by illuminated diagrams, activate pumps or slide-valves, determine the direction or speed of a switching locomotive or control switches and stages of a transformer in an electrical distributing substation. Centralized multi-station control systems, in which encoded control instructions are transmitted over the general distribution network, are the subject of a special display. A synopsis of the main techniques used in remote control engineering and a survey of the developmental history complete the section.

Radio Location and Navigation

Radio location and radio navigation play an important part in the safety of transport by air, by sea and space travel. Not requiring optical visibility of viewer and object, they enable the position and the speed of objects to be determined by means of radio equipment and also make possible the guidance of a vehicle to its destination on a chosen course.

The exhibition introduces the visitor to the fundamentals of position finding and to the relevant measuring techniques. Their application in directional wireless reception technology is illustrated in examples ranging from a simple frame direction finder to modern direction-finding systems. The significance to navigation of the transmission methods is made clear by instructional models of a rotating radio beacon and of all-weather landing with the beam approach beacon system, as well as by devices and graphs illustrating long-range navigation by the hyperbolic navigation system. The principles of distance measurement, height-finding and speed measurement are made intelligible by simple examples. The section ends with a survey of equipment used for the supervision and monitoring of air and sea traffic as well as with a display of radio location in space travel, animated by an illustrative model which explains position finding by means of satellites.

Radio and Television
(Sound and Picture Recording and Reproduction)

The light and colour values of points of a picture are scanned line by line for transmission and then may be converted – like sound waves – into electrical impulses. As such, they can be stored, transmitted and reconverted into their original form at the receiver. These procedures were the basic achievements for the most popular branches of telecommunications, namely radio and television. Sound and picture recording and reproduction techniques provide the high quality demanded by the converters at the beginning and end of the transmission path.

The first part of this section, dedicated to sound, presents the principles of the different electro-acoustic converters by models of microphones and loudspeakers. Then sound recording techniques are demonstrated by means of a record, compact disc, magnetic tape and film. Various studio equipment and radio receivers, as well as historic equipment, form the end of the part dedicated to sound. The second part begins with several demonstrations introducing the fundamentals of black-and-white television and – subsequently – those of colour TV. Equipment and graphs from the field of television picture recording and reproduction as well as video signal tracing supply further information on television technology. The final group in this section is a series of historic instruments from the period before 1940.

H. Schmiedel

Musical Instruments

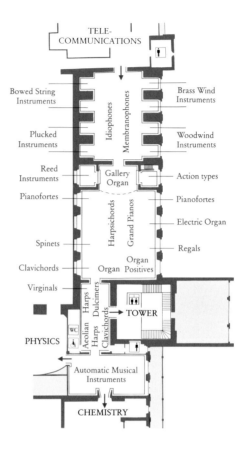

In order to make music audible, either human voice or appropriate instruments – the musical instruments – are needed. Whether they are the simplest possible, such as clappers, rattles or bull-roarers which man used as early as in ancient times, or whether they are the latest products of the electronics industry, they all are subject to the laws of physics and embody the technological achievements available at the time of their construction. This is why musical instruments have a legitimate place in a museum of technology.

From the conscious use of a tone, generated e.g. by a Stone Age bow-string, to digital sound generation, innumerable persons have endeavoured to advance the musical instruments. Styles and fashions gave birth to new types of instruments and made others fall into oblivion. Many of them were the result of an ingenious concept, a few only seem curious to us. Present-day western musical instruments, the evolution of which is shown here, are the result of continued development, based upon the traditions of professional and artistic craftsmanship.

The history of European musical instruments in the proper sense begins

View of the Music Room with the keyboard instruments
The Music Room, reserved for keyboard instruments, houses precious original instruments dating from the 16th century up until our time. In the front: a small Italian harpsichord of the 17th century with two 4' registers which sounds one octave higher than usual. Next to it: the most ancient harpsichord of the collection, built by Franciscus Patavinus in 1563. It is followed by another Italian harpsichord of the 18th century. On the musical gallery stands the earliest preserved organ of Southern Germany. Hans Lechner built it in 1630, with 10 registers, for the Maria Thalkirchen pilgrimage church. At the right: an organ positive from the region of Salzburg, 1693.

in the late Middle Ages. The major part of the instruments in use since the sixth century, the period after the great migrations of peoples, were inspired by the forms of Antiquity. Unfortunately, it cannot be ascertained any more in how far Celtic or Germanic instruments were popular, since they were made of non-lasting materials. There are, however, a few exceptions, such as finds of bone flutes and the lurer – bronze signal horns blown pairwise – which witness an astonishing mastery of bronze casting techniques.

The contact with Asiatic civilizations and with Islam brought a substantial number of new instruments such as the lute and zither types, shawns, trumpets and timpani, and – above all – the bow.

Another instrument of Antiquity, the organ (hydraulos) – the first proof of which dates back to Alexandria in the 3rd century – has to be mentioned here. This instrument, found in Spain in the 5th century, at the Franconian Court of the 8th century, in many churches around the year 1000 A.D., and now spread throughout the world as a gigantic instrument with thousands of pipes, is the best evidence of how intricately the threads of the history of art, of cultural history and of the history of technology are woven together.

In the 15th and 16th centuries, the development of occidental musical instruments in the proper sense began, starting from a new understanding of music which found its expression in polyphonic instrumental music. Bowed string instruments and wind instruments became diversified into groups which covered the whole pitch range from bass to treble. The keyboard, known from the organ, was transferred also to string instruments: the "keyed" instruments developed. In 1404 Eberhard Cersne mentioned the clavichord in his "Minne Regel", and several "technical drawings" and descriptions of the clavichord and harpsichord are preserved from the period around 1440.

1511 may be called the year of birth of modern instrumentology: Sebastian Virdung then published the first systematic treatise on musical instruments entitled *Musica getutscht und außgezoge*. In the same year, Arnold Schlick's treatise on the organ was published, and other books on musical instruments followed in the same century. They culminated in the *Syntagma musicum II* of 1619, by Michael Praetorius, which even today is considered the most important literary source about musical instruments of that period.

Information on the Exhibition

After Sebastian Virdung (1511) there were numerous attempts to classify the wide variety of musical instruments of all times and nations in one system. Based upon the scientific work of Victor Mahillon (1888), Erich M. Hornbostel and Curt Sachs developed a system of musical instruments which still is of universal validity today – despite some qualifications and extensions. It was an obvious choice for a technical museum to adopt this classification system since it is based on the type of sound generation.

The rooms of the exhibition only house some of the instruments from the total inventory of about 1400 items which characterize the musical practice or the instrument-making techniques of a particular period or region. Less typical forms and experimental constructions are accessible to scholars in the Reserve Collections.

In accordance with the main principle adopted for the collections of the Deutsches Museum, as many instruments as possible are demonstrated by playing, even though this brings about technical problems for the museum, such as increased wear. As a musical instrument is not only an object for daily use, but – in many cases – also a work of art, the visitors are not allowed to play the instruments themselves – in contrast to the practice of other departments. The demonstration of the musical instruments is reserved for specially trained staff.

Percussion, String and Wind Instruments

The central part of the room is occupied by a podium with manifold *percussion instruments* which are divided into two main groups:

1. *Idiophones* (autophonic instruments): rattles, clappers, jingle bells, cymbals, gongs, bells, chimes and others. The major part of these instruments come from non-European countries. In the group of Orff instruments, the first one, a trough xylophone built by Karl Maendler in cooperation with Carl Orff in 1927 is of particular historic value.

2. *Membranophones:* most of the drums shown here are also of non-European origin. The European instruments on display range from baroque timpani to a machine drum of the orchestra of the Royal Bavarian Opera (about 1860) and to modern percussion.

The right side of the room is reserved to *string instruments*. Six show-cases demonstrate the development of the following instrument types:

1. *bowed string instruments:* early, folkloric and non-European forms, such as a trumpet marine and hurdy-gurdy; instruments of the viola family (among which, a gamba by Paulus Alletsee, 1701); violas with resonating strings and their relatives; double-basses (among which, one by Franz Zacher, 1691); instruments of the violin family; rebec, special forms of the violin and some relatives; violin-making.

Hunting horn in F
Signature: "Iohann Heinricho/Eichgentobf in Leibzig Anno 1722" (O)
J. S. Bach used this instrument type – mostly in pairs – in a very impressive way for his 1st Brandenburg Concerto and for some cantatas. J. H. Eichentopf, whose instruments date from the period between 1710 and 1749, was one of the most famous instrument-makers of Leipzig. He built brass wind instruments as well as woodwind instruments.

Lute
Signature: "Gregori Ferdinand Wenger/Lauten- und Geigen-Macher in Augspurg. 1748" (O)
5 double strings and 1 single string. Tuning e.g. Gg cc¹ ff¹ aa d¹d¹ g¹. Original case.

Harps
The well-filled showcase illustrates the history of this instrument the origin of which dates back to prehistoric times.
Diatonic harp, of Southern Germany, 18th/19th century (O); *harp* from North Luzon, Philippines, about 1900, a type related to European models (former colony) (O); *hooked harp,* signature: "Caliard a Strasbourg", 18th century (O); single-action *pedal harp,* France, end of the 18th century (O).

Nine showcases give an insight into the historic variety of
2. *plucked string instruments:* primitive and early forms; East Asia; India; instruments of the tanbur type; lutes (among which, one by Gregori Ferdinand Wenger, 1748); guitars; mandolins, citterns; zithers. The left side of the room houses sixteen showcases dedicated to the *wooden and brass wind instruments:*
1. *Flutes* (among which early instruments by Theobald Boehm, of the middle of the 19th century, and a recorder by Louis Hotteterre with a head by Johann Christoph Denner, about 1700).
2. *Reed instruments:* bagpipes; instruments with single reed (among which launeddas from Sardinia, clarinets in the rare G tuning, a bass clarinet by Johann Heinrich Gottlieb Streitwolf, of Göttingen, 1833, saxophones from the workshop of their inventor Adolphe Sax); clarinets; instruments with double reed (among which: dulcimers, bombards, oboes, dulcians, bassoons, ranketts, crumhorns).

3. *Instruments with cup or funnel-shaped mouthpiece:* primitive and fol-kloric forms (horns of various animals; alphorns); fingerhole horns (cornetts, serpents and derived forms); replicas of wind instruments of Antiquity; trumpets (among which a trumpet fitted with "inventions" by Michael Saurle, early 19th century); trombones (among which instruments from Nuremberg of the 17th and 18th century); hunting horns (among which one by Johann Heinrich Eichentopf, 1722); bugles (among which a contrabass ophicleide in F by A. Barth, second quarter of the 19th century; remarkable also a "chromatic bass-horn" by Johann Heinrich Gottlieb Streitwolf, about 1830); development of valves.

Keyboard Instruments

The central room of the musical instruments exhibition is the so-called Music Room showing the evolution of keyboard instruments by means of originals and models dating from the 16th century up to our present times.

1. Clavichords: among which a fretted clavichord by Christian Gottlieb Hubert (1782).

2. Harpsichords: virginals; spinets; cembali (among which a virginal by Andreas Ruckers 1617).

3. Pianofortes: among which are a square piano by Sebastian Erard (1790) and an overstrung grand piano by Nanette Streicher (1834). The pneumatic-action player piano by Welte-Bechstein (1926) is also remarkable.

4. Organs: among which the most ancient is the organ from Southern Germany, preserved almost completely in its original state, built by Hans Lechner in 1630, and organ positives of the 17th and 18th century.

5. Reed instruments: regals; harmonicas; harmoniums; related forms. In the next room with the exit to the tower staircase, there are more *spinets* and *clavichords* of the 17th and 18th century (including a copy of the earliest preserved clavichord of Dominicus Pisaurensis, 1543) as well as *dulcimers, harps* (among which a double-action pedal harp by Sebastian

Barrel organ
Signature: "Xaver Bruder
Waldkirch im May 1869"
(O)
Sliding barrel with ten
pieces of music. 3 regis-
ters: stopped diapason at
8'; stopped flute at 4',
octave at 2'. 66 wooden
pipes for 22 tones; com-
pass C-e²; wind pressure
75 millimeters head of
water. 16 moving figures.

Virginal
Signature: "Andrea Ruckers me fecit Antwerpiae, 1717" (O)
Compass: C-f³, originally C/E-c³. The inner side of the top is papered with a picture showing a miracle which is said to have happened in Brussels in 1370.

Organ positive
Signature: "Anno 1693 den 12. Mai hab ich Niclaus Franciscus Lamprecht Orglmacher in Ötting diesses Werklein ferferdichet meines Alders / 38 Jahr / Gott gebe dass es zu seinem Lob und Ehr möge gebraucht werden". (O)
This organ formerly stood in St. Emmeram's chapel in Gersthofen near Augsburg.
Compass: C FᴰGᴱAᴮH c-c³. Slider chest, 3 registers: chimney flute at 4′ pitch, principal at 2′ pitch, quint at 1⅓′ pitch. 2 bellows with wooden ribs, treadle-strapped; wind pressure 45 millimeters head of water. Tuning pitch a¹ = 455 Hz.

Erard, about 1820), *Aeolian harps* and a glass harmonica (end of the 18th century), the sound of which may be heard from a tape.

Automatic Musical Instruments

The last room is dedicated to mechanical musical instruments:
1. Automatic musical instruments operated by barrels, discs or plates: this group includes the *Belloneon* with 24 trumpets and 2 timpani by Johann Gottfried Kaufmann (1805); the automatic trumpeter by Friedrich Kaufmann (1810); orchestrions, symphoniums, carillons and barrel organs, among which one with moving figures by Xaver Bruder of Waldkirch (1869).
2. Punch-tape automatic musical instruments: In addition to the Welte-

Bechstein player piano mentioned in the Music Room, the *Phonolizt Violina*, an automatic violin consisting of a piano and three violins built by Hupfeld about 1912, should be mentioned here.

Electronic Musical Instruments

The instrument group of *electrophones* is not accessible at present because of construction in progress.

F. Thomas

Automatic trumpeter
Signature: "Friedr./Kaufmann/in/Dresden 1810" (O)
The notes to be played are programmed on a barrel. By means of a lever system, this commands the valves which let the wind generated by two bellows get to 12 beating reeds. The sound of the reeds is modulated to the trumpet sound by means of the trumpet set to the mouth. The barrel and bellows are activated by a spring work.

Chemistry

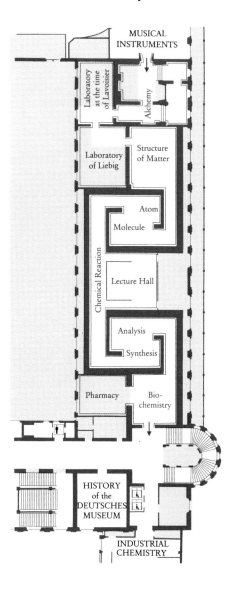

Chemistry is the subject of two different exhibitions in the Deutsches Museum: one of mainly experimental character, named *Chemistry;* the other, named *Industrial Chemistry,* contains exhibits which belong rather to the field of technology.

In Antiquity, chemical knowledge was mainly used for the production of medicines and of poisons. In addition, there were special techniques for gilding, used especially in temple workshops. This is also where the first attempts to imitate gold were made. Rudiments of the theory of chemical elements date back to the natural philosophy of Antiquity.

During the 1st century A.D., alchemy developed in Hellenistic Egypt, under the influence of ancient mythical ideas and Gnostic doctrine and in association with Aristotelian thought. The teachings of alchemy were taken over by the Arabs who continued to develop them.

During the Latin Middle Ages, alchemy spread throughout Europe. The medicine-oriented iatrochemistry of Paracelsus, too, was based upon alchemical ideas.

Apart from alchemy, there was also a largely theory-free technical branch of chemistry which was mainly applied in metallurgy. However, alchemy played an important part until the 17th and 18th centuries and was substituted only slowly by chemistry in the proper sense.

The first comprehensive theory of chemical reactions was provided in the 17th and 18th centuries by the phlogiston theory developed by Johann Joachim Becher and Georg Ernst Stahl. After the invention of the pneumatic trough by Stephen Hales, in 1727, pneumatic chemistry developed – primarily in England – and led to the discovery of numerous new gases. Above all, James Black, Henry Cavendish, Joseph Priestley and Karl Wilhelm Scheele took part in these discoveries. The chemical composition of water, too, was discovered and described. As a result of the research work done by Antoine Laurent de Lavoisier, the phlogiston theory was supplanted, towards the end of the 18th century, by the oxygen theory which ascribes the combustion of substances to the absorption of oxygen. Lavoisier also defined the element as a chemically indestructible matter and formulated the law of conservation of matter, which brought about the breakthrough in the quantitative approach to the study of chemical reactions. Together with his assistants, he created the chemical nomenclature, the essential part of which is still valid today.

Jeremias Benjamin Richter's law of constant equivalent weights (1791), Joseph Louis Proust's law of constant proportions (1797) and John Dalton's law of multiple proportions (1803) definitely established chemistry as a quantitative science. A theoretical explanation of these empirically determined laws was given in 1803 by Dalton who affirmed that matter was composed of atoms and that all atoms of a single element were the same, but different from the atoms of all other elements.

By the extensive determination of atomic weights, Jöns Jakob Berzelius tried to give an empirical base to this new theory. He also introduced many of the chemical symbols commonly used today.

The 19th century also brought about a considerable increase of knowledge in the field of organic chemistry, of which K.W.Scheele may be considered the founder; he was the first to isolate many organic compounds. In 1828, Friedrich Wöhler proved by the urea synthesis, and in 1845 Hermann Kolbe by the acetic acid synthesis, that – in principle – there is no difference between inorganic and organic matter. From 1831 to 1837, Justus von Liebig developed the accurate analysis of organic-chemical substances. Discovering the identical composition of cyanic acid and fulminic acid, Liebig, Wöhler and Berzelius created the term "isomerism" in 1831 and thus laid the foundation for structural chemistry. Of great help was the introduction of the valence symbol into chemical symbolism by Archibald Scott Couper (1857) and August Kekulé's discovery of the tetravalence of the carbon atom. In addition to Friedrich Rochleder and A. S. Couper, Kekulé developed the idea of the self-bonding of carbon atoms in 1857. In 1860, he postulated the ring structure of benzene.

Since Amedeo Avogadro's hypothesis was not accepted generally, ideas of the real equivalent weights and of the formulae of chemical compounds were unclear at that time. Not until the 1860 Chemists' Congress of Karlsruhe was the confusion ended by Stanislao Cannizzaro. In 1859, Robert Wilhelm Bunsen and G. Kirchhoff introduced the spectral analysis. In 1868/69, Lothar Meyer and Mendeleyev established the periodic system of classification for chemical elements. In the course of further development, more and more independent branches, such as biochemistry, industrial chemistry, radiochemistry etc., came into existence.

What is Chemistry?

Chemistry can be found in everything around us: in our own body, in all the things we can touch, in all objects our eyes can see. The growth of the flowers in spring, the brown colouring of the leaves in autumn, the baking of bread, the cooking of soup – really everything in this world is based upon chemical processes.

Nevertheless, we often experience chemistry as a strange thing, because its processes take place in tiny molecules and can be seen only when their products have accumulated to visible quantities. And the language of chemical formulae seems incomprehensible, even frightening, to the lay mind.

However, chemistry is absolutely omnipresent, and the number of identified existing compounds is estimated at about 15 million for organic chemical and at about 1 million for inorganic chemical compounds. Not a single day goes by without the discovery of several hundred new chemical compounds, either found in nature or synthesized in the laboratory. The task of chemistry is to study the substances of the animate and inanimate world, their composition and their properties, and to transform these types of matter into new substances with useful properties. The changes can be obtained by the exchange of atoms, or groups of atoms, in natural compounds (substitution), by decomposition of compounds, by assembling small and mini-molecules to bigger or comparatively gigantic molecules, or by suitable combination, repetition or variation of the processes mentioned above.

The prerequisites for such changes are: the knowledge of the composition and structure of the existing substances, which is sought by the methods of chemical analysis; quantitative ideas of the stability of the bonds to be dissolved or of the chemical valencies in the substance to be changed; and detailed study of the ways of reaction and of the laws ruling the production of a new substance with the desired properties.

Information on the Exhibition

The exhibition is divided into a historic section with 3 laboratories (alchemy, Lavoisier, Liebig) and an experimental section, in which the modern methods of chemistry are explained and demonstrated.

Alchemy

The task of alchemy was the refining and transformation of metals and other substances. The visible sign for the successful activity of the master was the purification of the disciple's soul. Thus alchemy was also a ritual act of worship which found its expression in ritual dress, in liturgical prayers and hymns. Alchemy originated in Hellenistic Egypt, about the

Alchemist's laboratory (R)
For many centuries, chemistry had to manage with very simple means. The resemblance with a kitchen is striking.

2nd century A.D., and represented a combination of various kinds of scientific, philosophic, mystic-religious and technical thought, into which also Gnostic, neo-Platonic and Stoic theories had been integrated. The alchemical methods not only had a symbolic character; the alchemist's activity also included experiments. He owned a laboratory, fitted with hearths, flasks, melting pots and distillation apparatus – besides an altar –, and he was familiar with the laboratory techniques and with the properties of the different types of materials.

Alchemy from the aspect of natural science was less important than from the aspect of human self-understanding. The laboratory work, the attempts of producing gold from base metals – such as lead, for example, – were not undertaken as an end in itself, anyway not by serious alchemists. While endeavouring to perfect metals, the alchemist simultaneously tried to achieve the perfection of his own soul. The lead therefore was a symbol for the unsaved soul, gold symbolized the redemption. The alchemist struggled to discover the self and to take possession of it in the belief that by doing so he would be able to redeem matter from its imperfect state. Thus he endeavoured to prepare the *philosophers' stone* which would be able to transform imperfect bodies into perfect ones by mere touch, like silver into gold. At the same time, the philosophers' stone was a symbol of the spirit of redemption, able to free the soul from all impurities. In Latin alchemy, the philosophers' stone was often identified with Jesus Christ.

Looking at the alchemical laboratory, the visitor can see different types of hearths. A showcase illustrates the evolution of the art of distillation from Antiquity up to the *moor's head* which was in use up until the 18th century. Alchemists believed that some mixtures had to be kept boiling over years, so they developed special receptacles for this purpose: the *pelican* and the *circulatory*.

In addition, the exhibition shows a *gallery furnace* for pharmaceutical work and a *Lazy Henry*, a special furnace construction for slow and uniform distillation. Glass fragments from the laboratory of the alchemist Johann Kunckel von Löwenstern, found during the excavation of his laboratory on the Pfaueninsel of Berlin, which was destroyed in 1686, complete the display on alchemy.

Chemical Laboratory at the Time of Lavoisier

In the 18th century, physical equipment, such as electrostatic generators, air pumps, pneumatic troughs and burning lenses, was also used in chemical laboratories. Important discoveries in the field of gas chemistry were achieved with these instruments.

As an example, a large lens manufatured by Ehrenfried Walter von Tschirnhaus about 1700 is on display here. At the right wall of the laboratory, there is an apparatus for the analysis of water on glowing iron. Standing in the niche of the right wall there is a small electrostatic generator similar to those then in use for the analysis of air by means of an electric spark. The centre of the room is dominated by a pharmacist's table from the monastic pharmacy of Andechs. On this table, there is a pneumatic trough of polished marble, of the type used by Lavoisier, as well as a simple burning lens for the ignition of substances in the interior

View of the laboratory at the time of Lavoisier (R)
18th century chemistry is characterized by the slow penetration of physical implements, such as lenses and electrostatic generators, into the chemical laboratories.

of the glass bell jars, which themselves stand in a pneumatic trough. At
the rear of the laboratory, a mighty hearth with chimney hood recalls
the type of hearth common in the second half of the 18th century, especially in France. Remarkable are the large bellows suspended under the
ceiling, from which the air was directed by pipes to the surface of the
furnace in order to produce particularly high temperature in the glowing fire on the plate.

18th century chemistry mainly dealt with the study of gases. In 1782, the
English scientist Joseph Priestley discovered the so-called *nitrous air* by
pouring nitric acid over brass cuttings. He discovered that this new type
of air was able to "imbibe" part of the normal air, namely the part which
supports breathing. So it was possible to determine whether the air was
breathable by this chemical reaction. This method was refined by Felice
Fontana who devised a special instrument for this reaction, the *eudiometer*, which was very popular. In 1805, Joseph Louis Gay-Lussac and
Alexander von Humboldt established the true oxygen content of the
air.

One of the great topics of 18th century chemistry was the attempt to
explain the phenomena of combustion. In the left niche of the rear wall
of the laboratory, two experiments made by Priestley and Scheele are
therefore referred to: the exhaustion of oxygen by the respiration of a
living mouse in a pneumatic trough and the burning of a candle in such
a trough. By means of a weighing instrument it is shown that the com-

bustion products of a candle are heavier than the candle itself. In 1789, Lavoisier decomposed mercuric oxide into mercury and oxygen in a goose-necked retort, then let the oxygen react with the mercury and thus obtained mercuric oxide again. Thus he clarified the role of oxygen in processes of oxidation and reduction. The terms of oxygen, reduction and oxidation were coined by him, as well as the nomenclature used in inorganic chemistry even today.

Liebig's Laboratory

The great rise of German chemistry began with the research work of Justus von Liebig. Liebig (1803–1873) was professor of chemistry in Giessen until 1852 and then lived in Munich until he died. Liebig completed the analysis of the elements, founded chemical teaching in the laboratory in Germany and worked out the theory of artificial fertilizing, in addition to numerous other studies. The exhibition shows a rather idealistic reconstruction of the Giessen laboratory fitted out with instruments from Liebig's laboratory in Munich. A Liebig drying apparatus, a small laboratory stove, a gasometer and two Liebig condensers, used by the scientist himself, can be seen there. The flat-bottomed flasks come from the laboratory of Liebig's friend Wöhler.

Old pharmacy, of about 1800 (R)
As an example of an old pharmacy, the monastic pharmacy of St. Emmeram's at Regensburg was reconstructed here. Its equipment combines originals from different pharmacies and is one of the most valuable collections of the Deutsches Museum.

Uranium in everyday household
Uranium was rediscovered in 1789 by Martin Heinrich Klaproth, after it had been used in the late Roman period to colour mosaics. Until Antoine Henri Becquerel discovered natural radioactivity in 1896, and since then up to the present day, uranium has found uses in the form of its compounds (uranyl salts, uranium oxide) as an ingredient in orange-yellow and black glazes, and as an additive to glass flux.
The yellow-green fluorescence of uranyl-ion which occurs in daylight and even more so in long wave ultraviolet light is a characteristic of the electron configuration around the actinide atom, uranium, and makes it thus – unintentionally – into a radioactive element common in everyday life.

A portrait of Liebig by the painter Wilhelm Trautschold dominates the room. The famous – and somewhat idealistic – representation of the laboratory, hanging at the left of the entrance, was painted by the same artist in 1842.

Three showcases show typical chemical instruments of the first third of the past century. They belong to the estate of Johann B. Trommsdorf. Among them, there are such instruments as a large travel oxhydrogen eudiometer as used by Alessandro Volta, an equivalent slide rule of the William Hyde Wollaston type and a pycnometer from the workshop of Goethe's friend Christian Gottfried Körner of Jena.

In the large wall showcase, instruments from the estate of Eilhard Mitscherlich are shown: among these, the goniometer which he successfully used for the discovery of isomorphism, and the remains of an apparatus for the determination of vapour density, which he used for disproving the law of A. Avogadro; nevertheless, this law is correct. The other half of the showcase is dedicated to equipment formerly owned by R. W. Bunsen: it shows some adsorptiometers, an indigo prism and his eudiometer.

Experiments Section

The experimental part of the department is divided into sections corresponding to a few important fundamentals: the structure of matter, atom and molecule, chemical reaction, analysis and synthesis, biochemistry. In every room, the visitor may activate a variety of push-botton reactions and demonstrations.

A lecture hall in the centre of the department provides the visitors with a short lecture with experiments (at 11.00 a.m. on weekdays). In addition to that, lectures on special subjects can be held upon request for large groups (please contact the management of the department for a list of lecture subjects and an appointment).

Among the historical highlights of this section is the table on which Otto Hahn set up an arrangement of original instruments such as he and Fritz Strassmann had used in December 1938 for the discovery of nuclear fission of uranium. The counterpart of this table is the laboratory bench with original instruments from the estate of Hermann Staudinger, the founder of the theory of macromolecular chemistry. The end and culminating point of the department is the historic pharmacy, a reconstruction of the monastic pharmacy of St. Emmeram at Regensburg. Part of the pharmaceutical containers on display came from St. Emmeram (blue and yellow coat of arms on white ground), the others from famous former pharmacies of Munich, Regensburg and Nuremberg. Nearly all vessels and drawers are still filled with original preparations. Portable and ship's medicine cases as well as a collection of particularly curious medicines, such as mandrake and Spanish flies, complete the display. In front of the pharmacy, there is a pharmaceutical hearth of the type which was commonly used in the second half of the past century, fitted with a water bath, distillation apparatus, drying closet, ointment mixer etc.

O. Krätz

Industrial Chemistry

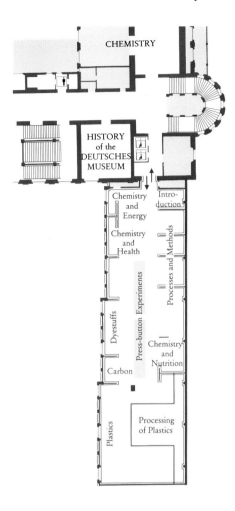

Industrial chemistry adapts the knowledge acquired by chemists in cooperation with scientists of other disciplines to the requirements of production. In most cases, many problems of chemical process technology have to be resolved before the discoveries of the chemists can be applied in large-scale production plants.

Until late into the 18th century, chemical products were manufactured in small quantities in workshops and small factories. With the rising industrialization and increasing population, chemical products were needed on a larger scale. Industrial chemical production began in 1746 with the setting-up of a sulphuric acid factory by John Roebuck in England. In 1791, Nicolas Le Blanc invented the process – later named after him – for the industrial production of *soda* which until then had to be obtained from the burning of sea plants or from the evaporation of soda lakes. In 1863, as much as 300 000 tons of this important chemical basic substance were already being produced. The great breakthrough of industrial chemistry, however, was achieved in the mid-nineteenth century with the discovery of coal-tar dyes. The production of the first coal-tar dyestuff *mauvein* by William Henry Perkin, in 1856, was a sensation of the London World's Fair. More aniline dyes, such as fuchsin, methyl violet, safranine and Bismarck brown were added in quick succession. The importance of colour chemistry for this period also can be seen from the fact that the *Patent No. 1 of the German Reich,* of July 2, 1877, was issued for the production process of a synthetic ultramarine dyestuff.

Dyes have been used since ancient times. For thousands of years, natural colours had to be obtained by strenuous and costly procedures from plants, animals or minerals. The use of precious colours often was a privilege of defined classes; purple, for instance, was reserved to high-ranking dignitaries. With the invention of synthetic dyestuffs and the foundation of numerous dyestuff factories all over the world in the second half of the past century, dyes in numerous shades finally became available to everybody.

Without the many products of the chemical industry, such as drugs, fertilizers, plastics, dyes and synthetic fibres, our present-day living standards would be unthinkable. Despite the problems caused by some chemical products, a life without the chemical industry can hardly be imagined for our world with its high population. It must be said, though, that chemistry has had its share in the high and still growing population figures, by its achievements in the field of medical care and improvement of foodstuff production by fertilizers. In solving the problems of the Earth's overpopulation, we will not be able to do without the help of the chemists and the chemical industry.

Information on the Exhibition

In the *Industrial Chemistry* department, which is housed next to the *Department of Chemistry,* there are two main sections:
1. the development and production of chemical products,
2. their application in various fields of life. Basic operations of chemical engineering, such as mixing, separating, agitating and conveying are explained by means of original equipment.

The subsequent group includes examples of processes used on a large industrial scale and their developmental history.

By means of industrial machinery in working condition, the production of plastic articles is demonstrated and explained twice a day. Following the suggested tour, the next section illustrates the application of the products provided by the chemical industry. In the centre of the department, there are stands with various experimental equipment and 18 press-button experiments on the different subjects which the visitor may activate one by one. Before the exit, a graphic synopsis illustrates the importance of the chemical industry to our economic system. The rapid progress in chemical engineering is reflected in the flexible arrangement of the exhibition.

Introductory Room

The initial materials like coal-tar, mineral oil and natural gas, minerals, air and water, as well as their transformation into basic substances for the production of plastics, synthetic fibres, dyestuffs, drugs, fertilizers and other chemical products are referred to here. A Frasch pump for the production of elementary sulphur is on display as an example of the obtaining of important chemical raw materials.

Processes and Methods

In these two groups, reactors and plants as well as basic operations of chemical engineering, such as mixing, separating and mass transport, are dealt with. Several highly interesting historic apparatuses witness individual developmental steps of the chemical industry. Thus the visitor can find in this group: an apparatus used by Walter Reppe for acetylene pressure experiments; two original pilot reactors by Matthias Pier used for the methanol synthesis and for the pressure hydrogenation of tars and oils; and the original of a tube contact reactor, Knietsch type, for the production of SO_3.

The subsequent original apparatus by Fritz Haber and Le Rossignol was the first successfully used for the combination of the nitrogen of the air with hydrogen and for their transformation into ammonia. Next to the Haber apparatus, an experimental furnace by Stern and Mittasch is on display; it was used for the testing of catalysts for the ammonia synthesis.

A sectioned reconstruction of a modern ammonia reactor follows and gives an insight into the technical dimension of this process. To this

Pilot reactor by Haber, 1908 (O)
By means of this original apparatus, Fritz Haber (Nobel prize 1918) and Le Rossignol obtained about 80 g of ammonia per hour from nitrogen and hydrogen. It was the basis for the patent application in 1908. It already contained the essential elements of the later industrial application. The realization of the process in large-scale industrial plants dates back to Carl Bosch who was awarded the 1931 Nobel prize, together with Friedrich Bergius. The Haber-Bosch process gave a strong impetus to high-pressure measurement and control techniques and to catalyst chemistry.

Ziegler's apparatus, 1957 (O)
Apparatus for the continuous low-pressure polymerisation of olefines, Ziegler type. By means of this pilot plant, the conditions of large-scale industrial utilization were studied. This process, for which K. Ziegler was awarded the 1963 Nobel prize, has gained great economic importance.

group also belong two models: one of a slagging gas producer and one of a steam cracker for the production of synthesis gases by the steam reforming process. These processes supply the hydrogen for the ammonia synthesis.

Opposite the ammonia group, there is an extraction column for liquid-liquid extraction systems and a cracking tower in continuous operation. Next to them stands Ziegler's semi-industrial pilot plant for the low-pressure production of polyethylene. It is followed by the sectioned original of an ammonia combustion furnace used for the production of nitrogen oxide as basic substance for the synthesis of nitric acid.

This group also deals with the history of nitric acid, sulphuric acid, potash and soda. The original cell used for chlorine-alkali electrolysis by the amalgamation process is on display here in combination with a diorama of an industrial production plant.

At the end of this group, the visitor can see a Söderberg electrode with the appropriate model of a phosphorus furnace, as well as the model of a plant for the production of NPK fertilizers.

Chemistry and Nutrition

A synopsis of the most important fertilizer types is given here. The significance of the individual substances for the nutrition of the plants is explained. In addition, this group emphasizes the importance of pesticides, plant protectives and preservatives.

Plastics

A wall with exhibits gives a survey of the ubiquity of plastics in technology and in daily life. The exhibits are divided into groups corresponding to the main types of plastics. By means of a functional model, the different methods of polymerisation used in the production of plastics may be activated by the visitor who need only press the appropriate buttons.

Processing of Plastics

In this extensive group of the exhibition, quite a few production machines in working condition are on display. They are demonstrated and explained at scheduled times; in addition to that, special guided visits of this section can be arranged for groups upon request. Among the processes to be demonstrated and explained are injection moulding, extrusion, blow moulding, deep drawing, powder coating and fluidized bed sintering, as well as welding, heat cutting and the processing of heat-shrinkable sleeves. In addition, models familiarize the visitor with the production of polyurethane foams and with glazing.

Carbon as Working Material

A self-contained group on carbonization and graphitization processes deals with the importance, production and application of their products; exhibits illustrate the topics in these fields.

Processing of plastics (P)
The machines used for the processing of plastics are demonstrated and explained by the Museum staff. The visitors may take the produced articles home.

Dyestuffs

Here stands the large model of the Leverkusen dyestuff factory of 1898. This factory was the first to be constructed according to purely technological needs of chemical engineering. In a nearby showcase, original samples and colour preparations by Paul Friedländer, Carl Graebe, Carl Liebermann, Peter Grieß, Adolf von Baeyer and a colour preparation of William Henry Perkin's mauvein are shown. In addition to them, historic samples of ultramarine and of various natural colours can be seen here. A wall showcase explains the significance and application of different dyestuff groups. In the adjoining niche, the importance of varnishes, plastics and adhesives in car construction is demonstrated by an exhibit.

Chemistry and Health

This group uses the examples of an artificial kidney and of a modern automatic analyser to exhibit the progress achieved in the field of medical care. The analyser gives an example of the advance in chemical diagnostic possibilities. The advance in the pharmaceutical field and in hygienics has global repercussions for the growth of the world's population.

Chemistry and Energy

The important role of chemistry in the storage of energy is illustrated by the original of an industrial fuel element. In addition to it, the complete cycle of battery manufacturing is reproduced by a graph and exhibits.

G. Probeck

Dyestuff plant, Leverkusen (M)
The memoir by C. Duisberg, of 1895, on the construction and organization of the Leverkusen works is a milestone in the history of the chemical industry. According to the guiding principles expressed therein, the factory was built in 1898 (the model on display was reconstructed from the original plans). The arrangement of the plant, which followed the ideas of the memoir, was based upon the requirements of modern chemical engineering. Remarkable for those times are the staff rooms and bathing facilities near to the production plants.

Suggestions for the continuation of the tour
You can now finish the tour of the first floor and continue to the left with the visit of the *Aeronautics* department, or else go up to the second floor by the main staircase first and have a look at the *Altamira cave* (p. 214), or get to the second floor by the winding staircase at your right and thus to the *Special Exhibitions* (p. 258).

Aeronautics

The early history of flight began hundreds of million years ago, when insects, saurians, birds and bats conquered the air. Ever since man consciously has observed nature, the bird's flight inspired his dream of flying and human flying experiments, although they kept failing for thousands of years.

Man only succeeded in becoming airborne when he left behind the bird's flight model and operated on entirely different technical principles: the two French brothers Jacques Etienne and Joseph Michael Montgolfier invented and built a hot-air balloon (according to the

First floor (old Astronautics Hall)
Additional maps of the Aeronautics Hall see p. 186, 192, 199, 200

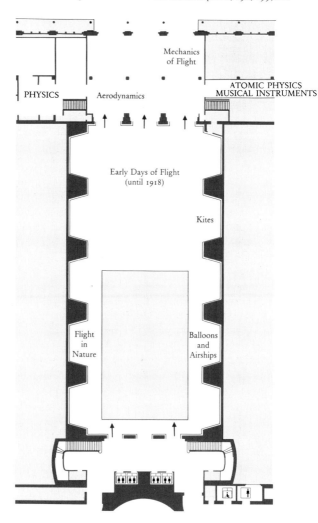

lighter-than-air principle), with which two men became airborne on November 21, 1783.

A few days later, the physicist Jacques Alexandre César Charles followed with a hydrogen-filled balloon. The successors of the balloons were the giant rigid airships of Count Ferdinand von Zeppelin, which operated a regular transatlantic airline service in the 1930s.

About a hundred years after the first balloon ascent, the study of the bird and the bird's wings, too, was crowned by success. Systematic study supplied the brothers Otto and Gustav Lilienthal with the decisive knowledge for the construction of the first gliding apparatus able to fly. With these flying machines, Otto Lilienthal learned to fly during the years 1891–1896; he was the first man to fly.

In the first decade of the 20th century, powered flight came about, starting with the first controlled motor flight of the brothers Wilbur and Orville Wright on December 17, 1903. But it was not until the utility of aeroplanes for warfare was discovered, shortly before and during the First World War, that aircraft construction and aviation in general received extensive support from the state.

The development of the aeroplane as a means of transport dates from the period after the First World War. It was based upon important wartime achievements, such as all-metal construction and high-power engines. During the twenty interwar years, an air traffic network spread over the whole globe and often made headlines by adventurous pioneer flights over mountain ranges, deserts and seas.

Because of the political tensions during the thirties the expenditures for armament rose considerably. This led to a rapid development of aviation technology in all fields: airframes, engines and propellers, navigating equipment (instruments, automatic pilots), ground facilities, airports, air traffic control etc. The extremely high standards to be met by the entire aircraft system required and promoted innovation in many fields of technology and science – and led to intensive interaction between both fields which is still in effect today.

During the Second World War, the aircraft gave warfare a new terrible dimension. Bomber aircraft brought inconceivable destruction upon industrial plants and civilians alike. From bombers and military transport aircraft derived the post-war long-range airliners which achieved non-stop transatlantic flight. The most important innovation was the jet engine which was made ready for series production during the war. The particular mode of operation of this engine type – continuous aero-thermodynamic process, purely rotatory masses – allowed a precipitous rise in power. The first aircraft with jet propulsion, a *Heinkel He 178,* which was fitted with a He S3B turbojet engine developed by Hans von Ohain, made its maiden flight as early as August 27, 1939, a few days before the Second World War broke out. Post-war fighters fitted with turbojet engines reached flight speeds of up to twice the speed of sound and altitudes of above 20 km. The corresponding change in commercial aircraft came in 1956 for the Soviet Union and in 1958 for the western countries. The new jet airliners – almost twice as fast and twice as big as the propeller aircraft in use so far – definitely established the aircraft as a means of mass transport. The introduction of wide-body airliners in the 1970s intensified this development. At present, i.e. in the 1980s, about 800 million passengers use the aircraft every year. In cargo traffic, aviation stands at the beginning of rapid expansion.

Information on the Exhibition

The visitor best begins his tour of the exhibition on the first floor. From the entrance hall, he goes up the right staircase and then turns left to the Old Aeronautics Hall (Early Days of Flight until 1918). Still on the same level, he continues towards the propeller aircraft with piston engine. After this section, he may decide whether he prefers to go *downstairs* by the staircases or the spiral staircase, passing by the mezzanines housing the air traffic control, flight control and navigation sections, and to finish his tour on the ground floor (jet aircraft, helicopters, gliders), or whether he would prefer to use the escalator *upstairs*, thus getting to the Astronautics department, and look at the exhibits of model aeroplane technology, rescue and safety in the mezzanines, then going down by the spiral staircase around the A4 rocket to the ground floor.

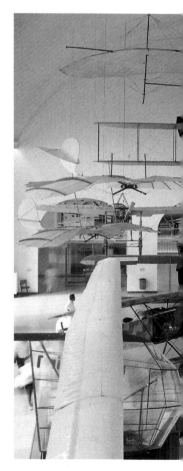

View of the Old Aeronautics Hall
At the left edge of the picture: gliding apparatus by *Otto Lilienthal* (O, R), whose experiments supplied the proof that man is able to fly. At the rear of the Hall: a biplane of the *Wright brothers* (O), developed from the aeroplane with which the first controlled motor flight was achieved in 1903. In addition to them, the early days of flight are represented by: *Blériot Typ XI*, 1909 (O); *Grade monoplane*, 1909 (O); *Etrich-Rumpler Taube (Dove)*, 1910 (O). On the floor, two examples of combat aircraft used in the First World War: left, the fighter *Fokker D VII*, 1918 (O); right (behind), the reconnaissance plane *Rumpler C IV*, 1917 (O) and above, a *Fokker Dr. I* triplane, 1917 (R).

Early Days of Flight until 1918

First floor

The early history of flight – from its beginnings until 1918 – is the subject of the displays in the *Old Aeronautics Hall*.

The early history of the aeroplane shown here begins with *flight in nature,* then deals with the first human flight experiments up until the achievements of aviation at the end of the First World War. Parallel to it, the history of the *Lighter-than-Air* crafts from the balloon to the airship is explained here. A separate group illustrates the developoment of kites from a colourful, exciting toy to an important technical device.

The history of air travel begins precisely on June 4, 1783, the day when the Montgolfier brothers first displayed a hot-air balloon in France. It was with a *Montgolfiere* that manned air travel began a little later, on November 21, 1783.

This is why the guided tour through the Aeronautics Department starts with the model demonstration recalling the details of this first balloon ascent.

Ascent of the first manned Montgolfiere (Di)
On November 21, 1783, the hot-air balloon named *Mont-golfiere* after its inventors made its first ascent with the world's first two aeronauts. It started from the garden of the La Muette castle near Paris and landed about 10 km away, after a flight of 25 minutes. The balloon consisted of painted fabric with paper decorations glued to it, a fabric-covered gallery of wickerwork and a fire grate in the interior which could be fired from the gallery.

The gas-filled balloon soon prevailed over the hot-air balloon. The attempts of making the balloons steerable and thus developing the airship from them failed until a suitable engine became available: the light high-speed Otto engine. The first operational airships were constructed about 1900. Besides the non-rigid airships, the construction of which was generally adopted for smaller crafts, the large rigid airships were developed by Count Zeppelin, Johann Schütte and Karl Lanz.

The airship gained its real importance as a means of long-distance transport. In 1909 the first air transport enterprise was founded: the *Deutsche Luftschiffahrts-AG.* After the First World War – in the 1930s – Zeppelin airships took up regular transatlantic service for the first time. By means of structural elements, models and pictures, a survey of the history of aviation is given in this part of the exhibition.

On the opposite side of the Hall, the variety of flight in nature is illustrated by flying seeds, insects, saurians and – of course – birds. Examples ranging from the simple parachute to highly complicated flying apparatus and to the perfected high-performance wing of soaring birds are shown here. Especially noteworthy is the bio-technical model, the inherently stable *Etrich-Rumpler Taube* (Dove, 1910) patterned after a tropical flying seed.

Films on the different types of flight in nature, and finally a film on the first muscle-powered flight of man, make it clear that – despite all resemblances – the ways taken by nature and those adopted by technology are different. Germany's first successful muscle-powered aircraft, the *Musculair I* (1984) by Günter Rochelt has found its place in the exhibition here.

All attempts to imitate the bird's flight failed until the cambered profile was revealed as the secret of the bird's wing. To document this historic step towards a scientific-technical solution of the flight problem, this section displays three experimental wings which Otto Lilienthal used for his lift measurements, as well as two gliding apparatus (1895/96) by means of which Lilienthal became the first man to fly.

The Wright brothers improved the aeroplane by the aerodynamic control and thus created the prerequisites for powered flight which they achieved for the first time on the December 17, 1903. The aircraft on display (1909) is the only preserved example of the first operational Wright planes built in series.

The rapid progress in aviation is illustrated by the first German powered aeroplane, with which Hans Grade won the first German flight competition in 1909, by the French aeroplane Blériot XI (the same type was flown by Louis Blériot when he crossed the Channel in the same year), and by the *Etrich-Rumpler Taube,* with which Hellmuth Hirth achieved the first long-range flight in Germany from Munich to Berlin in 1911. The technical standards at the end of the First World War are shown by two examples, the *Rumpler C IV* scout plane (1917/18) and the *Fokker D VII* fighter aircraft (1918).

Aerodynamics and Mechanics of Flight

First floor

In the passage to the New Hall, the essential physical fundamentals of flight, the working methods and experimental equipment of aerodynamics are explained in four groups:

1. the nature of airflow and air forces,
2. the beginnings of scientific research,
3. the development towards higher speed,
4. mechanics of flight (control and stability).

Demonstrations on these subjects are presently being set up.

Nose cap of the Zeppelin LZ 127 airship (O)
The LZ 127 *Graf Zeppelin* took off for her maiden flight in 1928. The *Graf Zeppelin* was the most successful airship of the Zeppelin series and became famous by spectacular flights – among others – across the North Atlantic, around the world and to the Arctic. Five Maybach engines with a power of 530 HP (390 kW) each gave the LZ 127 a maximum speed of 118 km per hour. The cruising speed was 100 km per hour. With a length of more than 230 m, the *Graf Zeppelin* was three times longer than the Boeing 747 *Jumbo Jet.*

Aircraft with Propeller/Piston Engine Propulsion

First floor

Immediately after the First World War, the construction of military aircraft was prohibited in Germany. This is why the first post-war development projects brought commercial aircraft types to the market.

First floor (New Aeronautics Hall)

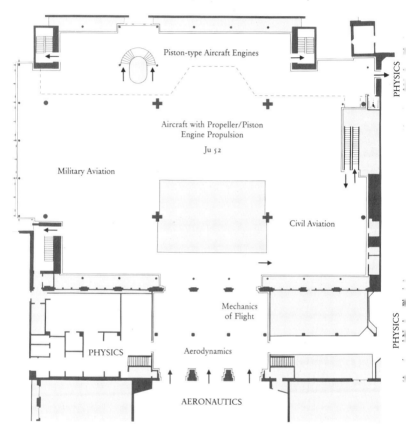

An outstanding example for this is the *Junkers F 13* with its corrugated metal skin. It can be seen at the right side of the Hall.

The *F 13* was the first aircraft to be built especially for air traffic. Its special construction (all-metal structure, low-wing cantilever monoplane, enclosed, comfortable passenger cabin) pioneered modern aircraft design. More than 300 aircraft of this type were sold worldwide and flown in mail, cargo and passenger services. Behind the *F 13*, a survey of the development of commercial aircraft and of air traffic is given by means of pictures, texts and numerous models. The central part of the Hall is occupied by the *Junkers Ju 52*. It came onto the market in 1932. With a production figure of more than 5000, it was Germany's most frequently built aircraft for military transport and civil aviation.

Junkers F 13, 1919 (O); above, *Messerschmitt M 17*, 1925 (O)
The *F 13* was the first true airliner. It was built in all-metal construction which then was still unusual. The sturdy aircraft could be found on all continents until the 1930s. The *M 17* sporting aeroplane with its low-power engine distinguished itself by good flying performances, a result of its extremely light construction. The *M 17* was the first light aircraft to cross the Alps.

At the left side of the Hall, towards the window front, the section on military aviation is housed. The *Bf 109* fighter, constructed by Willy Messerschmitt, represents the standards of aviation in the mid-thirties: extremely light stressed-skin structure, aerodynamic design, low drag coefficient, high-power engine. The final stage of the propeller aircraft is illustrated by the *Dornier Do 335*.
It reached a maximum speed of more than 750 km per hour, which made it the fastest series-produced propeller aircraft. It was not used in combat during the war. At the same time, the Luftwaffe put the still faster rocket-propelled and jet-propelled aircraft types into service.
The production of military and commercial aircraft doubtlessly accounted for the major part of aircraft construction figures. However, the production of smaller aircraft types (sporting, touring and training aircraft) also acquired considerable economic importance. Famous examples are on display here: the *Messerschmitt M 17* and the *Klemm 25*, both particularly light wooden constructions of the twenties (suspended above the *Junkers F 13*); the *Junkers Junior*, an all-metal construction; and the *Focke-Wulf Stieglitz*, an aeroplane with which competitions of flight acrobatics were won. The *Messerschmitt Bf 108* (1934) was considered to be the fastest touring plane of its time; the military liaison plane *Fieseler Storch* (1936) was famous for its slow-speed flying characteristics (both planes can be found in the left part of the hall). The *Dornier Do 27* (1956) was the first post-war model development by Claude Dornier; like the *Fieseler Fi 156 Storch*, it was intended for low take-off and landing speeds.

Piston-type Aero-engines and Propellers

First floor

The first aero-engines were adapted car engines (examples on display: *Wright/Bariquand et Marre, Daimler E4F*). As early as around 1909, engines especially designed for the propulsion of aeroplanes were put into service, such as the French rotary engines which were air-cooled radial engines with a fixed crankshaft and rotating cylinders. A functioning model is presented. This special construction remedied the cooling problems and ensured quiet running. The First World War brought a considerable increase in power figures. Just for comparison: *Oberursel U1* (1914), 110 HP and *BMW IV* (1919), 240 HP (1 HP = 0.735 kW). Postwar interest was increasingly focused on economical operation and

View of the New Aeronautics and Astronautics Hall, opened in 1984
The exhibition on the ground floor includes jet aircraft, gliders and helicopters. Propeller aircraft are on the first floor. Astronautics are housed on the second floor.

reliability, an important prerequisite for the use of engines in airliners. Water-cooled multiple-bank engines competed with air-cooled radial engines (for comparison: *BMW VI* and *Pratt & Whitney "Hornet"*). The German version of the Hornet built under license, the *BMW 132*, is fitted to the *Junkers Ju 52*.

The armament efforts before and during the Second World War drove motor construction to the limits of their performance. Power ranges of about 2000 HP were achieved. Examples: *Daimler Benz DB 601* (1937), 1100 HP; *Junkers Jumo 213* (1944), 1870 HP; *BMW 801 J* (1943), 1800 HP. The large engines of U.S. long-range bombers and long-range airliners of the post-war period, such as the *Pratt & Whitney R-4360* (1945), 3500 HP, and the *Wright R-3350* (1953), 3400 HP, show the final stages in the development of piston-type aero-engines.

Junkers Ju 52/3m, 1932 (O)
The *Ju 52* acquired worldwide fame because of its robustness and reliability. In the 1930s, it was the standard commercial aircraft of the Deutsche Lufthansa. However, the major part of the 5000 aircraft built were flown as transport aircraft during the Second World War. The high quality of this aircraft is proved by the fact that there are still a few Ju 52 in flying condition today.

Oberursel "U0" rotary engine, 1914 (O, D)
This rotary engine of the *Oberursel* type had a power of about 80 HP (67 kW) and was constructed in Germany in 1914. The essential advantage of rotary engines – in addition to their reliability – was their low weight. Disadvantages, however, were strong inertial and centrifugal forces, which tended to affect the manoeuvrability of the aircraft, and the relatively high consumption of fuel and lubricants. Rotary engines were used until the end of the First World War.

After the Second World War, jet engines supplanted the piston-type aero/propeller engines first in military aircraft and, during the fifties, also in commercial aircraft. One reason for this is that at high flight speed the blade tips of the rotating propellers reach sonic speed; the physical phenomena engendered cause a drastic drop in efficiency.

Besides the high-power engines for military and commercial aircraft, a broad range of smaller engines was developed mainly for sporting, touring and training aircraft. This field of industrial production still is of considerable economic importance now. About 15 engine types illustrate the development in this application field.

The element that converts the engine power to propulsion efficiency is the propeller. It is the airscrew efficiency which is decisive for the performance of the entire propulsion system.

The development of propellers is demonstrated by twenty-five examples. It began with simple twisted *metal-sheet paddles* and led to complex construction types of laminated wood, of light metal or of steel. An essential feature of propeller construction is the controllable pitch of the blades. A functional model shows the pitch control mechanism. The blade angles have to be adjusted according to the changing speed of flight and to the engine output in order to obtain the maximum efficiency. The control gear has to transmit high airscrew torques and to absorb strong centrifugal forces and alternating stresses.

Turbojet and Turboprop Engines

Ground floor

There is a fundamental difference between turbojet and piston-type aero/propeller engines. In the piston engine, the entire thermodynamic cycle – *suction of the air, compression, combustion and expansion* – occurs in one single cylinder, causing a relatively heavy piston to oscillate at high speed. The resulting high and alternating mass acceleration and vibrations make heavy constructions necessary.

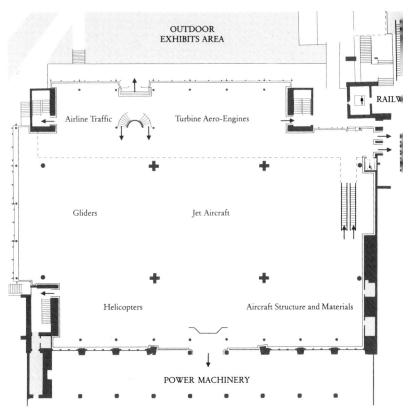

OUTDOOR
EXHIBITS AREA

Airline Traffic

Turbine Aero-Engines

Gliders

Jet Aircraft

Helicopters

Aircraft Structure and Materials

POWER MACHINERY

RAILW

In turbine aero-engines, by comparison, the process takes place in adjacent spaces, and only rotating masses are involved: the rotating compressor sucks in the air and compresses it to a high pressure. Fuel is injected into the combustion chamber and burnt together with the air. At constant pressure, the air is heated to a high temperature. The heated expanding air streams through the turbine at the rear of the combustion chamber and thus transfers part of its energy to it. The turbine turns the compressor. The remaining energy is converted to kinetic energy in the subsequent exhaust nozzle. The air leaves the nozzle in the form of an airstream with high velocity. The thrust figure depends on the airflow per second and on the speed difference between the air streaming in and out. Engines of this type are called turbojet engines.

Another possibility consists of using the remaining energy in a second turbine which drives a propeller. Engines of this type are called turbo-prop engines.

Jet engines revolutionized aircraft construction. The working principle described above, together with the advantage that it drops the propeller, too, made considerably higher output, greater altitudes and higher speeds of flight possible – far into the supersonic speed range. The first jet engines were developed in the thirties by Frank Whittle in England and by Hans Joachim Pabst von Ohain in Germany.

A reconstruction of the first Heinkel/Ohain engine *He S3B* is on display. On August 27, 1939, the world's first jet-propelled aircraft flew with this propulsion unit. During the Second World War, the first jet engines were put into combat service: the Junkers *Jumo 004* (fitted into the exhibited *Me 262*) and the *BMW 003* (a cutaway model is on display).

The English-American construction type then still differed from the German construction in several elements, the German engines mainly were pure axial-flow engines, the English engines still had a radial flow compressor. The cutaway model of the *Allison J 33* illustrates the differences. Substantial improvement of all parts of the propulsion unit, among which the controllable compressor blades *(General Electric J 79)*, not only increased the output of the engine (higher thrust), but also reduced the operation cost – a crucial point in jet engines. Two-shaft and three-shaft engines with a higher bypass ratio are examples of further developmental steps which made their use in commercial aircraft economical.

The standards of the seventies are exemplified by the *Turbo-Union RB 199* three-shaft reheat bypass turbojet engine (cutaway model) for the *Panavia Tornado* multi-role combat aircraft, by the *Pratt & Whitney JT 9D* front-fan bypass turbojet (cutaway model) for the *Boeing 747 Jumbo Jet* and by the *General Electric CF6* (beneath the wing of the *Air-*

Messerschmitt Me 262 A, 1944 (O); above: Messerschmitt Me 163 B, 1941 (O)
The fighter aircraft *Me 262* was the first aircraft with jet propulsion to be built in series and used in combat. The novel propulsion system made a maximum aircraft speed of 870 km per hour possible. The *Me 163* was a rocket-propelled fighter. Since the burning time of the propulsion unit was very short (five minutes only), the aircraft were glide landed.

bus), of similar construction. In addition to them, there are turbojet engines for vertical take-off and landing (VTOL) aircraft on display: the vectored-thrust lift/propulsion engine *(Rolls Royce Pegasus)*, suitable for both vertical take-off and horizontal flight, and the *Rolls Royce RB 162* VTOL turbojet engine of extremely light construction (fitted to the *Dornier Do 31* transport aircraft).

For reasons of economy, jet turbines are suitable primarily for very high cruising speeds – close to sonic speed and above.

Where high speed is less important, the well-proven propeller is still in use. In propulsion, however, the turboprop engines have superseded the piston engines and are used, above all, in military transport aircraft (*Rolls Royce Dart* and *Tyne* turboprops), in business aircraft *(Lycoming ALF 502)* and in helicopters *(Allison 250)*.

A few more aero-engines are on display at the end of the Power Machinery Department.

Jet Aircraft

Ground floor

The rocket-driven and turbojet aircraft of the Second World War introduce the visitor to the aircraft types of the jet age. On the German side, there were the *Messerschmitt Me 163* rocket-driven interceptor and the *Messerschmitt Me 262* turbojet fighter. Together with the *Bachem Natter* interceptor with rocket propulsion and the *Fieseler Fi 103* or *V1* (vengeance weapon 1) fitted with a pulse jet engine, they testify to the enormous expenditure in arms development during the war.

Ten years after the end of the war, fighters achieved more than twice the speed of sound (over 2000 km/h) and a multiplied destroying capacity. The *Lockheed F 104* (next to the *Me 262*) is an example of this new type of aircraft. In the late fifties, the *F 104 (Starfighter)* was taken over by the newly founded West German Air Force and produced under license in the Federal Republic of Germany from 1960 onwards. The reconstruction of the West German air industry and Air Force is closely linked to this aircraft.

An independent, technically demanding and financially costly development programme was set up by the Federal Republic of Germany in the 1960s and 1970s. VTOL combat and transport aircraft were developed in order to do away with the take-off and landing runways, that were many miles in length and vulnerable to bombing. Because of a change in NATO strategy, however, they never entered series production. The prototypes of all three projects, all of them technically successful, have been made available for the collections of the Deutsches Museum: the supersonic fighter *EWR VJ 101* (hanging above the *F-104*), the fighter-bomber *VAK 191* (in storage) of the VFW-Fokker group and the VTOL transport aircraft *Dornier Do 31* (in the courtyard of the Museum).

The first postwar civil aircraft development project of significance was started by the Hamburger Flugzeugbau GmbH (HFB) in 1964. Its target was a fast business aircraft with jet propulsion. The prototype *(HFB 320 Hansa Jet)* is on display here. Despite its advantages, only

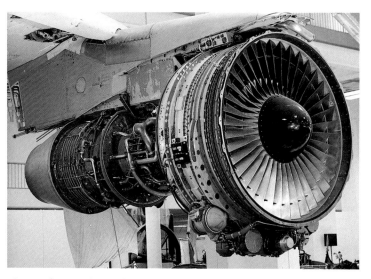

The main features of the *turbofan engine "CF6"* of the American firm General Electric, used in the European airliner *Airbus A 300*, are low operation cost and low noise. The engine has been in use in airline traffic since 1971 and produces a thrust of about 25 000 kilopond (250 000 N). The airflow rate is about 660 kg per second. The *CF6 engine* is also used in other aircraft types such as the *Boeing 747* and the *Douglas DC 10*.

Lockheed F-104 G Starfighter, 1960 (O); above: *Entwicklungsring-Süd VJ 101 C,* 1965 (O)
The *F-104 G* was the standard combat aircraft of the West German Air Force up until the 1980s. It was the first aircraft built in series that achieved more than twice the speed of sound. The *VJ 101,* an experimental aircraft, was developed as a VTOL successor of the *F-104 G.* The engines at the wing ends are turned to vertical position for vertical take-off.

Cross-section of the fuselage of the Airbus A 300, 1972 (O)
The wide-body airliner *Airbus A 300* is the result of European cooperation. The cabin houses up to 345 passengers. Cargo can be transported in standardized hold-containers. The maximum payload is 35 tons (metric).

40 aircraft were sold – not enough to make its production profitable. Civil aircraft construction in Germany (and Europe) got new impetus only at the end of the 1960s, with the start of the *Airbus* programme.

The development of the wide-body aircraft *Airbus A 300* was started by France and Germany against the apparently overwhelming U.S. competition. In this project and in the projects of its successors *A 310* and *A 320* some 47 000 persons are engaged, of which about 20 000 directly or indirectly (subsidiary industries) in the Federal Republic of Germany alone. In 1972, the *Airbus A 300* took off for its maiden flight. From this first *Airbus*, there are several parts on display here: a wing with the engine (from another aircraft) attached to it; the undercarriage; and a cross-section of the fuselage. The dimensions and technology of modern aircraft construction may be studied on these exhibits.

Helicopters

Ground floor

The development of the helicopter into an operational and reliable craft took longer than that of the aeroplane. Not until the thirties, when aeroplanes already flew transatlantic routes, did the first practical helicopters appear. This fact is due to the complicated mechanics of the helicopter, as lift and propulsion are produced and controlled by one constructional element only – the rotor (demonstration).

The first helicopter with good flying performance and manoeuvrability was the *Focke-Wulf Fw 61*. A free flight model, used in 1934 for the testing of the propulsion system, is on display here. During the Second World War, the helicopters were made ready for series production. This generation, and the first generation of helicopters developed after the war, were expensive to operate because of their complex rotor and propulsion systems which can be seen in a partly sectioned *Sikorsky S-55*. In the mid-sixties, when light and economical turboshaft engines supplanted the piston-type engines in aircraft propulsion, operation became less expensive. Glass-fibre reinforced plastics have been used as working materials for rotor blades since 1965 and allow the hingeless structure of the rotor, requiring less maintenance. The exhibited *BO 105* by Messerschmitt-Bölkow-Blohm (MBB) exemplifies this technology.

Gliders

Ground floor

Gliding is a flying sport in its purest form. Its development had a fundamental influence on aviation. The first successful flying apparatus were motorless gliders. They originated as experimental types for the investigation in the fundamentals of flight aerodynamics and mechanics (Lilienthal, Wright).

In the gliding section, the important steps in the development of gliding are explained. The first step towards gliding, however, is illustrated on

Messerschmitt-Bölkow-Blohm BO 105, 1969 (O); behind: *Sikorsky S-55*, 1949 (O)
The two exhibits represent two helicopter generations. The progress achieved in aircraft construction is shown by the empty weight. The modern *BO 105* with the same loading capacity of one ton and nearly equal engine power weighs nearly one ton less. This is the result of a new rotor system (hingeless rotor and rotor blades of glass-fibre reinforced plastics) and another type of engine (turboshaft engine).

fs 24 Phönix, 1957 (O)
The *Phönix* was the first sailplane made of glass-fibre reinforced plastics. This construction – prevailing in sailplanes of our time – combines the advantage of stability with small weight. Furthermore, it achieves a great accuracy of the profile, a prerequisite for laminar profiles with low drag coefficient.

the first floor (Early Days of Flight), by the glider of Otto Lilienthal (1895), who was the first man to prove that man was able to fly.

After the First World War, motorless flight was rediscovered as a sport and experimental field. The *Vampyr* (1921) achieved the step from gliding to the sailplane: flights lasting several hours became possible for the first time. In the late twenties, when the pilots learned to use thermal updrafts (demonstration), the flight performances grew rapidly. Gliding became possible even in the plains: winch launch and towed flight (diorama) supplanted the rubber cord start. The variometer – an instrument indicating the climbing speed and the speed of vertical descent of the plane – became the most important instrument of the glider pilots. During the thirties, gliding became a mass sport and served for training purposes in aviation. In addition to high-performance gliders, simple and sturdy training aircraft – such as the training glider *SG 38* (1938) – were built.

The traditional wooden glider construction reached its high point in the standard aircraft *Ka 6* (1958), the most popular German sailplane, and in the high-performance sailplane *HKS-3* (1955). A new developmental phase began when the *fs 24 Phönix* (1957) introduced plastic construction in combination with the modern laminar profiles into aircraft construction. While gliding developed into a high-performance technology, the seventies brought a return to the flying sport going back to the original simplicity: hang-gliders. As an example, the glider *Bergfex* (1975) can be seen. Just as the *ultralight* aircraft (on display *Ranger M.,* 1980) originated from the combination of the hang-glider with a small engine, the motor glider derived from the sailplane with auxiliary engine. The more powerful types of the latter, which can take off on their own, are closer to the light powered aircraft types. A successful demonstration of how solar energy or muscle power can be utilized was given recently by the experimental aircraft *Solair* (1980) and *Musculair* (1984), both types by Günter Rochelt (*Solair 1* is on display on the ground floor, *Musculair* in the old aeronautics hall.)

Aircraft Structure and Construction Materials

Ground floor

The exhibition of this section still is in the planning phase. It will be focused on the history and technology of aircraft construction with the following topics: development of 1. light-weight structures, from lattice-work to stressed-skin structure; 2. the materials (from bamboo to carbon fibre); 3. the construction methods and strength tests.

The subsequent phases of aircraft construction, from the first concept to operation in airline traffic, will be shown by the example of the European airliner *Airbus*.

First mezzanine (New Aeronautics Hall)

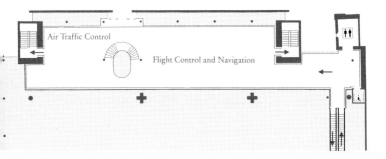

Flight Control and Navigation

First mezzanine

How does the pilot know his cruising altitude or speed? How does he find his way to the airport of destination? The railroads are railborne, the car follows the roads and the road signs. The aircraft, especially when in or above the clouds, perhaps at night and in fog, has no such established lines of reference. During deliberate or involuntary curve flight, when squalls or fall winds push the aircraft out of its flight path,

Compass LKE 12 "EMIL",
1936 (O)
This compass comes from the Airship LZ 129, the "Hindenburg", which exploded in Lakehurst on May 6, 1937 while landing. This type of Askania magnetic compass was part of standard equipment for airships and airplanes.

the human body is exposed to accelerative forces in addition to the force of gravity. As a consequence, the pilot's sense of position in flight is confused, often he cannot even distinguish up and down any more. Several devices, instruments and regulators have been developed in order to make air navigation and flight control possible for the pilot. A display of the entire field (with demonstrations) is under construction at present.

Air Traffic Control and Commercial Aviation

First mezzanine

The air space above industrial countries, along the airways of world traffic and in the area of great airports has become scarce.

Considerable expenditure in the fields of technology and organization is necessary in order to control aircraft of all imaginable sizes and speeds so that no danger for man or equipment can arise. This is true for general aviation (sporting, private and business aircraft), for regular airline traffic and for military aviation.

Burning torches lining the airways of night mailflight marked the beginnings in the twenties. Nowadays, a network of radio beacons, air information service stations and radar stations covers the Earth. Air traffic controllers of the national air traffic control centres control and monitor the air traffic.

A demonstration shows how pilots, air traffic controllers and passengers experience the phases of a commercial flight from take-off to landing: at a model airport, airliners take off and land on plexiglass rails. A slide show explains what happens.

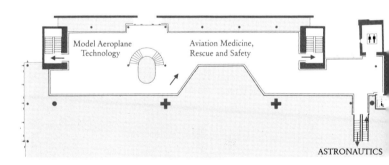

Second mezzanine (New Aeronautics Hall)

Aviation Medicine, Rescue and Safety

Second mezzanine

The conquest of the air brought about extreme physical and psychic stresses and manifold dangers for man. The parachute, used for spectacular show jumps from balloons in the 19th century, often became the last means of escape before crash. At high cruising altitudes – above 11 km – the air temperature drops to − 50 °C, the oxygen for respiration is insufficient. An artificial atmosphere must therefore be created in the cabin. In fighting aircraft, the pilot must be supplied with pure oxygen;

Ejection seat, 1967 (O)
The ejection seat is the main element of modern rescue devices in fighters. It ensures that the aircraft may be left in an emergency, at high speed as well as while at a standstill on the ground.

the cutaway model of an automatic oxygen system shows how this works. In fast curved flight, high centrifugal accelerative forces act upon the pilot. The limits of tolerance for man and the possibilities of protecting him by appropriate seat design and special suits are the subject of detailed study in flight medicine, which uses centrifugal machines for human experiments (demonstration of a model plant).

In high-speed fighters, the only means of escape from imminent crash is leaving the cockpit by means of the ejection seat. As early as during the Second World War pneumatically operated ejection seats were used and saved lives. The reconstruction of a Heinkel ejection seat is on display here. Nowadays ejection seats are highly complicated, fully automatic systems (ejection seat by Martin Baker, licensed construction by Autoflug). They are able to eject the pilot even from an aircraft standing on the ground, and will throw him up so high (by rockets) that he may safely land by parachute.

Not only military aircraft, but also airliners are equipped with a variety of rescue and safety devices; emergency slides, aviation life rafts and breathing appliances may be seen here.

Model Aeroplane Technology

Second mezzanine

Model aeroplane technology has played an important role in the development of aviation technology. Flight experiments with models, primarily those of the past century, served the study of basic problems in flying and the testing of new ideas. The English scientist Sir George Cayley (1773–1857) is considered the "Father of Aviation". In 1807, he presented a glider model by which he demonstrated in a convincing way how an aircraft should be constructed in order to perform stable flight: wings mounted to the front part, control and stabilization devices to the rear of the aeroplane.

Many other important personalities of the early history of aviation have achieved their contribution to the solution of flight problems by means of model aeroplanes. Among them are pioneers like William Samuel Henson and John F. Stringfellow (1848), Félix du Temple (1857), Alphonse Pénaud (he invented the rubber motor in 1872), Victor Tatin (1874), Wilhelm Kress (1885), Samuel P. Langley (1886), Frederik William Lanchester (1895) and Lawrence Hargrave (1888). Even Otto Lilienthal and the Wright brothers tested flight stability by models before they ventured to fly their apparatus themselves.

In the course of the 20th century, the model aeroplane technology has developed into an independent field and a demanding hobby. However, it has remained closely linked to aviation technology. The fruitful interaction between these two fields exists up to our times.

The displays on the history and technology of the model aeroplane cover an area of about 120 m² and include the following groups: 1. Model gliders, 2. Model motor aeroplanes and helicopters, 3. Model aero-engines, 4. Model aeroplane control, 5. Accessories, 6. Model rocketry.

W. Rathjen, G. Filchner, H. Holzer, G. von Langsdorff, M. Weidner

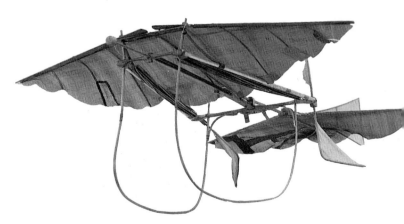

Hanging glider, 1887 (O)
A model by Wilhelm Kreß, named "Monoplan". Span: 860 mm; length: 940 mm.

Astronautics

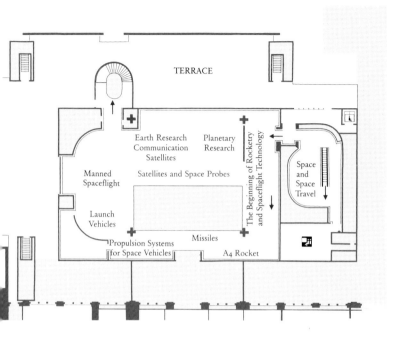

Technically speaking, astronautics is closely linked to aeronautics. However, they form two completely separate fields if their original aims are taken into account. The pioneers of flight wanted to fly, to move freely in the air like birds, whereas the astronauts aimed higher – away from Earth to the Moon, to Mars and even beyond to other stars. Their objective was the search for truth and for closeness to God. Just as the myth of Icarus' flight and fall symbolizes the human dream of flying, which dates back many thousands of years, the satire *"To the Moon and beyond"*, written by the Syrian, Lucian, about 120 A.D., shows that the idea of space travel, too, is very old and that human phantasy has never bothered about the limits of technical feasibility. Contrary to Lucian, who didn't care about technical problems, Jules Verne (1828–1905), in his visionary novels *From the Earth to the Moon* and *Round the Moon*, gave a rather detailed description of how he imagined the space craft, the launching site, the take-off, the trip to the Moon and the landing.

He was already conscious of the main problem of astronautics: in order to be able to surmount the gravity force of the Earth and to fly to other celestial bodies, the spacecraft has to be accelerated to the inconceivably high speed of 11.2 km per second (40000 km per hour). However, his suggestion of achieving this speed by shooting a gun of 270 m in length is not realistic; no living being would withstand this acceleration. The key to space exploration is the multistage liquid-propellant rocket, the only means that makes the take-off from Earth and the flight through outer space possible. The main credit for this discovery goes to three scientists: the Russian Konstantin Eduardovich Ziolkovski (1857–1935), the American Robert H. Goddard (1882–1945) and the German Hermann Oberth (born in 1894). Above all, Oberth's treatises *With the Rocket into Interplanetary Space* (1923) and *Ways to Space Travel* (1928) laid the foundations of space travel.

First experiments with rockets started in the twenties (take-off of Goddard's first liquid-propellant rocket on March 16th, 1926). In Germany, the military authorities took over the development of the artillery rocket as a long-range missile in the thirties. The construction of long-range guns had been forbidden to Germany after the First World War. On October 3, 1942, the first large rocket reached a height of about 84 km and thus touched the border of space. This rocket, named *A4* (aggregate 4) was the result of a ten-year development programme under the technical supervision of Wernher von Braun. Under the name of *V2* (vengeance weapon two) it attained regrettable fame two years later. It was used for the bombing of great cities such as London and Antwerp. After the Second World War, the increasing *Cold War* between East and West led to its rapid development into an intercontinental rocket carrying nuclear weapons.

On October 4, 1957, using a modified military rocket, the Soviet Union launched the first satellite, *Sputnik I,* into space – a sensation for the whole world and a shock for the United States. The U.S. pre-eminence was at stake. On February 1, 1958, the Americans caught up by means of a rocket developed from the *A4* by Wernher von Braun and his team.

In the 1960s, astronautics provided headlines in the world's press, and television let everyone participate in spectacular events: on April 12, 1961, the first man enters space – the Russian Yuri Gagarin; in March 1965, the first free space-walk – by the Russian astronaut Alexei Leonov. They were followed by collective flights, docking manoeuvres and, finally, by the flight to the Moon. On July 21, 1969, the American Neil Armstrong was the first man to step onto the Moon's surface. During the seventies, the U.S. carried out further Moon-landing missions; in the Soviet Union, flights to and stays in the Salyut space laboratories lasting several months became routine. In the 1980s, the Europeans, too, successfully got involved in manned spaceflight. In Autumn 1983, the American launch vehicle *Space Shuttle* placed the space laboratory *Spacelab,* the product of European development, into an Earth orbit. The German astronaut Ulf Merbold flew with the crew as a payload expert. One of the essential objectives of the *Spacelab* research programme was to find out if – and how – it was possible to make industrial use of the particular environmental conditions of outer space. In Autumn 1985, a Spacelab mission named *D 1* followed. The scientific part of the mission was financed and the responsibility taken over by the Federal Republic of Germany alone for the first time.

Less spectacular, but all the more significant from the scientific, economic and military aspects was the development of unmanned space flight of satellites. Meanwhile their success has put an end to the discussion of the significance and purpose of spaceflight.

Communication satellites transmit television productions and telephone

Astronaut, 1965 (R)
The first "space-walk" was achieved by the Americans during the Gemini 4 flight, on June 10, 1965: The astronaut Edward White floated free in space for 22 minutes, being linked to the spacecraft by a supply and measuring line.

calls. They switch dataflow between the centres of multinational companies, stock exchanges and large computer centres.

Meteorological satellites monitor the weather and its movements in the Earth atmosphere by automatic cameras and measuring sensors. Geodetic Earth orbiting satellites photograph and measure the pollution of the atmosphere, oceans and rivers. Their pictures help the cartographers in surveying the Earth.

Military observation satellites supply extremely sharp pictures of any selected place on Earth.

Navigation satellites relay accurate data for position finding to merchant vessels and warships.

Planetary probes have flown to nearly all planets of our Solar System, even landed on Venus and Mars, and have added considerably to our knowledge of the Solar System by the measurement data transmitted to Earth by radio.

Optical and radiometric telescopes mounted on satellites pierce the depths of outer space unhindered by the veil of the atmosphere. The extreme requirements to be met by the technology of the rockets, the spacecraft and their equipment have on the one hand caused an enormous expenditure; on the other hand, however, the results obtained by space research and development have been adopted by many other fields of technology (microelectronics, computer technology, new construction materials, systems engineering).

The development of manned space flight is aimed at a permanent Earth orbital space station which could be used as research laboratory, observation station, or even as a production plant for supermaterials or pharmaceuticals.

A manned flight to Mars has been in discussion for several decades. The return trip would last two-and-a-half years. The decision whether the flight should be ventured or not has not been taken yet.

Information on the Exhibition

The exhibition may best be reached by the escalators, from the first floor of the Aeronautics Department, and visited by the order of the sections described on the following pages. The exit is next to the *Manned Spaceflight* section and leads to the spiral staircase winding around the A4 rocket (V2).

Space and Space Travel

Visitors going upstairs by the escalator, coming from the Earth-centered world of aeronautics, are welcomed by mystical darkness in the introductory room of the Astronautics Department. Right in the beginning they are confronted with a juxtaposition of phantasy and reality. A wood engraving of the 16th century shows a scientist leaning a ladder against the celestial globe, thus symbolizing the craving for travelling to the stars. Next to him, an astronaut floats free in space: he could be American or Russian.

Further progress through the introductory room leads to topics such as *Cosmogony in Antiquity, The Evolution of Our Cosmogony of Today, Atmosphere and Space, Our Solar System* (scale charts of planetary orbits and comparisons of size and structure of the planets). The transition to the exhibition itself is formed by the topic *Phantasies and Utopias*, which again compares ideas with reality discovered later.

The Beginnings of Rocketry and Spaceflight Technology

At the beginning of this section, the physical fundamentals of rocketry – the so-called reaction principle (Newton's third law of motion) – are explained by means of simple demonstrations. A waterwheel of the Hero type (D) shows that this principle has been known for a long time. Powder rockets were used as fireworks and firesetting rockets in China and Europe since the 13th century, and have been in use as artillery missiles since the 19th century. During the twenties, the first practical experiments with rocket propulsion for space vehicles started in the Soviet Union, in the United States and in Germany (rocket-driven sledge and car by Max Valier, 1930; *HW 1*, 1931 first European liquid-propellant rocket by Johannes Winkler). The breakthrough towards usable giant rockets and the first launch of a rocket as a weapon is illustrated by the A4 (V2) rocket of Peenemünde.

Numerous types of rocket propulsion were used in guided missiles during the Second World War. Three examples are on display here: the *Rheinmetall R1* anti-aircraft missile (solid-propellant rocket), the

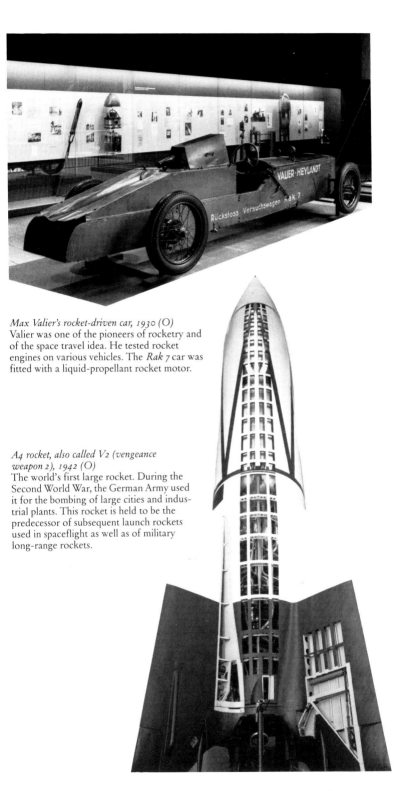

Max Valier's rocket-driven car, 1930 (O)
Valier was one of the pioneers of rocketry and
of the space travel idea. He tested rocket
engines on various vehicles. The *Rak 7* car was
fitted with a liquid-propellant rocket motor.

*A4 rocket, also called V2 (vengeance
weapon 2), 1942 (O)*
The world's first large rocket. During the
Second World War, the German Army used
it for the bombing of large cities and industrial plants. This rocket is held to be the
predecessor of subsequent launch rockets
used in spaceflight as well as of military
long-range rockets.

Kramer X4 (with a liquid-propellant rocket engine by BMW) and the *Henschel Hs 293* glide bomb (with a Walter rocket engine using hydrogen peroxide as propellant).

The entire rocket technology developed during the Second World War as well as all its subsidiary aspects (construction, propulsion, command, remote control etc.) was the point of departure for the further development of military long-range ballistic rockets and guided missiles, and finally the space-launch rockets in East and West.

Propulsion Systems for Space Vehicles

The different types of rocket propulsion units and their working principle (chemical, nuclear and electric propulsion), which were only presented briefly in the rocketry group, are dealt with in detail in this part of the exhibition. Several finished rocket engines developed in the United States, in Europe and Germany are on display: from the *Saturn* space vehicle, the *Rocketdyne H1 rocket engine;* the solid-propellant *apogee motor* by MAN; the HM 7 and Viking IV engines of the European *Ariane* launcher and small *hydrazine* thrusters for orbit and attitude correction. In a separate room, electric propulsion is explained by a demonstration; an original ion thruster *(RIT 10)* is on display.

Launch Vehicles and Launching Sites

The launch vehicles that carry satellites, probes and manned space vehicles into space are mostly derived from military medium-range and intercontinental rockets, exceptions being the *Saturn V* rocket, 110 m long, which flew the US astronauts to the Moon, and the European *Ariane* rocket. A series of models of the major rocket types is on display on a 1:25 scale and allows comparisons.

Space travel not only requires the rockets, satellites and spacecraft, but also the launching sites, control centres and an Earth-covering network of communication and trajectory monitoring stations. An idea of the dimensions of a launching site and of the vehicle assembly buildings is given by a diorama of the J. F. Kennedy Space Center, Florida, USA. This is where the *Saturn* Moon rockets were launched in the past and where the *Space Shuttles* are launched in our times. The launching site of the European *Ariane* (model) is in Kourou (French Guiana, South America).

Satellites and Probes

From the enormous variety of satellites and probes and of their scientific, economic and military tasks, four subjects form the major topics of the exhibition:

1. The first satellites and probes
Models of the first Soviet *(Sputnik 1)* and U.S. satellite *(Explorer 1)* and of the first international satellites *(Ariel, Alouette, Heos A)* point to the beginnings of technical satellite development programmes. Technological details may be studied in prototypes of the first satellites built in the Federal Republic of Germany *(Aeros* and *Azur).*

Earth receiver station for weather photographs, 1984 (O)
This station receives weather photographs from the European geostationary *Meteosat II* and from American and Soviet meteorological satellites on polar orbits. The photographs are read out by a monitor and can be printed.

2. Exploration of the Earth and weather observation

This section is focused around an Earth receiver station for satellite pictures of weather formations. Several times a day, the latest weather photographs from the European *Meteosat II* and from US and Soviet meteorological satellites are received directly and read out by facsimile printers and monitors. The extremely sharp cloud pictures show what a valuable tool spaceflight has become for climatology.

3. Communication satellites

Technically speaking, communication satellites are relay stations in space. They receive radio waves from Earth transmitter stations, amplify them and transmit them again. The corresponding Earth receiving station could be situated on the other side of the Atlantic Ocean. In principle, three satellites, placed into a geostationary orbit at a height of 36 000 km above the Equator, are sufficient to send information (telephone call, radio or TV broadcast) around the globe. The construction of a communication satellite can be seen in a few models and in the original *Symphonie* satellite on display. The *Symphonie* satellite was an experimental satellite developed in German-French cooperation. Because the Europeans have their own launcher, the *Ariane,* since 1981, they are able to place profitable communication satellites in space themselves and thus break the monopoly held hitherto by the Americans. European communication satellites *(ECS)* have already been put into space. The first German and French satellites for live TV transmission *(TV-SAT* and *TDF1)* will introduce a new phase in television from 1987 onwards.

4. Exploration of the planets

From the aspect of science, astronomy and astrophysics are the

Helios solar probe, 1974 (O)
Space probe to explore the Sun. Since 1974 and 1976, two Helios space probes orbit around the Sun on elliptical orbits. In 1987, Helios 1 still transmitted data to the Earth, though it was designed for a working period of only 18 months. The airworthy prototype is on display here.

branches to which spaceflight probably brought the most significant progress. The observation of the planets and celestial bodies from the Earth has up until now been disturbed by the atmosphere. Spaceflight offers scientists the possibility of placing astronomical observatories in space (on satellites) and of sending space probes equipped with cameras and measuring devices to the planets.

An impressive example is the *Helios* solar probe. Two such probes have orbited around the Sun since 1974 and transmit to Earth scientific data on electric and magnetic fields, emission of particles and photons by the Sun and from the depths of outer space.

Manned Spaceflight

Man's conquest of space has required an enormous technical expenditure.

Outside of the Earth's atmosphere, the environment is deadly for man. It lacks oxygen; the radiation of the Sun reaches the spacecraft unhindered by air; meteorites and cosmic radiation may strike the spacecraft. Also incalculable were the effects of weightlessness on the human body and the psychic stresses of space flight on the crew. During the re-entry flight through the atmosphere, the spacecraft had to be slowed down by the frictional forces of air alone, from a speed of about 28 000 km per hour to nearly zero speed. Despite these problems, both the Soviet Union and the United States carried out intensive programmes within only ten years, struggling for prestigious first achievements in the space race.

In 1961 the Soviet Union launched the first man, Yuri Gagarin, into a single Earth orbit; in 1969, two American astronauts landed on the Moon. To reach this target, the U.S. programme had employed a work-force of 300 000; the total cost was about 22 billion dollars.

The trip to the Moon has become a symbol of the apparently unlimited possibilities of technology.

The exhibition can give only a hint of the history and technology of manned spaceflight. A few items point to the technical aspect of the problems: a replica of the *Mercury* space capsule, the first American spacecraft, and two spacesuits used in the *Gemini* and *Apollo* space pro-grammes. These spacesuits even allowed astronauts extravehicular activities.

The model of the *Saturn v* rocket, the diorama of the Moonport in Flo-

Mercury space capsule, 1960 (R); behind: Gemini spacesuit, 1965 (O)
The Mercury space capsules were the first manned spacecraft of the United States. On February 20, 1962, John Glenn – the first U.S. astronaut – accomplished a three-orbit mission around the Earth in a Mercury spacecraft. The spacesuit in the background was worn by Frank Bormann during the Gemini vii spaceflight which lasted 14 days.

rida and an original oxygen-hydrogen booster of the second and third stage of the *Saturn v* also belong to this group.

Three dioramas illustrate the preparatory phase and the procedure of a Moon-landing mission: The first diorama shows the phase of rendezvous and docking of two space vehicles in an Earth orbit. Such docking manoeuvres take place according to laws completely different from those familiar to us on Earth, and therefore the astronauts had to be trained intensively for them. The safe control of the docking manoeuvres was an absolute condition for the successful carrying through of more complex space missions, such as the trip to the Moon or the construction of space stations.

During the Moon-landing missions, for instance, docking manoeuvres in Lunar orbit were necessary. The Lunar Module was released from the *Apollo* spacecraft here and then descended to the Moon's surface. After the lift-off from the Moon, it was docked again to the Command Module. This process is shown by a second diorama.

The central diorama is dedicated to landing on the Moon itself, namely to the fourth landing *(Apollo 15)* which was of particular scientific interest. In the proverbially hostile, desert-like Moon landscape, two astronauts are working. Their bulky, hermetically-sealed spacesuits nearly conceal the man inside. Numerous devices point to the comprehensive

Apollo 15 Moon landing, 1971 (Di)
Apollo 15 was the fourth successful U.S. Moon-landing mission. The astronauts David Scott and James Irvin stayed three days on the Moon and carried out a comprehensive scientific programme. A "Moon rover" was then used for the first time.

Suggestions for the continuation of the tour
In order to continue the tour of the collections, you go down the spiral staircase around the A4 rocket to the first floor. Here you can still make your choice: either you continue downstairs to the ground floor, or if you prefer to go ahead through the exhibition of *aircraft with propeller/piston engine propulsion* to the departments of *Telecommunications* (p. 146) or *Chemistry* (p. 164). Another possibility is to pass through the sections of *Aerodynamics/Mechanics of Flight* and *Early Days of Flight* to the elevators in the main staircase and to continue with the exhibitions of the second floor or go up to the *Planetarium* (p. 283).

scientific programme that the astronauts had to carry out on the Moon. Looking at this scenery, the visitor may get an idea of what a challenge it was to send men 380000 km away to this celestial body. A small stone from the Moon, on display in a showcase in front of the diorama, is a visible indication of what the astronauts brought back from the Moon – in addition to an abundance of measuring data and photographs. The present state of manned spaceflight is represented by the European Spacelaboratory *Spacelab* on display on the ground floor.

Space Technology

The high requirements to be met by the technology of the rockets, spacecraft and satellites made the development of new technological processes necessary. Examples are: micro-miniaturization of electronic components, ultralight materials and constructions, heat and cold-resistant parts and instruments, fully automatic measuring and control systems of top reliability (no maintenance is possible on satellites).

A selection of structural elements and devices developed especially for spaceflight are on display in showcases, among other items, parts from the heat-shield of the U.S. *Space Shuttle,* and dust protection shield of the comet Halley probe *Giotto.*   *W. Rathjen*

Altamira Cave

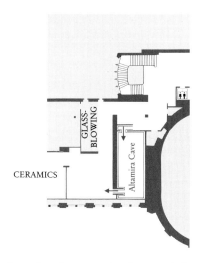

Finds of skulls and rudimentary implements led to the conclusion that man evolved from the series of the Primates some 600 000 to one million of years ago. Man of the Paleolithic period lived by hunting and by collecting fruit, mushrooms and wild vegetables. He used stone implements which have been partly preserved and indicate his ways of living. It is probable that he also used implements made of other materials, such as wood and bones. However, these have been lost by weathering over a period of many thousand years.

The condition of stone implements alone tells the story of a technical development: in the beginning, the stone was shaped only roughly, while – later on – it was worked into highly specialized tools like needles, knives, arrowheads, and in the Mesolithic period also into stone axes. Paleolithic men limited their production to implements and weapons needed for the daily struggle of life. The earliest expressions of worship and the arts can be traced back to the end of the Mesolithic period, but above all to the Neolithic period, the most famous being the paintings and engravings in the caves of Northern Spain and Southern France.

Information on the Exhibition

Before entering the room with the copy of the ceiling of the Altamira cave, the visitor is familiarized with the development of Stone Age implements by means of a chronological survey and a few examples. In the adjoining dimmed room, he finds the representation of a bison herd; the reconstruction of the ceiling painting found in the *Gran Sala* of the Altamira cave.

The cave of Altamira, near Santander in Northern Spain, was discovered in 1868. At that time, scientists took the wall paintings for forgeries. Not until the early 20th century, when similar cave-paintings were found in other parts of Northern Spain and Southern France and could be dated with accurracy, could this masterpiece be assigned to the Ice Age.

The colours are pigments occurring in nature. The painters used yellow, red and brownish ochres, and manganese earth and coal as black pigments.

The ceiling painting of the *Gran Sala* of the Altamira cave was copied using a complicated and costly process. It was finished in 1962 and preserves the opportunity to see the Altamira cave-paintings for visitors, after the cave itself had to be closed because the many visitors had endangered the preservation of this unique work of art.

Examples of other cave-paintings are on display in the wall showcases of the room, in the form of large-sized slides. Several copies of important artistic manifestations of the Stone Age, among which the *Venus of Laussel* or the *Lamp of La Mouthe*, are shown there.   *S. Fitz*

Glass-blowing

Until the opening of the Glass Department, the visitor can observe a glass-blower using the lamp.

Ceiling painting of the Altamira cave (detail)

Ceramics

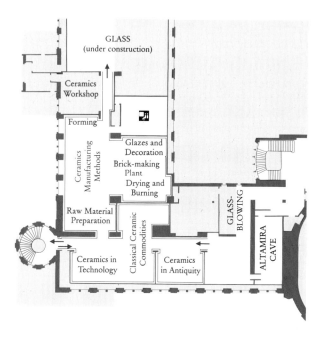

Ceramics are probably the earliest artificial working material known to mankind. The invention and earliest use of ceramics about 10 000 years ago is correlated to man's change to sedentary life, to the cultivation of plants and the domestication of animals. Because of their resistance to weather and high temperatures, containers made of ceramics have been in use as ideal storage and cooking vessels up to our times.

The raw materials for the production of simple ceramic items – the clays – can be found virtually everywhere, so the knowledge of the production method spread rather quickly from several independent centres. Around the birth of Christ, ceramics were known in nearly all parts of the world. In the beginning, the different simple forming methods didn't allow the production of ceramic products in large numbers. This changed with the invention of the fast-turning potter's wheel in Mesopotamia in the middle of the 4th millennium B.C. As early as in Antiquity, this fundamental invention – a parallel of the invention of the wheel – led to the setup of ceramic workshops with a production of up to 300 000 vessels; production figures of similar dimensions were equalled again only much later by the pre-industrial faience and porcelain manufactories of the 18th century.

The empirically acquired knowledge of the firing behaviour of different raw materials as well as their selection and preparation, and the continuous improvement of the kilns led not only to technical, but also to artistic mastery. The Attic black-figure and red-figure vases are striking examples of both.

During the 3rd millennium B.C., by a selection of particular clay types, it became possible in northern Mesopotamia to produce ceramics the ceramic body of which – in contrast to all ceramic types known hitherto – was not porous any more, but particularly hard. Independently, this ceramic material, named *stoneware*, was later brought to perfection in China by improved kilns with much higher firing temperatures. Based upon existing techniques, the production of ceramics with a white, transparent ceramic body – the *porcelain* – was achieved for the first time in China, about the 7th century B.C. The news of this invention rapidly spread throughout the Islamic culture area and reached Europe. The first (unintended) result of the attempts to find the secret of porcelain production was the invention of *faience* in the 8th century A.D. The coloured porous ceramic body of ceramic items was coated with a covering white glaze. Thus it was possible to obtain products which were similar to porcelain in appearance, but not so hard. For a long time, porcelain was a sought-after commodity of East Asian trade, a business which was carried on mainly by the Dutch. The decoration styles of Chinese porcelain had a strong influence on the decoration of European faience, especially on the products of the numerous manufactories of Delft.

The first European porcelain was invented in Meissen in 1708. Here, too, the first years of production bear the imprint of Chinese and Japanese decoration – a European style developed only slowly. Throughout the 18th century, porcelain and faience – the products of the manufactories – remained luxury items and reserved to the upper classes. Ceramics for the daily use of the people were made of porous earthenware, mostly coated with lead glaze, or stoneware in a few regions. They were produced in workshops organized by guilds. During the second half of the 18th century, a new ceramic commodity was first produced in English industrial plants and spread from there: the *whiteware*. This white porous – and therefore glazed – commodity rapidly supplanted the earthenware items in the household. This trend continued on a larger scale towards the end of the 19th century, when nearly everyone could afford to buy porcelain products, the manufacture of which had meanwhile been industrialized.

Because of their resistance to weathering, ceramics were used for building bricks, sewer pipes and water pipes as early as in the 4th millennium B.C. Structural ceramics in the form of building bricks and roofing tiles, sewage pipes, wall and floor tiles are in common usage today. Use was made of the resistance of ceramics to high temperatures in the construction of furnaces and the production of crucibles as early as in Antiquity, though the systematic production of fireproof ceramic products only began in the 19th century.

At that time, ceramics also gained importance because of their high resistance to chemicals. The stoneware in particular, which was both acid and alkali-proof, was one of the prerequisites for the 19th century development of the chemical industry.

The fundamental and new discoveries of natural science in the 19th and 20th centuries led to the development of novel materials in ceramics as well as in other branches of technology. The basic steps of the ceramic process: the *mixing of the raw materials – forming – drying – firing*, have remained unchanged in principle, but were adapted to the requirements of economic production. The physical and chemical testing of the raw materials, the mechanization of the forming processes and the technical-scientific optimization of the drying and firing processes have changed the characteristics of ceramic industrial plants. In former times, working in pottery was considered strenuous and injurious to health. Today the supervision of production plants and automatic conveying equipment has supplanted manual labour to a large extent.

The field of ceramics, which initially only used clayey raw materials, has expanded to a variety of additional inorganic, non-metallic materials in the past hundred years. Oxides, such as aluminium oxide, for instance, are raw materials of outstanding resistance to heat and mechanical wear. Silicon carbide and silicon nitride are particularly suitable materials for heat-stressed machine elements. Of growing importance are ceramic materials with particular electrical properties for capacitors, hot conveyors, semiconductor compositions and piezoelectric ceramics. Ceramic magnets fulfil numerous tasks in electro-technics, in mechanical engineering and in private households. The list of possible applications is endless and keeps growing in the wake of systematic investigation into these groups of materials.

Information on the Exhibition

The visitor will find four clearly distinct sections in this department, preceded by a survey of the historic development of ceramic materials and by an explanation of the term ceramics.

Ceramics in Antiquity

Beginning with the invention of ceramics and a selection of early examples, the exhibition deals with the spreading of ceramics throughout the world and with the different ceramics manufacturing techniques. The section dedicated to ceramics produced without the potter's wheel is followed by exhibits of ceramics thrown on the potter's wheel. A selection of mass products, such as oil lamps, anointing oil vessels and Roman utility dishes points to the widespread use of ceramics in Antiquity. Ceramic construction materials like building bricks, roof tiles and clay pipes have also been in common use ever since.

The decoration methods of ceramics in Antiquity are also dealt with in detail, the techniques of Greek vase-painting being one of the main groups in this section.

Classical Ceramic Commodities

The four classical ceramic commodities, i.e. *earthenware, stoneware, whiteware, porcelain,* are classified in accordance with the technical aspects of the raw materials used. In the group of porous ceramics with coloured ceramic body – called *earthenware* or soft pottery – unglazed items as well as objects coated with transparent lead glaze or opaque glaze containing tin, called *faience,* are shown. Earthenware is not only

Ceramics in Antiquity
Ceramics used for storage and transport are arranged in the middle of the room. Jars with two vertical handles fastened to the body and neck (called amphorae) were used mainly for the transport of liquids. They often are the only remains of sunken ships on the bottom of the sea. The big storage vessels with a wide mouth, the so-called pithoi, are still produced today in an uninterrupted tradition of more than two thousand years. They are built up from clay strips and fired in special kilns on the production site.

presented in the form of containers of all kinds, but also as an important material of structural ceramics, such as tiled stoves, wall and floor tiles, building bricks and roofing tiles.

Another section of the exhibiton houses the whiteware, which also has a porous, but white ceramic body and is coated by a colourless glaze.

In the nearby showcases, there is a juxtaposition of the two vitrified ceramic materials: stoneware (with coloured ceramic body) and porcelain (with white transparent ceramic body). Here, too, a short survey summarizes the historic development of these materials from their invention.

Ceramics in Technology

This section of the exhibition gives a survey of the possible fields of application of ceramics in technology. Except for a few fields, they have all developed from about the mid-nineteenth century onwards, but a great many only in our century. Ceramics with the property of electrical insulation, to which the porcelain insulator belongs as well as the spark plug, are compared to ceramic materials with semiconductor properties or piezoelectric ceramics. A material in common use today is the ceramic magnet.

The outstanding hardness of ceramic materials is utilized for wear-resisting parts of heavily stressed machines, e.g. for plain bearings, thread guides of textile machinery, tools for the wire drawing technology. Cutting tools which are superior in quality to the common tools made of steel or widia are another application. The constancy of the mechanical and chemical properties of several ceramic working materials qualifies them as promising materials for the construction of combustion engines with high operating temperatures.

In the exhibition, the very extensive application of ceramics in technology, namely refractory and chemical-resistant materials, is represented only by a few examples. A small group points to the role of ceramics in medicine, e.g. in artificial joints.

Ceramics for industrial use
In the front, at left, there are two stoneware pipes, manufactured in 1910 and 1980, the essential difference between them being the type of leakproof, but flexible pipe connection for which a satisfactory solution was found only in recent times.

In the front, at right, a case insulator of brown glazed porcelain for a 245 kV measuring transformer can be seen.

In the second row, at the left, there is a crankshaft grinding wheel with ceramically bonded corundum granulate; next to it, a coiled cooling pipe, both made of stoneware. Because of the demands made by changing temperatures, the ceramic pipe (15 m in length) has a loose bedding.

The stoneware acid container (right), of about 1900, holds about 1500 litres. In the 19th century, stoneware was the only material suitable for the storage and conveying of acids. For the same reason, conveyors for hot caustic gases and vapours – like the centrifugal exhaust fan in the third row (left) – were also made of acidproof stoneware.

Behind, (left) is a model (scale 1 : 5) of a washing and adsorption column lined entirely with acid-proof ceramic moulded bricks. Equipment of this type has been successfully used in the ceramic industry, especially for the production of nitric acid, for nearly 70 years.

Brickmaking press with pug mill, 1856 (O)

This machine is the prototype of the earliest brick-making press with a pug mill. It was invented and built by Carl Schlickeysen in 1856 and presented at the 1862 London World's Fair with great success. The press consists of a cylinder with a closed bottom and with a funnel-shaped mouth at the top. A shaft, which is concentric to the axle, with inclined cutters is rotating inside. The clay is filled in at the top, pressed down by the screw motion and simultaneously kneaded and homogenized. At the bottom of the cylinder, a continuous column of clay comes out at the mouthpiece attached to the side. The press was driven by horse-power.

Fully automatic miniature brickmaking plant (D, detail)
This plant in working condition corresponds to a fully automatic brickmaking plant at the technical standards of 1980. The clay, brought in by a feeding hopper, is formed to hollow bricks (30 × 45 × 30 mm). After a drying time of 20 hours, the bricks are fired at about 850 °C in a tunnel kiln. The passage time through the tunnel kiln is about 4 hours. In the picture, the wire cutters, which divide the continuous clay column into the individual bricks, can be seen, as well as a loaded transfer car.

The firing processes of the ceramic industry
The burning apparatus with two lenses (about 1700) in the front is ascribed to Ehrenfried Walter, Count of Tschirnhaus. As early as 1687, Tschirnhaus carried out first experiments for the production of porcelain. By means of firing apparatus (today, we would say: laboratory kilns using solar energy) he studied the melting behaviour of various rock types and minerals. In the rear, a cutaway burner area of a modern tunnel kiln and the arrangement of items on the car for porcelain glaze firing can be seen.

The Ceramic Production Method

Equipment, machinery, models and explanatory boards are shown in separate groups dedicated to the basic steps of ceramic manufacture. A synopsis of raw materials is followed by a group of machines required for the preparation of raw materials. The forming of ceramic items can be done either on the potter's wheel or by presses, lately also by complicated jigger machines. A selection of such tools and machines is on display.

The firing of ceramics mostly takes place in big kilns. A series of models summarizes the development of kilns in the production of ceramics. Surface finishing, too, plays an important role in ceramics. A few selected examples and specimens illustrate the various types of glazes and decoration methods used in ceramics.

A showcase offers a survey of the production steps in porcelain manufacture. Representing the procedure of production of all other ceramic products, miniature bricks are produced by a fully automatic model plant.

In addition to this, the visitor may observe the manual manufacture of ceramics in a workshop.

S. Fitz

Glass

Like ceramics, glass is one of the earliest artificial raw materials. Receptacles and coloured decorative glass objects made in the temple workshops of the Egyptians and Babylonians were excavated from the sand of the deserts. The invention of the glass-blower's pipe around the birth of Christ gave a strong boost to glassmaking. In the 19th century, Otto Schott's treatises contributed considerably to the development of glass as a technical material which, through scientific research, is constantly finding new areas of application.

Glass-blowing

Prior to the opening of the *Glass* Department, the visitor can watch a glass-blower using the lamp (next to the entrance of the Altamira cave).

S. Fitz

Bottles and receptacles (O)
Until the opening of a permanent exhibition there will be occasional special exhibitions on glass as a working material. The picture above shows items from the collection of Eugen Leiterer (1983/84).

Technical Toys

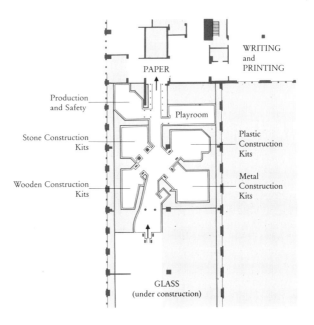

For more than a hundred years, technical devices and inventions have influenced the production of toys. Toys, which are generally scale models of our environment, also bring technology into the nursery: be it the historical steam engine of the 19th century or the computer-aided machine tool of our times. More and more, toy models reflect technical evolution. In the form of toys, technology becomes intelligible and understandable. An essential social task of toys consists in providing a key that children can use to make contact with the world of adults.

But not only children, even technicians, engineers and inventors play in many ways, as part of their work, trying to find new creations. So technical play is not wasteful, but often a preliminary stage of dealing with technology itself. This is why it is useful for the Deutsches Museum to investigate technical toys and to present them in exhibitions, thus fulfilling its task of familiarizing the broad public with the fundamental principles of technology.

Until the opening of a permanent exhibition, special exhibitions will be arranged. The exhibition *"Amazing building blocks"* (*"Bauklötze staunen"*) is presently on display.

Information on the Exhibition

Playing with constructional parts and the history of construction kits represent, in an exemplary way, the relationship between technology, architecture and games. The themes of the exhibition are: building and construction kits, their history in particular; technical, economic and social problems; production and safety. Upon written request in advance, school classes and nursery-school groups can try out various sets of construction kits.

Wooden Construction Kits

Playing with building blocks is certainly more than two hundred years old. During the 1780s, construction kits – i.e. constructional parts designed and arranged in boxes in a systematic way – appeared and soon developed into two different types: *thematic* and *elementary construction kits.*

Thematic construction kits serve the construction of houses, palaces, churches, fortresses etc. Well-known examples are: the constructional toys of the catalogue of the mail-order firm Bestelmeier (1793); the Münchner Kindl construction kits (after 1904); the architecture kit A-Ba-Ka (1919), as well as a series of construction kits from the Erzgebirge, designed by the firms S. F. Fischer, Emil Reuter, Carl Fritzsche, Louis Engel, Gotthard Drechsel (from the end of the 19th century on).

Elementary construction kits give the playing child more freedom in the choice of the building theme, offer a wider variety of design and lead to a more intensive experience and understanding of space.

Friedrich Fröbel (1782–1852), one of the most renowned educators of the first half of the 19th century and the initiator of the kindergarten system, created the basis for this kind of construction kits with his playthings which he was the first to use intentionally as toys and educational instruments. Although the construction kits made up only a single part of the playthings, they had a central importance. Designed in mathematically pure forms (ball, cube, cylinder and their divisions), they were conceived as the means by which the playing child as well as the adolescent could perceive and understand the structures of time and space and to develop a comparative and discriminating way of thinking. The Uhl and Kietz construction kits produced after the Second World War, which were widely used in nursery schools, revived Fröbel's ideas.

The instability of larger wood constructions soon prompted the inventors to seek connecting elements and techniques. As early as 1829, the Viennese Joseph Trentsensky was granted a patent for his building blocks which were stabilized by an assembly wire. Subsequently, pegs of wood or metal, sockets of sheet-metal (Minerva-Baukasten) or rubber were also used.

Other fixing possibilities resulted from holes, slits, grooves, projecting parts and the like in the building elements themselves. Well-known kits of this type are the Thuringia kits (after the turn of the century), Ingenius kits (of the twenties) and Dusyma kits (of the thirties). Even the Matador construction kit (1901) was based upon this connecting system; in addition, it was the first kit to allow rotary motion and thus made it possible to represent technical items in working condition – a novelty in wooden construction kits. In 1954 Hans Wammelsberger applied the combination of the perforated strut and screw, which had proved successful in metal construction kits, to wooden construction kits. He added cubes with threaded holes as well as screwdriver and spanner, all made of wood, and thus obtained his successful "baufix" construction set.

Stone Construction Kits

Otto Lilienthal is famous as a flight pioneer. The first stone building block system, sold worldwide under the name of "Anker Steinbaukasten" goes back to the Lilienthal brothers. The initiator of this development, however, was not Otto, but his brother Gustav Lilienthal, a committed architect and a friend of children.

The basic form of the stones is the cube with its divisions and multiples, as well as other simple mathematical bodies such as the cylinder and the pyramid. The colours developed by Lilienthal, a pale brick-red, yellow earth and slate-blue, correspond to the colours used in the architecture of the late 19th century. Adjustment to architecture led to a further differentiation of the blocks. After fruitless attempts to sell the kits himself, Gustav Lilienthal gave over his invention to Adolph Richter. This clever businessman had a patent issued in 1880 and marketed the "Anker Steinbaukasten" after having added construction patterns to it. Richter's stone building block sets form an elaborate system with complementary parts, which started as a small box of 19 blocks and led to a complete set of 3861 blocks, completed by numerous special versions such as the Anker kits for bridge construction (1901), the country house kit (1912) and the fortress kit (1916).

Anker Steinbaukasten, a kit of stone building blocks (O)
The Lilienthal brothers were the inventors of the Anker stone building block kits, of the project as well as of the production. Artificial stones in the colours used by the architecture of the period of promoterism – limestone, brick and slate – were to supplant the simple wooden building blocks. However, the sales failed to bring the desired profit. But as the development of the kit had consumed the savings of the Lilienthal brothers, the process developed for the construction of these artificial stones was sold to the Richter company of Rudolfstadt who had it patented in 1880.

The well-conceived system of building instructions, an extensive publicity and the "Richter Anker Steinbaukasten Verein" (Club) made the Anker stone building block set a worldwide success on which other manufacturers patterned their products: the Bing stone block set (about 1915) and the Domusto bridge construction set (1912). After the war, a series of additional stone block systems came onto the market, but soon disappeared again; the best-known of them were the Tetek construction kits and the Meadom kits.

Metal Construction Kits

More than 80 years have gone by since Frank Hornby (1863–1936) invented the first metal construction kit (1901). The moment was not pure coincidence. The rapid advance of industrialization and the expansion of the railroad network had inspired technicians to grand and mighty buildings. The belief in technical progress was unbroken and the time was ripe for the idea of a construction kit by means of which the technical environment could be copied in the form of models.

Hornby's Meccano metal construction kit consisted of perforated metal struts with screws and nuts as well as of shaft and axle as structural elements for rotary motion. Meccano was a worldwide success and became the model for other kits. The Walther company adopted Hornby's basic ideas for the Stabil construction kits and developed them further; the Märklin brothers bought the rights to the confiscated Berlin plant of Meccano Ltd. Until after the First World War, the structure of metal construction kits was influenced by Meccano.

New paths were opened by Trix, which used a three-row perforation for their struts, thus making manifold and stable constructions possible; by Metalo-Trigon with their triangular basic elements (1912) and by Dux with flat constructional parts (1939). "Meco" and "Meweka" systems left the assembly of structural parts to the user; they made available only the tools.

The metal construction kits reached their heyday during the inter-war period. After the Second World War, they had another revival, but their importance diminished rapidly after the introduction of plastic construction kits.

Plastic Construction Kits

The plastic construction kits overcame the narrow social borders drawn by earlier types: they are toys for everyone, for all ages and classes, boys and girls.

The first plastic construction kits, i.e. boxes with parts made of thermoplastic plastics, are products of the fifties. The first building blocks of "Idema", the first plastic construction kit of the Federal Republic of Germany, were modelled on the brick and made of bakelite. No connection was possible in construction. Only with the change from bakelite to polystyrene in 1959 did the inventor of Idema, Josef Dehm, achieve a stable joint between the individual parts. Children could now construct buildings, and wheels made static models movable.

Also based on the brick idea is Lego. Its inventor Godtfred Kirk Chris-

Industrial models – a new perspective for construction kits
On a small scale, "fischertechnik" models represent projects which later will be executed on a large scale.

tiansen combined all construction kits and created opportunities for all ages.

Whereas the described construction systems had been based upon the brick idea, Max Amsler conceived his "constri" system from the view of high-rise building construction. From the beginning it also included moveable models.

The launching of the Soviet Sputnik in 1957 started a race which led to an upgrading of natural science and technology also in schools. Imbedded in this trend of the time is Artur Fischer's invention (fischertechnik 1966) which allowed the representation of technical functions in a realistic way. A series of construction kits has been produced for the special requirements of workshop teachers (ut series 1969/1971).

If so far the objective was to copy technology on a model scale, the latest industrial models constructed with fischertechnik systems go beyond: technology is designed, i.e. the models built by construction kit techniques are themselves models for technology.

Production and Safety

From the beginning, the production of construction kits required high accuracy. Very early, machines were used. Mechanization and automation led to the injection moulding process still used in the production of plastics. This method makes accurate, rapid and cheap production of constructional parts possible – a prerequisite for widespread use.

Within this section, the production of wooden and plastic constructional parts and the mechanical and chemical safety of toys are dealt with.

G. Knerr

Paper

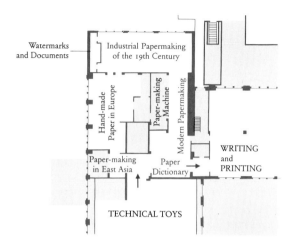

Watermarks and Documents

Industrial Papermaking of the 19th Century

Hand-made Paper in Europe

Paper-making Machine

Modern Papermaking

Paper-making in East Asia

Paper Dictionary

WRITING and PRINTING

TECHNICAL TOYS

The first indication of the invention of paper was found in the Chinese historical work *Hou Han Shu* which describes the later Han period (25–220 A.D.). According to this chronicle, the Chinese government official, Ts'ai Lun, informed the Emperor in the year 105 that he had succeeded in making paper from tree bark, hemp, old rags and fishing nets. During the 8th century, the Arabs in Samarkand learned paper-making from the Chinese. Over the course of several centuries, their knowledge spread as far as Europe.

The earliest mention of papermills on European ground dates back to the 12th century (Xativa, Spain).

From these beginnings up to the 19th century, there was very little change in paper-making techniques. The raw materials used were rags from vegetable fibres (cellulose) such as linen, hemp and cotton. The rags were decomposed into their individual fibres in stamping-mills. The single sheets were scooped out of the liquid fibre suspension, then pressed between felts and air-dried.

A small papermill with one dipping vat normally had about ten to fifteen workers who produced up to 5000 sheets a day. It is said that in about the year 1600 there were between 150 and 200 paper mills in the different areas of Germany, and in about 1800, some 1300 vats with a total of 15000 workers. In the German territory, paper mills were often set up by free imperial towns, sovereigns and monasteries and then leased to papermakers.

During the 14th century, paper gradually supplanted the parchment which had been common until then. Paper consumption in the scriptoria of monasteries, administration and in the private sphere was correspondingly small in the beginning. This situation changed with the introduction of letterpress printing about the middle of the 15th century. Of the 180 copies of the *Gutenberg Bible* with 42 lines per page, 150 were already printed on paper and only 30 on parchment. Because of its lower cost and better printability, paper became the material prerequisite for cultural development and the mercantile system. Already in the 15th century, news had been printed on flyers. The first periodical newspapers came into existence about 1600. During the 16th century, books were already printed in runs of thousands. More and more persons were instructed in writing and reading; the number of those who were interested in books – and also could read them – grew rapidly.

It is easy to understand that this soon led to a shortage of rags which had for a long time been the only raw material of paper-making. However, all efforts to find a substitute were unsuccessful until wood was discovered as fibrous material in the 19th century. In 1843, Friedrich Gottlob Keller suggested using shredded wood (ground-wood pulp) for papermaking – newsprint, wrapping papers and cardboards of today have a ground-wood content of up to 90%. It was not until the second half of the 19th century that a fibrous material of nearly equal quality as rags was found in the cellulose, obtained by chemical disintegration of wood (Benjamin Chew Tilghman: sulphite pulp, 1886/87; Carl Ferdinand Dahl: sulphate pulp, 1882).

Only by the utilization of wood as fibrous material could paper and cardboard attain their present-day importance as packing materials. Up to the 18th century, the major part of the paper production was used for writing and printing. The idea of conserving fibrous materials by adding disintegrated waste paper to the fibre suspension also dates back to the 19th century.

A revolutionary change in papermaking was caused by the invention of the endless screen papermaking machine by the French engineer Louis-Nicolas Robert (1798/99), the working principle of which is still valid for the latest machines. The trail blazing idea was to pour the fibre suspension onto an endless moving screen and thus to produce paper rolls, as opposed to individual sheets. This change from intermittant to continuous production has led to the development of machines that produce up to 2000 m of paper per minute, with sheet widths ranging from 6 to 9 m.

The significance of such output figures may easily be understood considering that the 1980 consumption of paper and board was 155 kg per person in the Federal Republic of Germany, which is equivalent to a total of nearly 10 million tons.

What is Paper?

Paper is a mat of plant (cellulose) fibres. Not taking into account the mechanical entanglement, the coherence of the fibres results from chemical bonds (hydrogen bonds) which form between the hydroxyl groups of the cellulose molecules during the papermaking process. These bonds are so strong that the tensile strength of paper can outdo that of ordinary structural steel, taking into account the specific weights.

The Period of Hand-made Paper

The first part begins with the forerunners of paper – *papyrus and parchment* – and with the paper of primitive tribes, the so-called *tapa.* Tools from a Japanese paper-making workshop illustrate the paper-making process used in East Asia.

Japanese paper-making tools, about 1900 (O)
Japanese paper is made from inner bark fibres which are prepared by beating instruments (at left). From a wooden vat (middle) the paper sheet is scooped out by means of a bamboo mould, which is attached to a hinged frame.

Ox-head watermark in paper from Germany at the end of the 14th century (O)
Watermarks were the trademarks of the early papermakers. They are produced by a wire form sewed onto the sieve of the paper-making form. This then shows itself when the paper is held to the light as a thinner, lighter mark.

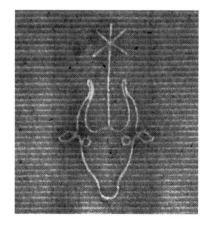

Paper-mill equipment of the "hand-made paper period" (O)
The rag-cutter of about 1800 from Zettelsdorf near Bamberg and the 16th century (?) stamping-mill of Fabriano (Italy) served the preparation of rags. The hollander from the August Plöger paper-mill of Schieder (Westphalia), dated 1845, is a mill for the disintegration of the fibres. Such beaters emerged in Holland in the late 17th century and gradually supplanted the stamping-mills which so far had been common in Europe. The wooden screw press was used as early as in the 17th century, in the Moulin de la Combe-Basse (Auvergne, France), for pressing the water out of the wet paper sheets bedded between felts. In Germany, a pile of 181 sheets, called "Pauscht", was usually pressed at once.

European papermaking, beginning in the 13th century and nearly unchanged up to the 19th century, is characterized by millwork. This can be seen from original equipment, such as the rag-cutter, stamping-mill, hollander and screw press, from different paper mills as well as from models of a water-powered paper mill of Westphalia and of a Dutch paper mill, driven by wind power. Moreover, the exhibition houses a great number of different types of moulds (18th and 19th century).

The individual phases of the papermaking process are represented by four dioramas based upon copperplate engravings from the *Encyclopédie* by Diderot and d'Alembert, Paris, 1751–1780, and from *Descriptions des arts et métiers,* Paris, 1761–1789. The hand scooping process is demonstrated daily; it contributes to a better understanding of how the paper sheet is made from the liquid fibre suspension.

The exhibition of old papers with watermarks and of various documents illustrating the history of paper is housed in a dark room in which the light-sensitive exhibits are protected against damage by lighting of only 50 lux.

The Beginnings of Industrial Papermaking

The foundations of the modern papermaking industry were laid in the 19th century. The invention of the papermaking machine started

Hand scooping (P)
In the background, original 18th and 19th century moulds and T-pieces (for drip-drying of the wet paper sheets) can be seen.

Paper-making machine, France, 1820 (O)
This machine formerly belonged to Claude Sauvade, the owner of the Moulin de la Combe-Basse (Auvergne, France).
This machine, probably the earliest endless screen machine preserved, is an improved version of the paper-machine invented by Louis-Nicolas Robert in 1798. The fibre suspension flowing from the wooden pulp chest is dewatered on the screen; the wet roll passes through a pair of roll presses. Since the machine has no dryer, the wet paper is wound on to a reel, then has to be cut and air-dried. The machine has a power of 2,2 to 2,9 kW (3 to 4 HP), a speed of about 5 m per minute and is driven by a waterwheel (view from the drive side).

Paper 233

mechanization in the production of paper. The use of wood instead of rags, which had become rare, was trail-blazing for industrial paper-making.

The French endless screen machine of about 1820 probably is the most important exhibit in this second part. As far as we know, no other museum owns a papermaking machine of the same age and excellent condition. Another matchless exhibit is the small wood grinding machine which Friedrich Gottlob Keller used for the production of ground wood in his experiments of 1843. The progress of the 19th century is also illustrated by models of ground wood mills and material preparation machines, as well as a drying cylinder of 1859 weighing over 2 tonnes, from B. Donkin & Co., London. Only since 1820, when Thomas Crompton discovered mechanical drying by means of steam-heated cylinders, has the production of paper in rolls been possible. This was a prerequisite for the operation of roll printing presses.

The introduction of substitutes for rags and the production of paper grades for defined purposes made a classification by quality standards necessary. The prerequisite for such a standardization was appropriate testing methods. A small collection of paper testing apparatus of the late 19th and early 20th century is on display in a showcase.

Modern Papermaking

The Deutsches Museum always tries to show the latest technology in addition to the historic development. This, however, is possible only to a

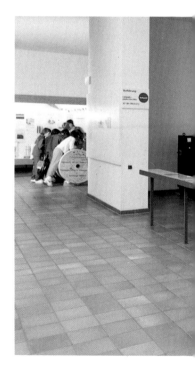

Endless screen paper-making machine, laboratory scale,
built in the Escher-Wyss training shop of Ravensburg in 1956/57 (O, P)
This machine is 7 m long and produces about 2 m of a 25 cm-wide paper roll per minute. (Presentation three times a week.)

limited extent, not only because of the rapid changes, but also because most of the machines are too big to fit into the exhibits. The raw and auxiliary materials used today are shown in the form of samples; their production can only be illustrated by the following models: continuous grinder, refining plant for the production of woodpulp, cellulose digester, continuous digestion plant and waste paper de-inking box.

In front of the showcase containing the basic materials there is an experimental paper-making machine which may be considered a model of a modern papermaking machine in working condition. The low speed of about 2 m per minute allows observation of the formation of the paper web on the screen and its passage through the press and dryer section in slow motion.

It is evident that the experimental paper-making machine cannot give the same impression as a visit to a paper mill. Even the projection of slides on the wall behind the paper-making machine or films of the production plants give an insufficient idea of the overwhelming aspect of such high-speed machines which produce up to 500 tons of paper per day.

At the end of the third room, a wall showcase houses a *Dictionary of Papermaking* comprising about 80 different grades of cardboard and paper in alphabetical order, giving a description of their essential properties. Only a fraction of all existing paper grades are included; the criterion of selection was not the economic importance of the different grades, but the attempt to demonstrate the variety of paper as a material and of its applications.

L. Michel

Writing and Printing

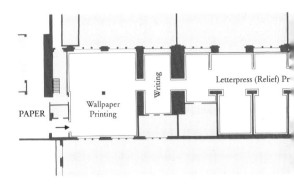

Writing was developed about 6000 years ago in different countries. In the beginning, the script was scratched, pressed, chiselled, painted or written on walls, objects, stone, metal, wood or clay tablets, and on leather, parchment and papyrus. About 1400 B.C., the Phoenicians used the first alphabetic script which consisted of 22 letters. As well as the Semitic scripts, the Arabic, Cyrillic, Greek and Latin scripts developed from this script. The earliest examples of reproducible print are found in Chinese one-side prints and block-printed books from the period of about 600 A.D. (prints from an engraved wooden block).

Johannes Gutenberg (1395/1400–1468) invented a reproducible method of printing which made possible large numbers of identical prints at low cost. This was the technical prerequisite for the public access to books, for the rise of newspapers and periodicals and generally for the – until then inconceivable – circulation of written information. Perhaps only a few other inventions have had such an extraordinary impact upon civilization and society.

Printing with individual, movable metal type presupposed a casting process – the principal item of Gutenberg's invention – as well as a press, printing ink and some knowledge in paper handling. Within a few years, Gutenberg had printed the 42-line Bible, which is still considered one of the masterpieces of the printing art. The first printers combined the activities of the punch cutter, type founder, compositor, publisher and bookseller. The different branches started to become independent after 1500.

One of the first independent type cutters was Claude Garamond (1480–1561), whose type faces are still in use today. Anton Koberger (about 1440–1513) of Nuremberg owned the first large-scale business with 24 presses, 100 journeymen and 16 bookshops. Gutenberg's system was so perfect that it existed nearly unchanged until 1800, i. e. for more than 350 years.

A revolutionary change in the reproduction of pictures and illustrations was brought about by copperplate engraving, a process which was introduced in the early 15th century. It became the favourite technique along with woodcutting and developed to the dominant illustration

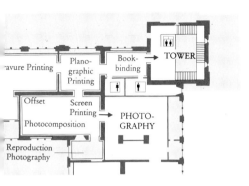

method, together with etching and its variations, like dry needle, aquatint and soft ground etching. In the form of engravings and etchings, the artwork of many artists could reach a broad public.

The growing demand for printed books, the increasing number of printed copies, the advent of newspapers (the first daily newspaper was published in Leipzig in 1660), and the desire to be kept informed could no longer be coped with by means of hand presses with a printing rate of about 300 sheets per hour. The first cylinder printing machine was constructed by Friedrich Koenig in 1811 and marked the dawn of mechanization in printing.

The struggle for higher printing speed, demanded by the spreading newspapers, fostered the construction of cylinder flat-bed machines (1000 to 1500 impressions per hour), of the perfecting presses (for simultaneous recto and verso printing) as well as of high-speed presses with several printing units (4000 impressions per hour) and finally led to the introduction of the reel-fed rotary presses (8000 impressions per hour) in 1865.

The platen presses, which emerged during the second half of the 19th century, filled the gap between hand and cylinder presses. They were designed for the printing of small numbers.

Although casting machines coped with the production of increasing numbers of print types, composition itself remained hand labour despite numerous attempts of mechanization. The decisive invention was made by Ottmar Mergenthaler who introduced the *Linotype* line composing and casting machine (1883–1886); this machine, together with the *Monotype* single-type casting and composing machine (1885) and the *Typograph* (1890), dominated the market until the advent of photocomposition in the 1970s.

Whereas the essential effect of the innovations in text printing, achieved during the 19th century, was an increase in the printing speed, illustration printing broke new ground. In 1796, Alois Senefelder invented lithography, the first process of planographic printing. Chromolithography, a process developed from it, was the first to offer the possibility of printing colour prints true to the original.

During the second half of the 19th century, the following new methods of colour reproduction evolved out of the progress in photography and chemistry:

Collotype printing, developed by Joseph Albert (Munich, 1868), photogravure (heliogravure) printing, by Karl Kliĉ (Vienna, 1879), photochrome printing, by Orell Füßli (Zurich).

Worthy of special mention is Georg Meisenbach, of Munich, who from 1882 to 1889 developed a method of decomposing continuous tone originals into halftone dots and transferring them to zinc plates. A few years later, the processes of three-colour and four-colour reproduction were mastered by letterpress (relief) printing, gravure (intaglio) and offset (planographic) printing, the latter being an offspring of lithography.

The technical progress achieved in the 19th century mainly reduced the cost of printed products. In addition to the light illustrated press, the informative daily newspapers, advertising posters, leaflets and catalogues, appeared inexpensive book series and pocket books. The book clubs and guilds, which had come into existence after the First World War, recruited millions of new book readers.

Today many traditional printing processes merely serve artistic purposes. So far, letterpress printing still is the realm of newsprint, but web offset is already supplanting it even there. The magazines and catalogues with high circulation figures (e.g. the *Spiegel*, about 1 million; the *Stern*, 1,8 million; *Quelle* catalogue, about 8 million copies) are printed by web-fed gravure cylinders with 45 000 revolutions per hour.

Nearly all other printed works, ranging from books to packing material, are printed in offset. Sheet-fed offset machines achieve up to about 10 000, web offset presses up to 25 000 impressions per hour. A substantial change in composition and picture reproduction took place when electronics invaded the printing industry. In the 1970s photo-composing machines, in which the types are stored either in the form of black-and-white negatives or as encoded digital information, have supplanted the mechanical typesetting machines. Even picture reproduction is now done by means of electronic equipment – the so-called scanners. They make it possible to produce colour reproductions ready for print straight from the original in a single operation.

Information on the Exhibition

This department, opened in 1965, shows the different printing methods in sections marked *letterpress, gravure, planographic* and *screen printing.* Moreover it deals with the development of writing and of composition as well as with reproduction photography and bookbinding. The demonstration of composing and printing machines in the department is intended to make the understanding of the often complicated processes easier.

Before the visitor reaches the *Writing* section, coming from the *Paper* department, he has to cross a room with a provisional exhibition on wall paper printing, comprising patterns of old wall papers, tools used in hand printing and a wall paper printing machine (Julius Fischer, Nord-hausen, about 1900).

The Development of Writing

In the first room, writing implements, materials and script samples of Antiquity are shown. The reconstruction of a monastic scriptorium with a writing monk illustrates the only text reproduction method known in the Middle Ages.

The typewriter emerged only in the second half of the 19th century. A selection of typewriters illustrates the most important phases up to the modern automatic typewriters. Of particular interest is a Chinese typewriter, of 1959 vintage, with 2314 individual characters.

Relief Printing (Letterpress)

The most ancient printing method belonging to relief printing is wood-cut. It is explained by means of an illustration showing Saint Rochus, the work of an unknown artist of about 1530, and the original printing block used for it. Korean type and prints of the 17th and 18th century, Japanese coloured woodcuts of the 20th century (shown in combination with the printing blocks, implements and inks) as well as a woodcut larger than life-size *(Epheben 1965)* by Professor HAP Grieshaber indi-cate the worldwide application of this technique.

Wooden screw press, signed in the screw: "Canstat 1790" (O)
Signature of the base: "Gemacht in Reutlingen von Christian Adam und Sohn Franz Kurz vor Gebrüder Mäntler Hof – und Canzley Buchdrucker in Stuttgart. 1811." On this letterpress printing press, the oldest in the Deutsches Museum, the "Schwarzwäl-der Bote" was printed in Oberndorf on the Neckar during the last century.

"Columbian Press", iron lever press, London, 1826 (O)
This press, built by George Clymer, Philadelphia, in 1810 is distinguished by easy handling, since the eagle-shaped balance weight discharges the heavy platen.

The original part of Johannes Gutenberg's invention of letterpress printing (about 1450) were the tools for the production of letter matrices and the hand casting instruments. The period of early prints is represented by a copy of *Schedel's World Chronicle* of 1493 as well as by a page from the 42-line *Gutenberg Bible* and the *Catholicon* (1460). Looking at the 18th century printing workshop with – partly original – equipment, lead melting furnace, casting devices, composing frame and a wooden press, the visitor can get an idea of the professional life of printers who, at that time, carried out by themselves all steps of the process – from type casting to printing.

The fact that the printing technique remained much the same until well into the 19th century is illustrated by a wooden screw press (signed by Christian Adam and his son Franz Kurz, Reutlingen 1793) and a *Columbian* iron lever press by George Clymer (London, 1826).

The model of the first cylinder press in working condition documents the epoch-making invention by Friedrich Koenig. He constructed the first flatbed cylinder press jointly with Andreas Friedrich Bauer in London in 1811.

The machines on display are a hand-operated flatbed cylinder by Helbig and Müller (Vienna, 1842) and a *Planeta* by the Dresdener Schnellpressenfabrik (Coswig, 1910–1920). With a small model in working condition, the Augsburger Maschinenfabrik made publicity for the first German web-fed printing press at the 1873 Vienna World's Fair.

Three letterpress printing machines, which were 'modern' at the opening of the exhibition in 1965, namely the *Original Heidelberg* automatic platen press, the *Original Heidelberg* automatic cylinder stop press and the automatic cylinder *Albert-Export-Ala*, Frankenthal, stand at the end of the series of sheet-fed letterpress printing machines.

The increase in printing speed achieved in the 19th century required faster, i.e. mechanized composition. Rare exhibits from a series of less successful experiments are the typesetting machines by Charles Kastenbein, of 1871, and that by Joseph Thorne, of 1884. In contrast to them, the *Linotype* line composing and casting machine, invented by Ottmar Mergenthaler in 1883, was a worldwide success. A machine of this type,

Linotype 6C Quick composing machine, Berlin, 1965 (O)
Ottmar Mergenthaler of Hachtel (Baden-Württemberg) developed the first usable line composing and casting machine in Baltimore (1883–1886). The key-selected type matrices stored in the magazine are assembled into lines that are justified by the insertion of space bands and then filled with molten lead. When the single lines are formed into columns, the composition is ready for print. The Linotype composing machine had worldwide success until photo-composing machines conquered the market in the 1960s and supplanted lead composition.

built in 1965, as well as a *Monotype* single-type casting and composing machine (England, 1965) can be seen in operation.

The invention of the halftone screen by Georg Meisenbach (of Munich) brought about a revolutionary change in picture reproduction for letterpress printing. The printing plate on display together with the patent no. 22 244 of April 21st, 1883, was produced by the inventor himself.

Gravure Printing

Copperplate engraving, introduced in the 15th century, and etching, which emerged some time later, are both manual gravure techniques. The display of implements, printing plates and prints aims at the explanation of these methods and of their variations – dry point engraving, etching, roulette, soft ground, aquatint and heliogravure. A diorama produced in the workshops of the Deutsches Museum shows the work in a copperplate printing shop of the 17th century. A very precious exhibit is the wooden copperplate press from northern Germany which dates back to the first half of the 19th century.

Heliogravure, a process invented by Karl Kliĉ in 1879, is considered a forerunner of modern gravure printing. The first sheet-fed rotary gravure press, developed in 1910 by Karl Blecher in cooperation with the Kempewerk of Nuremberg, represents an important step towards mass gravure printing. Gigantic gravure rotary presses are nowadays used for the printing of magazines and catalogues with high circulation figures.

Planographic Printing

Lithography, which uses prepared limestone as print carrier, was invented by Alois Senefelder in the years 1796–1798 as the first planographic printing method. From Senefelder's workshop originated the pole press (1797) and a small portable press (1818), both lithographic hand presses. In addition to them, the wooden lithographic hand press by Johann Mannhardt (Munich, 1848) and the metal one by Karl Krause (Leipzig, 1906) deserve special attention.

A collection of printing plates represent the different lithographic techniques including chromolithography, a process developed by Gottfried Engelmann in Paris in 1837.

A small wooden press dates from the early days of collotype which played an important role especially in the reproduction of paintings. The first application of collotype printing was made by Josef Albert in Munich in 1868.

The offset process is related to collotype and lithographic printing in so far as it is also based upon the mutually repellant property of grease and water.

The first rotary offset press with three cylinders (plate, rubber-covered, and printing cylinder) came onto the market in the United States about 1900. The first German machine was built by Caspar Hermann in Augsburg. Today offset is the most common process and equally suitable for text and illustration printing as well as to the printing of packing material. The sheet-fed single colour offset press by *MAN-Roland* (Offen-

Alois Senefelder's pole press, 1797 (O)
This lithographic hand press, which largely consists of original parts was built by the inventor himself. The stone is prepared for print, a sheet of paper is put on top of it, and the leather-covered printing frame is then swung to cover it. The scraper, which is attached to a long pole, is pressed down by a footboard and then pulled over the leather covering. Alois Senefelder (b. 6/11/1771 in Prague, d. 26/2/1834 in Munich), not only had found a simplified method of illustration printing by inventing lithography, but also laid the foundation for offset printing.

Two modern *Offset printing machines (O)* ready for operation and demonstration
In the front: Heidelberger GTO 52 single colour offset press, by Heidelberger Druckmaschinen AG, Heidelberg, 1982. Maximum sheet size 36 × 52 cm. Maximum printing rate 8000 sheets per hour.
In the rear: Roland Favorit RF 01 single colour offset press, by M.A.N.-Roland Druckmaschinen AG, Offenbach am Main, 1980. Maximum sheet size 46 × 64 cm. Maximum printing rate 10000 sheets per hour.

bach am Main, 1980) on display here is in working condition and prints up to 10000 sheets per hour.

Screen Printing

The far-reaching possibilities for the use of screen printing in the printing of objects (even on uneven surfaces like those of tableware etc.) were recognized and developed for industrial application only in the 1950s. The stencils and screens, a screen printing machine for printing flat surfaces (by Holzschuher, Wuppertal, 1965) and the *Rondomat* (by Albert, Frankenthal, 1971) for the printing of cylindrical, cone-shaped, spherical and flat bodies are exhibited in order to explain this procedure.

Reproduction Photography

The enlargements, line and screen photographs as well as the colour separation necessary for the printing of illustrations are made by means of process cameras, the working principle of which is based upon the photographic camera, or by so-called scanners which scan the original line by line. An example of the former type is the *Super-Autovertikal 60* camera by Klimsch (Frankfurt am Main, 1964), and of the latter, the *Chromagraph* electronic scanner by Rudolf Hell (Kiel, 1968).

Photocomposition

The conversion of a type pattern to electrical values as well as their storage and recall was only possible when the prerequisites had been made available in the field of electronics. In the 1960s, the first electronic phototypesetters appeared on the market and finally supplanted the hot-metal machines. In the *CPS 2000* automatic photosetting machine (Berthold, Berlin, 1980), exchangeable negative face carriers are used for the exposure of the photographic film. Other phototypesetters copy the face of the letter onto the film by means of an electronically controlled cathode ray. The structure and working scheme of a *Digiset* phototypesetter is illustrated by the functioning model by Rudolf Hell (Kiel, 1978).

Bookbinding

The exhibition only deals with "classical" bookbinding. The sewing press, trimming plane and gilding tools as well as the screw press (by Johann Mannhardt, Munich, 1866) belong to the implements used by bookbinders in centuries past.

L. Michel

Photography

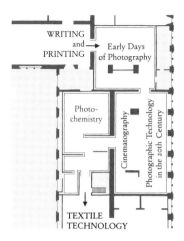

For a long time man had wished to find a technical process enabling him to picture objects in a lifelike and objective way without using the drawing pencil and paintbrush.

1839 is considered to be the year of the birth of photography. On August 19 of this year, the physicist Francois Arago presented the process developed by Louis-Jacques-Mandé Daguerre (1787–1851) to the *Académie des Sciences* of Paris. The so-called "daguerrotypes" were photographic positive pictures of unicum character, obtained from copperplates coated with silver and sensitized by iodine vapour. The reproduction from negatives typical to photography became possible only when in 1851 Frederik Scott Archer published the wet collodion process, which also allowed shorter exposure times than that for daguerrotypes. In the beginning, photography was practiced less by artists, such as Nadar (his true name was Felix Tournachon 1820–1910), than by photographers with mainly commercial interest. André Adolphe Disdéri (1819–1890) in particular had a feel for the popular craving to be portrayed according to one's status, which he met by photographic portraits in appropriate poses and surroundings.

An essential step forward in the technical progress was the suggestion in 1871 of Richard Leach Maddox (1816–1902) to use the silver bromide gelatine coating which still is in common use today. With the silver bromide gelatine dry plate it became much easier to take photographs: no bulky equipment had to be carried along as with the wet collodion process which required laboratory treatment of the plate before and after exposure.

It was again commercial interest that found ways and means to give the general public access to the thrilling experience of a self-made picture. The decisive step in this direction was achieved by George Eastman (1854–1932) who introduced the rollfilm (with celluloid base in 1889, with paper base shortly before) and "The Kodak" box camera with 100 rollfilm exposures. Nothing could have expressed the simplification of photography better than the publicity slogan *"You press the button, we do the rest"* of that time. Simultaneously, the rollfilm, with its shorter exposure times and the possibility to take pictures in quick succession, opened an important new field of application: the topical photoreport.

Further development was characterized by a trend to smaller, handier and less complicated cameras; the *Leica* 35 mm camera – introduced in 1925 – is a milestone in this development. 35 mm photography, the cameras of which now rank at the top of technical perfection, gave the photographer better possibilities of participation in the events, by snapshots and shooting picture sequences.

Experiments with colour photography date back to the early days of photography. However, the first method to gain significance was three-colour photography, a process developed by Frederic Eugen Ives (1856–1937) and patented in 1888. It produced three black- and white pictures of a subject using a red, green and blue filter (like in colour separation for colour printing) and then superimposed them by three projectors fitted with the corresponding filters. In addition to this indirect method, another process started a new phase of development: screen photography, introduced by the brothers August and Louis Lumière in 1904, which used coloured starch grains instead of the colour filters of the Ives process. These *autochrome plates,* introduced in 1907, were followed in 1916 by a similar colour screen plate marketed by Agfa. The real boom in colour photography, however, first started in the thirties, when diapositive films were brought to the market by Kodak (1935) and Agfa (1936). These films consist of superimposed layers of different colour-sensitivity. The photographic negative-positive process was first introduced by Agfa in 1939.

Daguerre camera, 1839 (O)
made by the optician Giroux of Paris in the "year of the birth of photography". Plate with seal and inscription: "Aucun appareil n'est garanti s'il n'en porte la Signature Mr. Daguerre et le Cachet de Mr. Giroux. Le Daguerrotype Exécuté sous la Direction de son Auteur à Paris chez Alph. Giroux et Cie, Rue du Coq St. Honoré No. 7".

Probably the most important photochemical innovation of the postwar period was *Polaroid 95*, the world's first instant camera presented by Dr. Edwin Land in 1948.

Technically speaking, cinematography may be considered a special branch of photography which is characterized by the shooting and subsequent screening of pictures in rapid succession, thus giving the spectator the illusion of motion. This is why its forerunners were glass plates with photographs taken in quick series, aimed at the study of movements (Eadweard Muybridge, 1872). To make a film, however, presupposes a substantial supply of filming material, and this was available only with the rollfilm (first construction of a motion picture camera by Lumière, in 1895).

In the beginning, the films could only be accompanied by gramophone sound. The optical sound recording system, which records the sound track next to the picture, was introduced in 1922 (Triergon optical sound-film camera).

In Germany the first movies were made in 1912/1913 *(Der Andere, Der Student von Prag).* As early as in the First World War, the possibilities offered by movies both for documentation of the war *(Wochenschau)* and for propaganda had been discovered. After about 1927 the sound film began to substitute the silent film which was then in its artistic heyday.

In 1936 the first colour short movie was produced in Germany (Carl Froelich *Das Schönheitsfleckchen);* longer colour movies followed after 1941.

Information on the Exhibition

The exhibition is housed in three rooms: the first and second inform the visitor of the historic development of photographic equipment for pictures and filming; the third room mainly illustrates the photochemical processes.

Early Days of Photography

The first – dimmed – room is dedicated to the early days of photography (1839 until about 1900). A particularly important item illustrating the history of photography is the earliest Daguerre camera imported to Germany, which was made by the optician Alphonse Giroux of Paris from 1839 on according to Daguerre's instructions.

As a sample of this process, a so-called daguerrotype (positive picture on a silver-coated copperplate) made by Lebrun in 1840, is on display together with the camera.

Also from this period dates a remarkable all-metal camera by Peter Wilhelm Friedrich Voigtländer (1841) with the world's first specially made lens for a photographic camera (in the third room).

Among the cameras used in the wet collodion process (advantages: shorter exposure times in comparison with daguerrotype and the possibility of reproduction), the following should be mentioned: the panorama camera by Thomas Sutton (about 1860), with a wide angle objec-

Voigtländer all-metal camera, 1841 (O)
with complete daguerrotype outfit, i.e. with cassettes, plates, iodizing chest and chemicals for the development. The conical camera is mounted to a tripod and bears the signature: "Voigtländer & Sohn in Wien, Nr. 84".

tive consisting of a system of water-filled lenses, and the *Dubroni* by Jules Bourdin (about 1867). The latter may also be considered the first instant camera, because the entire treatment of the picture carrier (sensitizing, exposure, development, fixation) takes place in the camera case.

Based on the industrial production of dry plates from the 1870s on, photography increasingly spread among amateurs. This is illustrated, for example, by the Steinheil detective camera (about 1890), the Krügener *Electus* (about 1890; second version of the first German twin lens reflex camera); by the single lens reflex camera of Dr. Adolf Hesekiel (about 1895) and the *Nettel-Deckrollo* (about 1905).

From the same period dates a series of special cameras, such as the so-called secret cameras in the form of books (e.g. book camera by Krügener, about 1888), binoculars (e.g. Goerz *Photo-Stereo-Binocle*, about 1906), walking-sticks (*Ben Akiba*, built by A. Lehmann, about 1903), pocket watches (*Ticka* by A. Houghtons Ltd., about 1907), as well as cameras which were worn hidden under the waist-coat (button-hole camera by Stirn, about 1888, the most common secret camera). Other cameras on display: three-colour camera (A. Miethe-Bermpohl, about 1902); a camera mounted on a carrier-pigeon (*Doppelsport* by J. Neubronner, ca. 1902), *Bosco* automatic portrait camera by C. Bernitt, about 1894); panoramic cameras (*Liesegangs Rotationsapparat*, about 1895, and *Ernemann Panoramic Camera*, of about 1907; both cameras are equipped for panoramic shooting); multiplicating camera (*Royal Mail* by W. Talbot with 15 objectives, about 1907); stereo cameras (by Ernemann, about 1909).

Photographic Technology in the 20th Century

The second room houses displays illustrating the history of the measurement of exposure time, flashlights, shutters and lenses. The same room also accommodates more recent rollfilm cameras, of which the following should be mentioned:

1. Sub-miniature cameras, such as the *Minox* (VEF Riga, about 1937/size 8 × 11 mm) and *The Kombi* (A. Kemper, about 1893/size 28 mm in diameter;

2. Miniature cameras, using perforated 35 mm motion picture film, like the *Minigraph* (Levi-Roth, about 1915), the *Sico* (Simons & Co., about 1925) and the *Leica I* (E. Leitz, about 1930);

3. Medium size cameras, such as the *Prominent* (Voigtländer, about 1933/size 6 × 9 cm), the *Pupille* (Auf. Nagel, about 1934/size 3 × 4 cm) and the *Hasselblad 1600 F* (Victor Hasselblad, about 1948/size 6 × 6 cm);

4. Large-size cameras, like the *Clack I* (H. Rietzschel, about 1901/size 10 × 12,5 cm).

Cinematography

The second room shows exhibits belonging to cinematography. The transition from the individual picture to the motion picture is illustrated by the *camera for instantaneous shots in sequence* by Friedrich Wilhelm Kohlrausch (about 1894), which, however, was hardly sold, because Lumière's *Cinématographe* came to the market in 1895. This camera – in

"Cinématographe" by Lumière, 1895 (O)
First motion picture camera, used also as projector for the developed films.

"Panzerkino" (cinematographic projector) by Oscar Messter, 1912 (O)
For synchronous reproduction, this projector could be coupled with a gramophone. In 1914, there had already been several sound-slide shows with the so-called biophone.

contrast to Kohlrausch's – used rollfilm and soon prevailed because of its light weight and handiness.

Among the cinematographic cameras, the 35 mm *Kine Messter* (O. Messter, about 1899), the *Filmette II* (Ertel-Werke, about 1923) and a collection of amateur cine cameras for narrow film from the period between 1920 and 1977 deserve special mention.

Cinematographic projection is represented by three 35 mm large projectors: one from the early days, the *Panzerkino* (Messter, about 1912), the lamp house of which had an asbestos covering and was separated from the fully encased driving mechanism; a projector with the first *Triergon* optical sound camera (about 1923); and, finally, a large modern cine projector (Bauer, about 1977). In addition, a selection of narrow film cameras of the period from 1920 to 1977 is on display.

Photochemistry

The third room is dedicated to photographic processes and modern laboratory technology. Among the exhibits that serve to explain the processes, the Voigtländer all-metal camera with complete daguerrotype outfit (1841) and a fully automatic printer by Agfa (about 1976) with an output of up to 8000 prints per hour are worthy of particular attention.

H. Kühn

Textile Technology

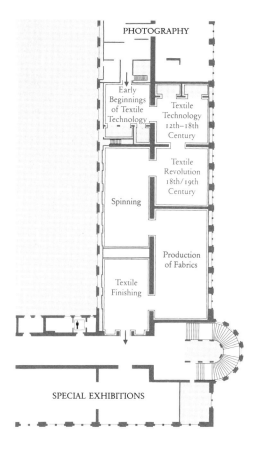

Today, it is no problem for man to adapt to the changes of climate at any time. All of us have an exchangeable "second skin": our garments. They add to our well being, because they assist the body in temperature regulation and in controlling its moisture content. They add to our living space, because they make us independent from the influences of weather and climate. Garments, however, also offer an opportunity for the expression of our personality and tastes.

In which evolutionary phases did man conceive and apply textile technology?

The hairiness of the human body slowly diminished in the course of man's evolutionary history and thus offered less protection against the influences of the climate. The hunters and fruit gatherers originally dressed in animal hides and cloths of plaited grass.

Presumably, the production and use of such primitive garments led, in a first phase, to the further development of textile techniques such as *plaiting and sewing* with the bone needle, long before *spinning and weaving*.

The textile techniques in the proper sense – spinning and weaving – presuppose suitable fibrous materials and implements. The hand spindle and the warp-weighted loom were invented with ingenious simplicity.

According to the prevailing opinion, this leap ahead in technical evolution was achieved only after the change from nomadic hunting and fruit gathering to sedentary life. Agriculture and stockfarming made possible the cultivation of plants, e.g. of flax and cotton, as well as the breeding of sheep – thus fibrous materials became available for textiles. This opinion is confirmed by textile finds: Excavations in Catal Hüyük, Turkey, have produced the earliest finds of textiles, fragments of woolen fabrics, mats of woven marsh grass, weights used in weaving and spinning whorl; their age is about 8500 years. Remains of woven flax fabrics, ascribed to "Fajyum A", the civilization of Ancient Egypt, are about 7000 years old, fragments of cotton fabrics from West Pakistan about 5000 years old. Silkworm culture, too, has been known in China for nearly 5000 years.

It follows that in these civilizations hand-spindles for the spinning of fibres into yarns and the warp-weighted loom for the weaving of the yarn have been in use at least since the Neolithic period. The communal dwellers used them for the production of textiles for their own requirements.

Essential technical improvements were only achieved in the late Middle Ages. The spinning wheel and the treadle loom made the production of textiles easier and faster and allowed a greater variety of patterns. In the medieval cities of Europe, the handicraft textile industry developed out of the production for one's own needs. Oriented by the principles of market economy, small industrial textile enterprises produced for the continually spreading trade. The rapid increase in population figures and the accompanying rise in demand for consumer goods of all kinds favoured the set-up of large textile manufactories and the system of the commissioned cottage industry in the 18th and 19th century. Wage-earning male and female workers produced textiles by means of the spinning wheel and hand loom, either in the manufactories or at home, and the manufacturer or retailer marketed the products.

The industrial revolution, i.e. the change from manual to industrial production, began with the mechanization of the spinning and weaving processes in the 18th and 19th century and with the first use of the steam engine in a mechanized spinning mill in England in 1785. Most of the labourers of the period – above all, of course, the spinners and weavers – saw their living menaced by the new machines, and it came to riots against those who had either invented the machines or put them into service. Despite all resistance, there was no stopping the technical development. The new machines, together with better power sources continuously improved both technically and economically, and led to the setting-up of more and more textile factories. Organised according to rigorous principles of thrift, mass production and marketing began all over the world. The growing pace of industrialization in the 19th and 20th century led, first, to the mechanization of the textile processes in mass-production, then to automation and – from the seventies onwards – to the introduction of microelectronics into the textile industry.

Information on the Exhibition

In 1961, the Textile Technology Department was newly arranged. In six rooms, it shows important phases of the technical history of textile techniques, such as spinning, weaving, hosiery, knitting, felting and textile finishing, from Antiquity up to our times.

Early Beginnings of Textile Technology

The exhibition begins with the fibrous materials known in Antiquity: flax, raw silk, cotton and wool. The principle of hand spinning, the straightening and separating of the – previously entangled – individual fibres and their twisting into yarn, is represented in a schematic way. Several hand spindles give examples of this most original, simplest spinning device. In the middle of the room, there stands a warp-weighted loom, a reconstruction true to the original. Looms of this type, which have been known since the Neolithic period, were still used in Lapland around 1940. The principle of weaving, i.e. the crossing of warp and woof threads, is explained by texts and graphs.

Along one wall, the milling and washing of cloth (wool fabric) according to a wall painting of Pompeii can be seen. Beneath are illustrations of milling and Kirghiz felt-making. Remarkable is a Turkish carpet loom with a carpet that has about a million knots per square metre.

Textile Technology, 12th to 18th Century

The hand spinning wheel represents the next step in spinning. The hand spindle and the hand spinning wheel work by the *intermittent spinning process.* Great progress was made by the invention of the flyer spinning wheel, of which several versions are on display. It was the first implement to permit simultaneous spinning and winding. In two niches, there

Warp-weighted loom (R) with vertical, weighted warp threads. Finds of weaving weights from the 7th/6th millennium B.C. make it seem probable that the warp-weighted loom was in general use as early as in the Mesolithic period.

are reconstructions of a wool combing shop of the 18th century and of a weaving shop with a more than 200 year-old weaving loom from the Fichtelgebirge. They represent the development of the specialized textile industry and of the beginning of manufactories and commission weaving. Of decisive impact on the emerging textile industry was the invention of the "flying shuttle" by the Englishman John Kay in 1733. One loom in this room is fitted with a device of this type. The flying shuttle ran on rollers and was driven to and fro across the loom by pulling a picking cord, the result being an essential increase of the weaving speed. The consequence of the rising production figures was that it was not possible any more to produce enough yarn for the weavers by means of the spinning wheels common at that time – the term "yarn hunger" emerged – and new spinning machines had to be developed.

The "Textile Revolution"

During the 18th and 19th century, the change from hand labour to industrial production was finally achieved by extensive mechanization and division of labour.

The exhibition houses several reconstructions of the earliest spinning machines: a carder, a speed frame (the so-called lantern frame) and a flyer spinning frame used for roving as well as for spinning, all of them developed by the Englishman Richard Arkwright, and a Jenny spinning machine of 1860, similar to the famous *Spinning Jenny* invented by James Hargreaves in 1764.

An epoch-making invention in weaving was made by the Frenchman Joseph Marie Jacquard in 1805. By the jacquard apparatus named after him, the individual warp threads of the loom are raised or lowered independently by means of cards which are perforated according to the weaving pattern; thus the desired pattern is woven. The model of a jacquard machine for demonstration purposes and a carpet loom with jacquard attachment are on display in this section. Moreover, a ribbon loom as well as a roller loom and a slurcock loom, both used in knitwear production, the latter very similar to the stocking frame developed in 1589 and brought to near perfection by the Englishman William Lee.

The display ends with a small block printing shop and a series of hand blocks of the type used in the first half of the 19th century.

Textile Technology of the 20th Century

The room, like the technical field, is divided into the production of yarns (spinning), production of fabrics (e.g. by weaving, knitting, hosiery, felting) and textile finishing (e.g. dyeing, textile printing, processing). The display thus gives a survey of the development in the textile industry achieved by mechanization and automation during the 20th century.

1. *Production of yarns.* The operations taking place in the cotton mill and worsted spinning mill, called *passages* by the professionals, may be activated by push-buttons. In simplified form, demonstration models show the individual phases of operation of the different spinning machines and the resulting change in the structure of the raw materials – cotton

"Jenny" spinning machine, of about 1860 (O)
The original Spinning Jenny was invented by James Hargreaves in 1764. In the beginning, the simultaneous spinning of 16 threads, a few years later of up to 80 threads,
was possible with this machine.

Partial view of the "Textile Revolution" room
In the middle of the picture, there is a hand-operated carpet loom with jacquard
attachment, of about 1860 (O). The jacquard attachment, invented in 1805 by Joseph
Marie Jacquard, the son of a silk weaver of Lyon, serves pattern weaving.

Partial view of the "Modern Weaving" room
In the front, there is a power loom with gripper shuttle, 1964 (O); in the rear, a jacquard automatic multicolour loom, 1961 (O).

and sheeps' wool – from the random structure of the fibrous material to the fine-spun thread.

Another classical spinning method is demonstrated by a small spinning machine: the production of the *rove* and its processing to carded yarn may be observed a live demonstration. The latest development, the so-called "open-end spinning" is represented by a rotor spinning machine illustrating the principle of OE spinning.

A two-for-one twister and a showcase with textile testing apparatus also belong to the exhibits in this room.

2. Production of fabrics. The weaving section starts with the theme of preparation. The preparatory phases of weaving include, above all, spooling and the threading of the warp beam. The machines required for these operations are on display partly as originals, partly as models. In the area of weaving, there are two mechanical looms of older types and two automatic looms of the latest generation: a cloth weaving loom by Schönherr, of 1891, and a jacquard automatic multicolour loom by Saurer (1961), both with the traditional system of weft insertion (shuttle with weft bobbin), as well as a gripper loom by Gabler (1928) and a power loom with gripper shuttle (1964). The weaving section ends with a large showcase illustrating the three basic weave types with their variations as well as a few special weave types.

The knitting/hosiery section begins with displays on yarn preparation and the loop formation in knitting and hosiery, followed by the most important flat-bed and circular knitting machine types by which nearly all types of knitwear, from fine underwear to coarse shawls and ski pullovers, can be produced. In addition to them, there are two warp knitting looms and a rib circular knitting machine; the fabrics of all three are used for the production of underwear and sports overalls, for example.

Finally, there is a display of felt-making, i.e. the compression of undressed single fibres by heat, pressure and moisture to a textile fabric with a wide range of applications.

3. *Textile finishing.* The term finishing or processing encompasses all kinds of treatment which textiles have to undergo after leaving the weaving, hosiery or knitting machine. *Bleaching, dyeing, printing and high-grade finishing,* for instance, belong to these finishing processes. In high-grade finishing, i.e. by synthetic resin finish, the textiles receive various lasting properties which add to their wearing qualities, such as resistance to creasing, water resistance, dimensional stability, easy-care and flame-retardant characteristics. A large display board and a series of model textile finishing machines illustrate the finishing processes, whereas the three dioramas of a *high-grade finishing shop,* a *yarn dyeing shop* and a *screen-printing shop* give an idea of the working rooms in the textile finishing industry. During the demonstrations (daily at 3 p.m.) nearly all devices and machines of the Textile Technology department can be seen in operation.

H. Tietzel

Coptic tapestry, 3rd to 4th century
The multicoloured threads of the woof are not carried across the entire span of the material, but instead only as far as the colour is needed in order to compose the desired pattern.

Special Exhibitions

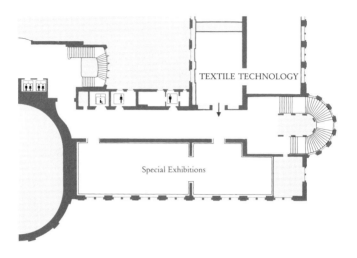

In this hall with an area of more than 300 m², opened in the summer of 1985, special exhibitions are arranged in continuous succession.
For details please contact the information desk in the entrance hall or consult the quarterly programme.

Suggestions for the continuation of the tour
The tour of the second floor ends here. Unfortunately, an uninterrupted tour of the third floor will be possible again only after the opening of the *Computer Science and Automation – Microelectronics* exhibition (p. 273).
Thus you may either go up the western spiral staircase to the third floor and visit the *Agriculture* department (you have to pass through the department in order to get to its historical section), or you go to the main staircase, with a view of the historical aircraft and ships, and continue your tour from here visiting the *Weights and Measures* department (p. 270) or the *Astronomy* department on the 5th floor (p. 279).

Agriculture

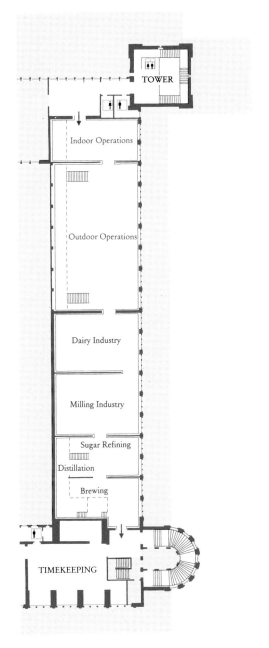

Agriculture is defined as the economic land utilization by farming and plant cultivation as well as by animal breeding, aimed at the production of foodstuffs and raw materials. The subsidiary industries which have developed from agriculture and are closely related to it, such as the dairy and milling industries, brewing, distillation and sugar manufacture, therefore also belong to this field. The first step towards agriculture, to systematic farming, was achieved by man in the Paleolithic period (16 000 B.C.) – as the latest archeological finds in the delta of the Nile tell us. From hunting and fruit collecting – i.e. from a gathering economy – he progressed to agriculture, i.e. to a reproducing economy. Animal husbandry, however, of the type still practised by nomadic tribes today, is considerably older.

The technical advancement in the field of agriculture, which is characterized by a powerful mechanization and motorization in our century, has produced a new field of technology – agricultural engineering. It has supplanted hand and animal labour in agricultural, forest and horticultural enterprises and aims at transferring it to machines, thus helping all those who cultivate the land as well as to provide the daily bread to all people by an increase of food production. The world population of today exceeds 4 billion, of which about 3 billion get sufficient food and over 1 billion are starving. Scientists reckon with a figure of about 7 billion for the year 2000. Supposing that about 5 billion of this total will get sufficient food, there will be about 2 billion starving.

Of the 4 billion living now, nearly two-thirds do agricultural work. Agriculture therefore still is the most important economic branch of mankind.

Information on the Exhibition

After heavy damage during the war, the department of Agriculture was reconstructed with an area of 1230 m² from 1960 to 1962 and opened on May 7, 1962. During the reconstruction phase, displays of several new fields of science entailed constrictions for a few older departments of the Deutsches Museum. So agriculture had to be reduced to three-quarters of the former area and concentrated primarily on the technical aspects.

Out of the abundance of rural culture, a few particularly valuable objects were acquired and thus could be preserved for posterity, at least in the Museum, in view of the especially rapid technicalization of agriculture in the past 100 years.

The department of Agriculture itself is divided into indoor and outdoor farming. Whereas the section on indoor farming shows the application of technology to the different operations inside the farmhouse, the outdoor farming section illustrates the technical development of soil cultivation. Sowing and harvesting are illustrated from the earliest documents known to us until present-day technology.

Indoor Operations

A rustic past envelops us, if we look at the authentic model of a farmhouse from the middle of the past century displayed in this room. It contrasts with a model of a modern farm standing opposite. Many hands are busy on this 40 hectare farm with a variety of animal husbandry and crops.

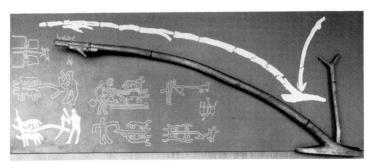

The plough of Walle, (R)
The original of the plough of Walle was found by peat cutters in July 1927, in a moorland 4 km northwest from Aurich, belonging to the community of Walle. It is now in the Museum of the Land of Lower Saxony in Hannover. The plough of Walle belongs to the type of the hook plough, also called sole plough. An oaktree supplied the main parts grown in one piece: the leg of about 3 m in length and the lay or ploughshare of about 60 cm in original length. A detailed study of the rock paintings of south Sweden gives some information of plough shapes, yoking (e. g. neck yoke) and the type of draught animals, oxen or horses.

The model of a modern, highly mechanized agricultural enterprise of equal size is characterized by the specialization in a few products. The daily work is done by only a few persons and well-selected machines in a rational way. The development of the milking machine, the thresher and of feed preparation machinery is represented by a few valuable exhibits.

Outdoor Operations

If we leave the farmhouses and turn to field work, we arrive at a room designed as a barn, illustrating the history of the tools and machines used in soil cultivation, sowing and harvesting. The earliest tool of man – the digging stick – marks the beginning of a development which has lasted many thousands of years and includes such phases as hoes, primitive sole and breaker ploughs, up to motor ploughs, mounted ploughs and quarter-turn reversible ploughs. Models give a clear idea of the plough shapes and yoking methods at all times in different countries. A variety of cultivators, harrows and land rollers is on display at the end of the series of model tillage machinery.

Much shorter, but not less interesting is the development of sowing implements and machines. The Chinese sowing plough, along with the Indian seed-drill made of bamboo, probably is the earliest sowing implement known. The drill invented by Locatelli, in 1663, leads over to the row seeders and drills. A particularly significant exhibit is the Finnish sowing machine, more than a hundred years old. An instructional model of a modern drill with 72 gear switching positions completes this section.

An impressive display shows the mechanization of corn harvesting, from the flintstone sickle to the combine harvester, with the gradual substitution of the tedious, time-consuming and costly hand labour by mechanized equipment.

The contrast between an accurate replica of the world's first reaper of

Tool carrier of about 1960 (O) in the outdoor farming section
This tool carrier was the first on which all implements could be mounted and removed by one person in a minimum of time and without great effort. Without using tools, the implements may be fitted to three working areas – in the front, between the axles and behind – and put into service independently of each other. The tool carrier in the picture is fitted with a beet harvester.

1831, and a modern self-propelled combine harvester is striking. A model of a winch-drawn beet harvester of the twenties contrasts with a tool carrier fitted with a beet harvester.

The cutaway model of a modern chaff-cutter as well as various models of green-crop and roughage harvesting machines point to the mechanization of fodder crop harvesting.

The Dairy Industry

The dairy industry had acquired great importance already with the nomads and nations of Antiquity. The earliest document of the dairy industry is the temple frieze of Al-Ubaid near Ur, dating from 3100 B.C. In this section, as well as in the following four sections, the central theme is not the production, but the processing of an agricultural product into other foodstuffs.

When entering the room, the visitor faces an Alpine dairy hut which is over a hundred years old. This is not coincidence, for it was the will of the founder that determined that the Deutsches Museum should be life-like in the type and variety of its displays, which aim at appealing both to the intellect and to the senses of the visitor. The strenuous muscle work, as it was traditionally done in Alpine dairy huts, is now done by means of appropriate conveying equipment, cream separators, butter churns, extensively mechanized cheese factories, refrigerating and heating equipment as well as by milk condensing and drying plants.

The Milling Industry

The milling industry is one of the earliest trades. It probably started with mills driven by animals, the animal treadmills. It continued with the

Sowing machine from Finland, around 1840 (O)
Until about 30 years ago, this approximately 140 year-old sowing machine still was in use on the farm of Eino Törmänen, some 20 km south of the polar circle. It is the task of a sowing machine to sow the various kinds of seed, according to their type, undamaged at a constant depth, with constant row spacing and uniform seed spacing in the row. The instructional model illustrates the mode of operation of a recent sowing machine with cam wheels and a 72-step gear. The gear allows the control of the number of revolutions of the feed roller within wide limits. Along with the hinged hopper bottoms and locking levers, this enables the sowing of the right quantities of the seed – from the smallest to the largest. The combine harvester, a fully automatic grain harvesting machine, allows the reaping and threshing of the corn in one single operation.

Dairy hut from the Valepp,
Tegernsee district, 1830 (O)
Alpine pastures are called "Almen" in Bavaria and Austria, and "Alpen" in the Allgäu, in Vorarlberg and in Switzerland. This hut was used as an Alpine herdsman's cottage (Alpine cheese dairy) up to 1926. During its last years, it was used as a stable for young stock. In addition to the work room, which can be seen on the picture, it had a living room and the stable. The dairy hut came to the Deutsches Museum without its furniture and implements. Later, it was fitted out with cheese-making and butter-making implements from the dairy cooperative of Auffach (Wildschönau, Tirol).

invention of the watermills, around 120 B.C., and subsequently with the various types of windmills in the first half of the 7th century. Industrialization in the milling industry began with the construction of the first automatic mill by Oliver Evans in 1795. An important invention was that of a mechanical sifting device, missing in medieval mills. The earliest mention of a mechanical sifting device dates from 1115 and is found in the description of the abbey of Clairvaux. Another improvement of flour sifting was achieved around 1800, by the boulter cylinders also introduced by Oliver Evans. After 1850, the centrifugal sifters were finally adopted. The replacement of the set of millstones by the roller mill, which took place in the second half of the 19th century, was certainly one of the most important events in the history of the milling industry.

Brewing

The *Blue Monuments* or *Monuments bleus* are considered the earliest documents of the brewing industry. The scripts of these clay plates of

Oil mill from Lohrhaupten, Spessart, about 1750 (O)
In addition to proteins and carbohydrates, fats belong to the three basic foodstuffs. This is why fats and, of course, oils were sought after and considered valuable goods for thousands of years. The oil mill shown in the picture was driven by a waterwheel and used for the processing of oil plants, such as rape, garden poppy, bigseed (flax), hemp and sunflowers, nuts and beechnuts. One (metric) centner (50 kg) of rape, for example, yielded 24 litres of oil.

the early Sumerians (4th millennium B.C.) describe the preparation of a libation from millet and another grain type – probably emmer. The brewing methods of history – the *cold beer* of the Egyptians, the *stone beer* of the Germanic tribes and the *Ossetian brewing method* – are explained by means of model displays. From the Middle Ages up to modern times, brewing was a home industry practised by individual families. In the middle of the 19th century, the first didactic books on brewing, based upon the results of scientific research, were published, and the technology of brewing progressed quickly.

The central part of a modern brewery – the brewing plant with its copper domes – dominates the room and illustrates the high degree of automation achieved in a modern bottling plant. Malthouse equipment, the clarification of the wort, the brewer's yeast and the fermentation, storage and racking are additional themes for the display of originals, models and illustrations. An illuminated diagram reproduces a "tour" through a modern malthouse and brewery.

Distillation

The term alcohol is derived from the Arabic *(al-Kuhl)* and means *the finest.* The Latin word *spiritus* means *spirit.* The alcoholic liquid was given these names because of its high volatility. The Arabs are said to have made a distillate from wine – the brandy – as early as around the year 1000 A.D. In the beginning, it was used only as a medicine. In the middle of the 14th century, *brandy (distilled wine)* was already a sought-after commodity of trade and an often misused luxury.

In the distillation section, the visitor can find a few outstanding exhibits from the history of the production of alcohol by distillation from potatoes, grain, fruit and roots as well as of the production of liquors and spirits.

Sugar Refining

For many centuries, sugar was made only from sugar cane, a tropical plant. The cultivation of sugar cane has been known in India since 400 B.C. The model of a West Indian sugar cane boiling plant illustrates the processing of sugar cane in sugar refining. The discovery of the sugar content of the sugar beet, and decades of selection were made by Andreas Sigismund Marggraf and Franz Carl Achard (1747–1801). A model of the world's first operational beet sugar factory of Krayn, in Silesia, shows the equipment and the processes used for sugar production. The latest state (1975) of the development in this field is represented by the model of a complete beet sugar factory with a daily production of 200 (metric) tons of sugar.

K. Rohrbach

Timekeeping

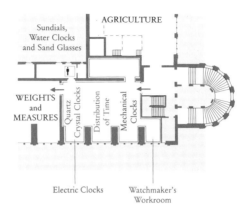

The change of day and night is a natural measure of time. Human societies have subdivided these periods. The Roman division, i. e. the division of day and night into separate series of 12 day and 12 night hours, was adopted in the Middle Ages. Corresponding to the seasons, the day hours were of unequal length: in summer, the day hours were longer, the night hours shorter, and vice versa in winter. However, the end of the sixth hour was identical with noon (12 o'clock in our chronology) throughout the year. The introduction of our present hour system with hours of equal length (equinoctial hours) accompanied the advent of mechanical clocks, with striking works, early in the 14th century. In the beginning, in the Holy Roman Empire, there were several possibilities of counting equinoctial hours: The *Small Hours* corresponded to our present system. The *Great Hours* divided the day into 24 hours, starting to count either at sunset (Italian Hours) or at sunrise (Bohemian Hours). In both cases, the starting point varied during the year. The *Nuremberg Hours,* used in the free imperial city of Nuremberg, were

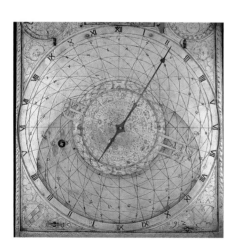

Dial with different hour marks (O)
Signature: "M.A. 1592"

counted in two sets, starting in the morning or evening. In summer, a maximum of 16 day and 8 night hours was counted (thus midday was at 8 o'clock, midnight at 4 o'clock). In winter, it was vice versa. Only with the abolition of the status of a free imperial city, after the Napoleonic wars, and the integration of Nuremberg into Bavaria was the system of the Nuremberg Hours abolished.

All these counting systems indicated local time, which depended on the geographical position of the place. When the railways spread as new and fast means of transport, the local times were standardized in the Deutsches Reich. As a first step, the local times within a politically independent territory were adapted to the time at the local seat of the court (railway time); the second step was the introduction of standard time which unified time in a large territory: Central European Time (CET) was introduced in 1892/93.

Information on the Exhibition

Turret Clocks

Since the 13th century, several attempts had been made to replace the water clock with its many faults, by a wheel gear clock with slow and uniform operation. By the 14th century, turret clocks with striking works had been installed in all major towns of Europe; they were the optical and acoustic regulators of public life in the communities. The turret clocks on display here were built between 1562 and 1905 and illustrate the change of the clock movement systems from the recoil escapement to the detached escapement.

Mechanical Clocks

Early in the 14th century, clocks with wheel gears emerged and made the measurement of time independent from celestial bodies (nevertheless, the sundial remained a common time-piece up to the 18th century) and from weather (in the north, water clocks could freeze). From the very beginning, mechanical clocks were combined with mechanical striking works for the acoustic indication of time. The struggle for more accuracy continued. The invention of the pendulum as a regulator of the gear rate (published in 1658) made the clock an instrument of astronomical observation. With the "chronometer", invented by John Harrison (1759), it became possible to fix a ship's position at sea accurately.

Sundials, Sand Glasses and Water Clocks

The Earth revolves daily around its axis, the pointer of a sundial therefore has a shadow that moves in the opposite direction from the Earth's rotation, or changes direction, and can mark the hours on a scale. Water clocks and sand glasses show the emptying of a material in a vessel on linear scales and thus the *flow* of time.

The shadow of the sundial reflects the eternal motion in the sky; waterclocks and sundials, however, only indicate short periods of time.

Turret clock with striking work for hours and quarters (O)
from the church of the monastery of Fürstenfeld, near
Fürstenfeldbruck, made in 1721 by Brother Andreas
Bardl, in operation until 1904.
This clock has a so-called anchor escapement of the
type invented by Robert Hooke in 1676. Remarkable is
the bearing of the shafts on anti-friction cylinders,
intended to reduce the friction, as well as the form of the
pendulum bar. Other details which cannot be seen on
the picture are: both striking works for hours and quarters are regulated by locking plates which let the knife-
edge of the locking-lever fall back only after the corresponding number of strokes. The hammers of the tower
bells were activated by large rope-operated pin wheels.

Master clock of a clock system
manufactured by Siegmund Riefler, 1905 (O)
Master clocks of this type had an electric winding device
and were set up in the clock cellars of observatories and
institutes of geodesy in order to be protected against
shocks and fluctuations of temperature. The pendulum
of invar steel oscillates in a hermetically sealed glass cylinder; variations of air density therefore do not affect
the oscillation time of the pendulum, so the daily error
of this clock is less than 0.01 second.

South German Table Clocks and Automata

The free imperial cities of Augsburg and Nuremberg were independent city republics; their independence was based upon the "refinement of raw materials", i.e. on the production of fine arts and crafts. In them there flourished many strictly regulated crafts, including that of the watchmaker. In addition to the time-pieces built by the watchmakers, mechanical wheel gears also operated movable parts, thus representing scenes of human or animal life. The "Bequest of Werner Brüggemann" shows the variety of this south German production.

K. Maurice

Figure clock "Bear Driver", around 1580/90 (O)

Weights and Measures

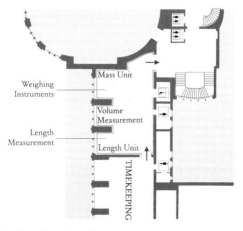

A prerequisite for all types of measurement is the determination of a unit which can be compared to the quantity to be measured and the result expressed in figures.

As early as in the civilizations of Antiquity, the representatives of lengths, volumes and masses were defined as units. Their validity, then and in the following centuries, was more or less limited to certain territories and periods. During the 17th and 18th centuries, the abundance of different values for yard, foot and pound finally led to a chaotic situation in the European countries. Despite equivalent names, the measures varied in size according to the place, often even according to the commodity type. The French National Assembly, in 1790, in order to put an end to this inconvenience, initiated standardization by an international system of measures, which was to be based upon an invariable natural measure and approved by all nations for all times. As the natural measure, upon which all other units were to be based, the unit of length was defined as the ten-millionth part of a meridional quadrant of the Earth. It was given the name "metre". In the confusion of the French Revolution, a clearly organized decimal system of measures was set up on this basic unit, giving definitions also for the units of area, volume and mass measurement – the metric system.

Several decades went by from the first provisional definitions of the French Revolution period until the introduction of the metric system on a broad basis. In order to accelerate its introduction and to bring the system to perfection, an international convention – the Metric Convention – was set up and signed by 18 countries in Paris in 1875, and the International Bureau of Weights and Measures was founded. Its first task was to find new standards for length and mass measurement, which were more appropriate than those of 1799: an International Prototype Metre and Kilogramme, made from the resistant alloy platinum iridium.

The first General Conference on Weights and Measures approved these standards in 1889, and accurate copies of them were distributed to the signatory states. Along with a series of further copies of decreasing accuracy, they form the basis of the national measuring and calibration systems.

The *International Bureau of Weights and Measures,* in cooperation with national institutes of other countries, is currently working at perfecting the definition of the measuring units in accordance with the requirements of practice and the possibilities of science. The result of these efforts was, in 1960, the creation of an international system of units, the *Système International d'Unités (SI),* which – in addition to the units of length, mass and time – defined three more base-units, namely those of electric current, thermodynamic temperature and of light intensity. This international system of units has been binding in the Federal Republic of Germany since 1970. In 1971, it was complemented by the base-unit for the amount of substance.

Information on the Exhibition

In this department, the development of the length unit and mass unit is shown, leading from the innumerable different yards, feet and pounds of former times to the metre and kilogramme.

Several demonstrations, some of which may be activated, introduce implements and devices used in length and volume measurement, in the comparison of masses and weight evaluation. The displays also reflect the evolution towards more accuracy, easier and faster determination of the measuring values, and the independent display and further processing of the values. The significance of limits of error in calibration and of tolerances in interchangeable manufacture are also referred to.

Unit of Length

In defining the length unit, a material standard – such as the *standard metre* of Paris – has been substituted by a defined multiple of an optical wave length. Thus the length unit is easily divisible and can be reproduced at any time.

A lamp container for the production of the length unit by means of a krypton 86 spectroscopic tube (1961) gives an idea of the complexity of the equipment needed for producing the radiation used in the definition of the metre.

Length Measurement

Originals and demonstrations of the most important measures of length, and types of measuring devices and instruments are on display here. The accuracy of measurement possible with these instruments can be seen by the visitor and compared against the tolerances required in modern replacement technology.

Volume Measurement

Development of volume measurement led from simple capacity measures to direct-reading devices, indicating volume by means of rotating hydrometric vanes, or measuring-chambers filled automatically, etc.

Self-indicating scales
In the front: an inclination scale with switching device for increasing capacity up to
10 kg (1961); in the rear: a built-in dormant weighing platform for weights up to
3000 kg (1961); the children are standing on the platform of a floor scale, from
where the weight forces are transmitted by a lever system to the weighing device and
indicated there.

Mass Unit

The mass unit in the metric system is the international *prototype kilogramme.* The original, a platinum-iridium cylinder of 39 mm in diameter
and height, is kept at the *International Bureau of Weights and Measures* in
Paris.
All calibrated weights, and the scales of weighing instruments, are indirectly compared with the kilogramme prototype.

Weighing Instruments

The balance is supposed to be the oldest measuring device. Its development is shown by examples ranging from the simple beam scale to
punched-card controlled weighing instruments.   *H. Schmiedel*

Computer Science and Automation – Microelectronics

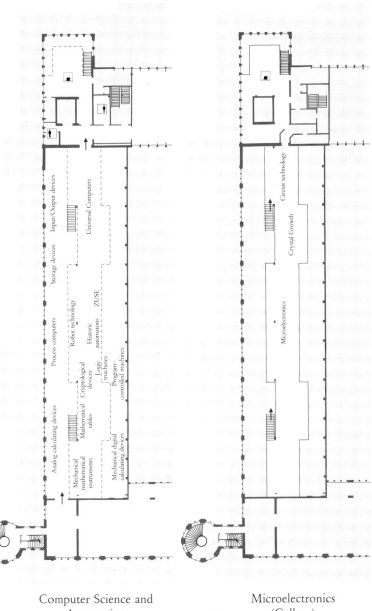

Computer Science and
Automation

Microelectronics
(Gallery)
Opening 1989

Analog calculating devices

Mechanical
mathematical
instruments

Mathematical
tables

Cryptological
devices

Process computers

Robot technology

Logic
machines

Historic
automatons

ZUSE

Program-
controlled machines

Mechanical digital
calculating devices

Storage devices

Input/Output devices

Universal Computers

Circuit technology

Crystal Growth

Microelectronics

Mathematical instruments and calculators witness a development which in this century culminated in computer science and automation technology. Based on the fundamental difference between digital and analog computation, a wide variety of designs and forms has been developed.

Computer science deals with the processing of coded information – numbers, symbols, and measurements. In connection with this, automation technology involves information processing by means of programmed machines. Microelectronics has shrunk these machines (which were still monster-sized in the middle of this century) to small, inexpensive, fast, dependable chips, which use very little energy.

The developments in the last fifty years have caused century-old traditional mathematical instruments to fall into oblivion. This applies to the

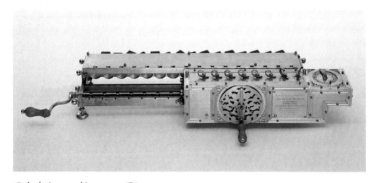

Calculating machine, 1923 (R)
designed by Gottfried Wilhelm Leibniz, conceived about 1670, built about 1700
(INV 56956)

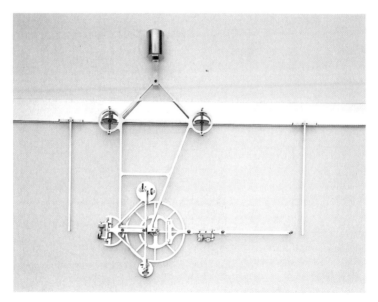

Integrator "AMSLER Type No. 4", 1906 (O)
Instrument No. 456 (INV 7591)

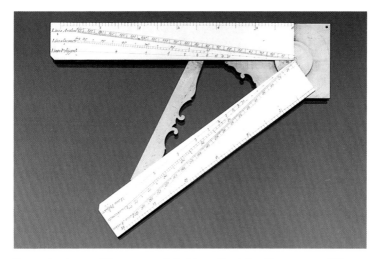

From a drawing set: *Silver sector* made by Georg Drechsler, Hanover *1775 (O)*
(from INV 65490)

Automaton –
Preaching Monk, about 1540 (O)
Southern German or Spanish
(INV 84/18)

Cypher machine "ENIGMA", about 1940 (O)
Marine model with 4 rotors (INV 84/584)

slide rule (itself based on the auxiliary means of the logarithm) and the hand-operated calculating machines. Even high-precision instruments such as the planimeter, integrator, and integraph appear to be almost at the end of their century-long history. Their substitution by constantly improving universal program-controlled electronic computers has already happened or is only a matter of time.

In addition to the presentation of now-historic instruments, the development of program control and the concept of universal alphanumerical computers make up the focus of the exhibit. In the exhibit on microelectronics, the production of chips and their base material, silicon, is dealt with.

Subjects

Mechanical mathematical instruments,
Analog calculating devices,
Process computers;

Mechanical digital calculating devices,
Mathematical tables,
Cryptological devices,
Logic machines;

Historic automatons,
Program-controlled machines,
Robot technology;

Universal computers,
Circuit technology,
Storage devices,
Input/Output devices,
Crystal growth;

Microelectronics.   *F. L. Bauer*

Detail of a relay box *from the program-controlled computer "ZUSE Z 4", 1942–44 (O)*
(INV 74692)

Detail from the central processing unit of "PERM", 1952–55 (O);
i.e. Programmed Electronic Reckoner Munich (INV 87/256)

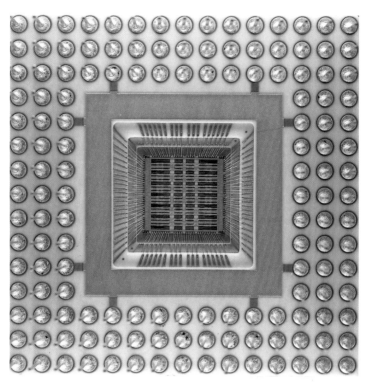

Mounted chip "SIEMENS SA 100 E", 1986 (Photo: Siemens AG)

Wafer with 1-Mbit chips, Siemens, 1987 (Photo: Siemens AG)

Astronomy

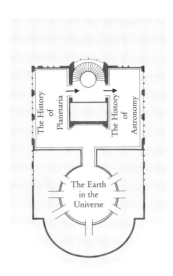

The History of Planetaria

The History of Astronomy

The Earth in the Universe

Astronomy is one of the oldest branches of science. There were three basic human needs that prompted investigation of the universe. The first was the need to worship (in Antiquity, the planets were thought of as divine beings), and the second was the need to produce a calendar that would facilitate industry, trade and communication. The third was the fact that the stars were important for orientation on land and at sea.

In ancient Greece systematic observation of the sky led to the composition of star catalogues and to the first mathematical theories for the prediction of planetary motions. The astronomical knowledge of that period was compiled by Ptolemy of Alexandria around 150 B.C. The tradition of this cosmology determined the cosmological and astronomical ideas of the Middle Ages. The central idea was that the Earth was the stationary centre of the universe.

A new age of astronomy began with the discoveries of Nicolaus Copernicus, Johannes Kepler, Galileo Galilei and Isaac Newton, who turned away from this view. Copernicus showed that the planetary motions, which seem so complicated, may be understood as simple orbits in a system with the sun in the centre and with the planets revolving around it. Based on the excellent observations Tycho Brahe had made of celestial motions, Kepler succeeded in proving the elliptical shape of the orbits, with the sun at one of the foci. Galilei was the first astronomer to use a telescope for the observation of the sky; support for the Copernican heliocentric system was provided by his observations. Newton finally explained all celestial motions by the principle of universal gravitation, thus linking astronomy and physics. Today we know that our solar system is part of a giant spiral nebula formed of 100 of billions of suns (stars). In the universe billions of such spiral nebulae (also called galaxies) exist.

Information on the Exhibition

The astronomy exhibition illustrates the evolution of astronomical knowledge, from the earliest beginnings – which date back to the Babylonians – to several recent discoveries concerning the structure of the universe.

Evidence of early astronomic investigation in Mesopotamia is indicated by astronomical symbols on archeologic finds like *stelae* or stone documents from the Babylonian period. Examples of such finds are shown in the replicas of a Babylonian stone document with star symbols (715 B.C.) and a three-piece Babylonian frieze with representations of the zodiac (about 1000 B.C.). The stars were thought of as deities who determined human fate.

More detailed information is available on the instruments used for astronomical measurements in Ancient Egypt. The exhibition shows reconstructions of a sidelight sundial (about 1480 B.C.), of a clepsydra (about 1400 B.C.) and of a sidereal clock, also called *merghet* (about 600 B.C.). The reconstruction of the ceiling relief from the temple of Dendera (Upper Egypt, 22 B.C.) deserves special attention.

The advanced knowledge of Greek astronomers is illustrated by the measurement of the Earth's diameter by Eratosthenes (about 275–194 B.C.), and by the measurement of the moon's distance by Hipparchus

Ceiling relief from the temple of Dendera, Upper Egypt, 22 B.C. (R)
This relief was discovered in 1798 by an officer of the Napoleonic army, on the roof of a sepulchral chamber in the ruins of the Isis temple of Tentyra, a formerly important town of Ancient Egypt, near the fellah village of Dendera (north of Thebes). The centre of the relief shows the zodiac with the 12 zodiacal signs, surrounded by animal deities (animals and walking men) symbolizing constellations which were used to determine the time during the night.

Astronomical clock with planetarium and celestial globe, 1744 (O)
Signature: "Phil. Gottfr. Schaudt in Ontsmettingen Balinger Amts im Württembergischen".

(about 190–120 B.C.). The simplicity and handling of the instruments used at that time can be seen from reconstructions of an obelisk *(gnomon)*, the *dioptra* of Hipparchus and a *triquetum* of Ptolemy.

The *astrolabe* – of which a few originals are on display in the wall show-cases – and the *quadrant* were important astronomical instruments of our civilization before the telescope was invented. The large *azimuthal quadrant* by Georg Friedrich Brander, of 1760/61, is worthy of special attention.

Sendtner's large planetarium for the Ptolemaic system ends this first epoch of the history of astronomy; at the same time it points to the beginning of change in cosmological ideas caused by new discoveries. Whereas hitherto the Earth had been considered the centre of the universe, it became more and more evident, after the end of the Middle Ages, that the Earth was orbiting the sun and that it was the latter which is the centre of our planetary system (Copernican system). A significant cause of this development had, no doubt, been the discoveries of Kepler (1571–1630), which led to the formation of Kepler's three laws. Kepler's second law is illustrated by a demonstration. Another contribution to the formulation of a new system was made by Galileo (1564–1642), whose observations with the – then newly invented – telescope were revolutionary for his time (a reconstruction of his second telescope is on display here). Galileo's view through the telescope produced facts which had not even been dreamt of until then. Thus he saw mountains and valleys on the moon, an infinite number of new fixed stars so far hidden to the naked eye, that Jupiter had moons, sun spots and that Venus had phases like our moon.

A diorama of the observatory of Johannes Hevelius (1611–1687) is an example of an early observatory of modern times. The telescope was developed from an instrument of mere observation to an accurate measuring instrument. Another diorama shows Ole Römer (1644–1710) at his *machina domestica* for the measurement of meridian passages. Moreover he was the first to determine the velocity of light.

Because of the limited space available, it has not been possible so far to show the history of astronomy up to the present. The *position of the Earth in the universe* is the subject of a dimmed circular room from which different cosmic objects may be viewed through several tubes.

A special exhibition on the mechanical representation of cosmological systems completes the tour of the department. It shows planetaria, armillary spheres, telluria and lunaria from the period between 1700 and 1825, a small selection of historic celestial globes, Sendtner's planetarium for the Copernican system (the counterpart for the Ptolemaic system is shown in the first section of the exhibition) and a table planetarium by Abraham and Jacob van Laun (about 1825). The Zeiss projector Model 1 of the planetarium, which was built by Zeiss at the instigation of Oskar von Miller and installed in 1925 for the opening of the Deutsches

Copernican planetarium in armillary sphere, 1754 (O)
Signature: "Se Monte et se Vend chez Desnos, Rue Sᵗ Julien le Pauvre. Quartier de la Place Maubert a Paris, 1754 . . .". According to the Copernican cosmology, a small gilt sun forms the centre of the model. Little cardboard discs, attached to rotational rings, symbolize the planets Mercury, Venus, Mars, Jupiter and Saturn. Similarly, the Earth is a small Earth globe, and the moon is revolving around it in the form of a small cardboard disc. A broad band of fixed stars and the meridians complete the model.

Ptolemaic planetarium in armillary sphere, 1754 (O)
Signature: ". . . Se Fait A Paris Chez Desnos rue Sᵗ Julien le pauvre . . .". The centre of this small model of the universe is formed by an Earth globe around which two cardboard discs, sun and moon, are orbiting. A broad band of the fixed stars and the meridians of the astronomical coordinates (horizontal and equatorial) complete the model. Such models were made in large numbers and used for instructional purposes.

Zeiss projector Model IV, 1960 (O)

In the projection planetarium, an artificial sky with 8900 fixed stars up to a magnitude of 5.5 is projected, showing the stars perceptible to the naked eye in the most favourable conditions. The diameter of the hemispherical dome is 15 m. The projector allows a quick motion effect, reducing the lapse of a day to a minimum of 4 minutes, a year to a minimum of 11 seconds.

Museum in Munich – the world's first projection planetarium – has meanwhile acquired historic value.

The Astronomy Department was destroyed completely during the Second World War. The present exhibition is only a provisional solution. We hope soon to be able to present an enlarged and fully rearranged exhibit on astronomy which will show our valuable historical original instruments and will treat the most up-to-date findings of modern astrophysics.

Planetarium

Situated on the central axis of the Museum, above the entrance hall and the Hall of Fame, is the planetarium. The image of the starry sky is pro-

Zeiss refractor in the western dome (observatory), 1924/25 (O)
Diameter of the objective: 300 mm;
Focal length: 4960 mm;
Magnification: from 50 to 1000 times (at choice);
Field of vision, according to the rate of magnification: $1° \ 16'$ to $2' \ 43''$;
Angle of resolution: $0.4''$;
Diameter of Resolution $\approx 14.^{m}5$.

jected onto a dome: the apparent motion of the stars is speeded up, the orbits of the planets and of the moon become perceptible and the constellations of both the southern and northern hemispheres are shown. With the help of special effects and horizontal projection, it is possible to take the visitor on a journey through our solar system or into outer space. The heart of the planetarium is the computer-programmed Zeiss projector M1015. This projector enables lectures on different subjects and at different levels to be given.

Observatory

The observatory also belongs to the Astronomy Department. It is housed in the western dome, accessible by mounting the western staircase. It is fitted with a Zeiss telescope of 30 cm aperture and 5 m focal length. Admission and demonstration are possible only by previous appointment.

G. Hartl

INDEX